A Pan-African Theology:
Providence and the Legacies of the Ancestors

Josiah Ulysses Young III

Africa World Press, Inc.
P.O. Box 1892
Trenton, New Jersey 08607

Africa World Press, Inc.
P.O. Box 1892
Trenton, NJ 08607

Cover design by Ife Nii Owoo
Book design by Jonathan Gullery

This book is composed in Stone

Library of Congress Catalog Card Number: 91-75600

ISBN: 0-86543-276-7 Cloth
0-86543-277-5 Paper

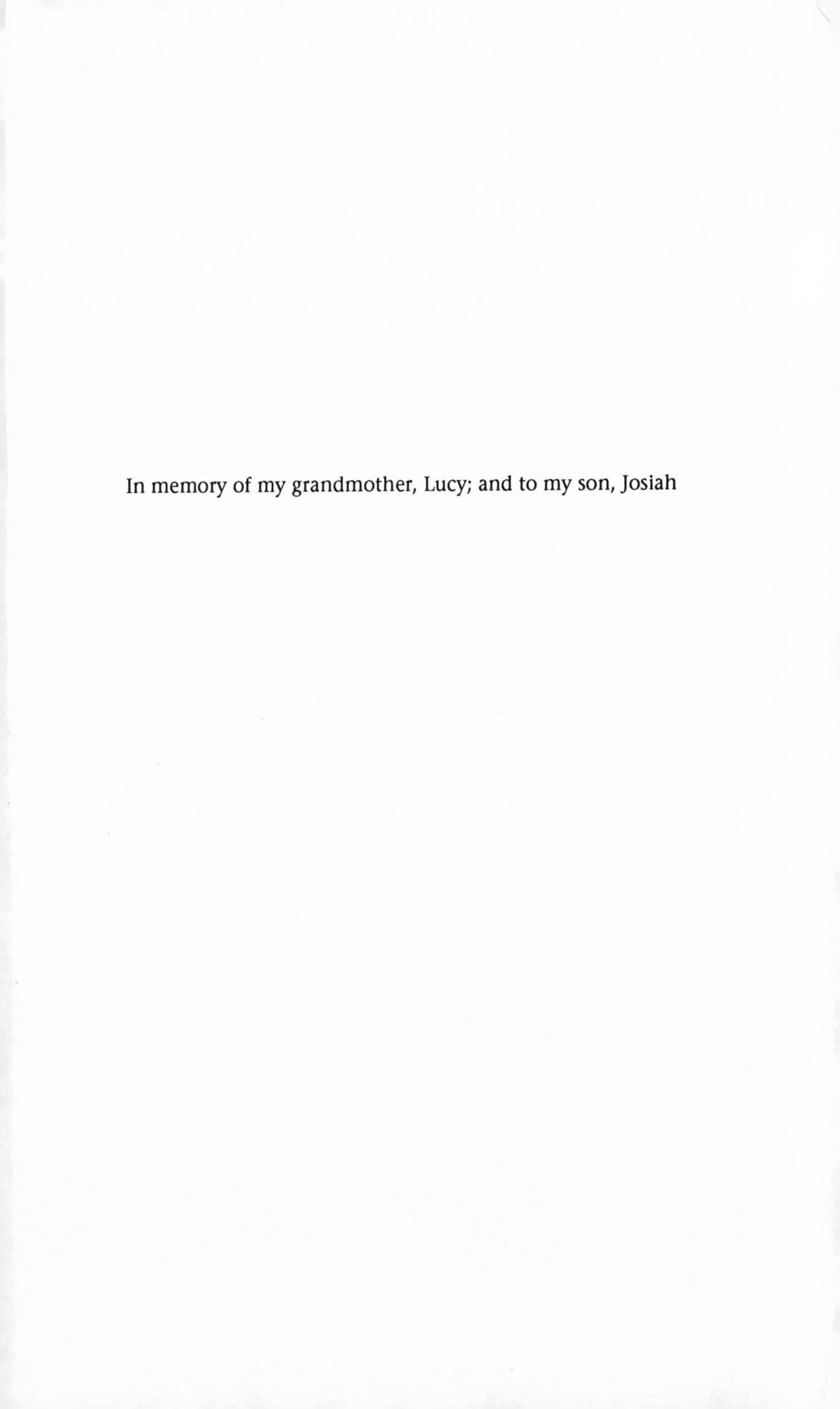

In memory of my grandmother, Lucy; and to my son, Josiah

What is Africa to me:
Copper sun or shining sea,
jungle star or jungle track,
strong bronzed men, or regal black
women from whose loins I sprang
When the birds of Eden sang?
One three centuries removed from the scenes his fathers loved,
Spicy grove, cinnamon tree
What is Africa to me?

— Countee Cullen, *Heritage*

Table of Contents

Preface:
What Africa is to Me

Within the providence of God, I, an African-American, attempt to explore in this book the redemptive, Pan-African implications of the African heritage. Africa invokes my sense of the theological implications of Amilcar Cabral's statement that Pan-Africanism "is a means of returning to the source."[1] Africa—despite its massive misery and awesome poverty—is a visible source of invisible ancestral legacies emblematic of the humanity of God.[2]

Ancestral legacies also connote contradictions, sometimes within a single individual, between alienation from and continuity with African heritages. The ancestors are not only progenitors of Niger-Congo heritages, they are also progenitors who separate themselves from those heritages. Thus, ancestral legacies refer to an inheritance entailing both the living memory of the ancestors' spirituality and the alienation from this memory as a result of slavery and colonialism.

In terms of alienation, ancestral legacies signify the thought of Eurocentric blacks such as Alexander Crummell. Indeed, alienation refers to internalization of mores that deform black consciousness into a crippling neurosis.[3]

In terms of continuity, ancestral legacies signify African peoples' redemptive resistance to "praxes of domination."[4] The "centrifugal force" of this popular resistance is redemptive, largely because it is hurled from values autonomous of the Eurocentric West.[5] These dynamic African values enshrine reverence for black life in a contemporary spirituality that appropriates elements of the past. Fundamental to this spirituality are continuities of the living and the dead, continuities sustained in successive generations.[6]

"Ancestral legacies," moreover, is a *symbolic* and therefore *mythic* idiom. To quote Mircea Eliade, "Perhaps the most important function of religious symbolism..*is its capacity for expressing paradoxical situations*, or certain structures of ultimate reality, otherwise quite inexpressible [emphasis added]."[7] In contexts that present continuity and alienation, the ancestors, as "great cultural symbols," heighten valorization of continuity—the "archaic" spirituality that sustains the liberation struggle.[8]

In its mythic dimension, the legacies of the ancestors signify a leitmotif that recreates the liberating meanings of the struggles of the African people. To quote Cedric Robinson, "without myths, that is without meaning, consciousness is set adrift into terror."[9]

This book seeks to focus black consciousness in terms of a hermeneutic inimical to the terror of Eurocentric praxes of domination. In the tradition of the ancestor Edward W. Blyden, I seek to define a Pan-African theology unvitiated by oppressive values. My goal is to articulate a perspective in "that fixed point of intellectual space where [a black theologian] stands to view the struggles, hopes and sufferings of his people."[10]

This book is a libation, so to speak, to the sacred memories of my ancestors buried in the United States and in the sacred richness of Africa's soil, whose names, languages, and gods I have yet to know.

Introduction: A Breakdown of Sections and Chapters

Part 1 of this text, entitled "Heritage: Return to the Source," constitutes Chapter 1, which explains the epistemic foundations, terminology and methodology I will employ in defining a Pan-African theology.

Part 2, entitled "Ancestor Theology: Legacies of a Pan-African Theology," is comprised of Chapters 2 and 3 and explores the historic contradiction in the idiom "ancestral legacies" in more detail. Part 2 is devoted to critical analyses of seminal clergy of the antebellum and postbellum periods who understood God's action in history in terms of a theodicy that defined Providence. Focusing on their understanding of Providence, I will abstract from these analyses issues to be developed in the third part of this work in a manner I think is significant for Pan-African Christians today.[1]

Part 3, entitled "The Invisible and the Invisible: the Providence of God," is a constructive exposition based on a hermeneutical paradigm of the Ecumenical Association of Third World Theologians (EATWOT).[2] The paradigm is tripartite and constitutes the dynamic circle of social and religio-cultural analyses that condition interpretations of Scripture and tradition.[3] In Chapter 4 I discuss the significance of social analysis in terms of the process of liberation and with a critical focus on the black underclass and the African peasantry. Chapter 5 discusses Pan-Africanization in terms of religio-cultural dimensions of the Pan-African experience. Focus here is on the relation of African traditional and black religions. I will also show in Chapter 5 that modalities of Afro-American music facilitate fresh conceptions of Pan-Africanization by way of a fresh conception of black religion. Chapter 6 discusses the meaning of revelation and Scripture, developing conclusions of Chapters 4 and 5. The meaning of the providence of God is reexplored in Chapter 7. I suggest that God, whose image has always been borne by the "old Africans," in Christ draws the African people close to the Divine. Joining the invisible to the visible, sanctifying the continuity of the ancestors, Providence restores a certain equilibrium facilitated by love of God and the African people. Focusing on the sanctifying work of the Spirit of transformation, I will also suggest in Chapter 7 the way in which blacks with a Pan-African consciousness must struggle practically for liberation.

Acknowledgement

One who thinks he is self-sufficient "is like the puppy who swings himself around and farts into a blazing fire with the aim to put it out." The ancestors compel me to acknowledge those who have helped me produce this book.

I should like to thank Kassahun Checole, Lynora Williams and Patricia Allen, of Africa World Press, for their support of my work. Steve Vecchietti retyped the manuscript for me and thus greatly facilitated its readiness for Africa World Press. Raymond Washington graciously photocopied many drafts.

Thanks are also due to my wife, Pamela Monroe. Her critical reading of the manuscript undoubtedly expedited its publication. In my quest to express why Africa's survival is indispensable for the world's redemption, Pamela, in having faith in me, has helped me keep the faith.

Several of my colleagues took time from their schedules to read and discuss the manuscript: Kelly Brown, James Cone, Donald Berry, James Logan, Philip Wogaman, John Godsey and James Shoeshire. I must thank Marjorie Suchocki for her belief in my work and unfailing encouragement. Emanuel Obiechina, my friend, and mentor in the Pan-African connection, talked at length with me about the project and encouraged me to seek its publication.

My mother Jacqueline also read the manuscript. I really appreciate her on-going interest in my work and edifying approval of my efforts. I must also honor my father, Josiah. His sagacity and blessing are legacies of the ancestors who sustain my love of truth and freedom.

I began to forge ideas for this book while teaching at Colgate University. There, students, such as Diane Stewart, Holly Smith, James Grooms, James Green, Adam Clark, Nicol Turner, Haley Thompson, Carla Beckford, Elizabeth Grossman, David Crittenden—and others—patiently listened to my ideas with respect. They continue to inspire me; they give me a vision of the "new humanity."

Finally, I must thank my son, Josiah Monroe Young. He has been very understanding and patient, although I spend too many weekends writing. This will soon change, "Mugu Muga."

A Pan-African Theology:
Providence and the Legacies of the Ancestors

Part 1
Heritage: Return to the Source

1.

Elements of a Pan-African Theology

Upon what would a theology of Pan-Africanism rest? How would it stand [epistemologically] and around what doctrinal themes would it revolve....I must explore these questions, at least provisionally.

Josiah Young
Black and African Theologies: Siblings or Distant Cousins?

In this chapter, I will discuss the epistemology, the methodology, and terminology of this book under the following headings:

1) Epistemic Foundations: Limitation of a Perspective;
2) Pan-African Theology: The Negation of Totality;
3) Pan-African Traditions;
4) Liberation & Pan-Africanization: Leitmotifs of a Pan-African Theology.

The Epistemic Foundation: Limitation of a Perspective

The fundamental critical principle of this text entails exegeses of ancestors of Pan-African theology. Their thoughts provide indispensable sources for construction of a contemporary Pan-African theology aware of its genealogy. The legacies they have bequeathed to African people must be critically evaluated; their theological insights must be developed in terms of the providence of God. These systematic issues are inextricable from the following ecclesiological goals: (1) to serve black churches in Africa and the Americas by way of a theological reflection that links the liberation struggles of the Pan-African community, and (2) to mark a certain development of black and African theologies from a Pan-African perspective.

The ancestors on whom I focus are clergy of the nineteenth century, Alexander Crummell and Edward Blyden. The list of ancestors of Pan-African theology is long. Maria Stewart, James Pennington, Majola Agbebei, James Holy Johnson, Samuel A. Crowther, Daniel Coker, Henry NcNeal Turner, Marcus Garvey, and others all deserve study. But I have chosen Crummell and Blyden, because, for my purposes, they embody the contradiction of ancestral legacies critically structuring my sense of the Pan-African experience.

Not unlike the way Africans have traditionally acknowledged their debt to their ancestors, I acknowledge my debt to Blyden and Crummell from whom the idea of Pan-African theology is in large measure taken.[1] And like the way in which Africans such as the Akan honor their ancestors with food and drink, I honor Crummell and Blyden with critical engagement of their thoughts. It is in that sense that the ancestors "are not under the earth," but "with us in the crowd." I propitiate them by attempting to contribute to the development of a Pan-African theology they presaged. Failure to wrestle with their ideas would result in a certain disequilibrium. A mere parroting of their ideas will be unacceptably chauvinistic to Africans. Lack of sustained analysis of their legacies weakens an historic bridge for a transatlantic theology. Neglect of these ancestors encourages ideological confusion and an ahistoric approach to theological reflection. Indeed, to quote Enrique Dussel: "Historical interpretation without a precise categorical framework [alienation and continuity] can fall into an historicism without a guiding hypothesis and, above all, without conclusions that elucidate a national and popular praxis of liberation."[2]

My analyses will set the contexts in which the ancestors reflected theologically, but are not merely confined to the context of the nineteenth and early twentieth centuries. Rather, the views of these ancestors encounter contemporary perspectives. The dialogue of the past and the present, the living and the dead, heightens appreciation of the themes of alienation and continuity within the Pan-African experience.

Black and African Theologies: Siblings of the Transatlantic World

The constructive principle of the text entails the abstraction and synthesis of perspectives of theologies of Africa and the United States. Indeed, this book is the sequel to my *Black and African Theologies: Siblings or Distant Cousins?* In that text, I proposed that a Pan-African theology is the logical, "transcontextual" discourse for those theologians of African descent whose interests are truly complementary.[3]

Fundamental to the development of my proposal are the black theologies of the United States and South Africa, already embarking upon a Pan-African enterprise, and a group of African theologians whom I call the new guard.[4] Among them are Mercy Oduyoye, Jean-Marc Éla, Engelbert Mveng, Eboussi Boulaga and Barthélemy Adoukonou. Allow me to digress briefly in order to explain the epistemological distinction between the old and new guards of African theology and its importance for Pan-African theology.

The New & Old Guards

The new guard draw close in praxis to black South African theologians, eschewing both the old guard's problematic focus on indigenization and exclusion of themes of liberation.[5] Giving too little attention to virulent problems of neocolonialism, the old guard focused on the *Christianization* of select aspects of African traditional religion. The old guard sought not to *Africanize* in a way truly emergent from popular culture, but to Christianize in a way dependent upon Eurocentric values and metropolitan support.[6] Indeed, the old guard's focus on African traditional religion was a modified continuum of a colonial missiology, which tended to view the primal religions of Africa from the bias of Euro-Christian worldviews.[7] The old guard reified the autochthonous meanings of ancestral values and failed to gauge the liberating meanings of those values resistant to colonial presences, particularly as found within the African independent churches.[8] Distinguishing themselves from black theologies of South Africa and the United States, the old guard did not define themselves as liberation theologians.[9]

Focusing on the problems of neocolonialism, the new guard, particularly Éla, Oduyoye, Englebert Mveng and Barthélemy Adoukonou, define themselves as liberation theologians.[10] They are critically conscious of Africanization — a process in which Christianity is absorbed into and transformed by African traditional cultures — at work in certain independent churches.[11] The new guard does not confuse Africanization with Christianization. Rather they view the two in distinction from each other, but in terms of an essential interrelation.

Contiguous with my interest in certain ancestral legacies, I examine the activities of the new guard in order to assimilate their paradigms of "Africanity" within dimensions of the African-American experience. Focus on the new guard's insights is critical as they have returned to the source, the black poor of Africa. In touch with the foundations of national cultures, the new guard's theology reveals the essential complementarity between political agitation and religio-cultural sensibility from which revolutionary resistance emerges.[12]

The new guard, moreover, such as Engelbert Mveng and Jean-Marc Éla, have aligned themselves with black theologians of South Africa and provide epistemological support for a Pan-African theology focused on liberation.[13] These theologians evince a solidarity in their commitment to a praxis emergent from popular culture and radical political theory.

Pan-African Theology: Negation of a Totality of Meaning

I do not argue that all theologians of African people subscribe to a Pan-African perspective. This text is neither definitive of, nor authoritative for the Pan-African implications of black religion. Black religion, from which much of this theology takes it substance, is a varied phenomenon. Although this Pan-African theology is significantly Christian, systematic reflection on Pan-African religion need not be defined in Christian symbols. One thinks immediately of Dr. Maulana Karenga and the *Husia*.[14] Black Muslims and black Jews could produce Pan-African theologies. Certainly, appreciation of the distinctions among religions of the Pan-African experience is necessary for any Pan-African discourse. A Pan-African theology must be malleable in the face of these distinctions, otherwise it can never effect a coalition of praxes of liberation, which is its goal. This theology seeks to valorize what blacks have in common: African descent, cultural modalities, and, especially among the poor, radical similarity in socioeconomic suffering. To insist inflexibly on the alleged ultimate values of a worldview makes transcontextual dialogue impossible and brings praxes of liberation into unprogressive conflict.

I focus on the transatlantic dimension of blacks of Africa and the United States. I am more familiar with the black experience of the United States and African history and culture than I am with the experiences of blacks of the Caribbean and South America. (I do, however, devote an entire chapter to a seminal progenitor of Pan-African tradition, Edward Blyden of St. Thomas, and know that much of Pan-African theory is owed to Jamaicans, i.e., Marcus Garvey and Harold Moody; and to Trinidadians, i.e., Sylvester Williams, C.L.R. James, and George Padmore.)[15]

I embark on no procrustean enterprise. I do not represent the totality of the Pan-African experience, which is a varied experience of oppressed women and men of diverse geopolitical contexts. I do not subscribe to the view that the African people have the same destiny. I have no way of knowing whether that is true. The African people are too diverse to assume teleological homogeneity. Within the Pan-African experience, material contradictions undermine the view that African people penultimately have the same destiny. *A Pan African Theology: Providence and the Legacy of the Ancestors* is limited in scope and narrowly defined, but emerges from Pan-African traditions.[16]

Pan-African Traditions

The seminal Pan-Africanism was the Pan-Africanism of the slaves.[17] Fundamentally, Pan-African traditions emerged from the slave cultures of the New World, from a condensation of values resistant to the oppressive power of Eurocentrism. These values were continuous with the cosmologies of the ancestors as they were emergent from essentially African worldviews.[18] Despite the distinctions among Africans enslaved from diverse areas of Africa, their cosmologies were similar enough to facilitate in the Americas a Pan-Africanism that gave impetus to both the forging of New World cultures and rebellion.[19]

The American matrix, which accounts, then and now, for differences among Africans and African-Americans, does not obscure the fact of an autonomous clustering of Pan-African values. As Sterling Stuckey explains, "when African values were drawn on, there was no necessary opposition between being African and having command of or responding to the values of another [American] people."[20] According to Stuckey, "small numbers of Africans were sufficient to constitute the 'critical mass' for the retention of essentials of African [traditional] religion in slavery." Moreover, initiation of youth into African-American culture, "rich in artistic and spiritual content...guarantees its presence in consciousness, and to a considerable extent, in behavior, for a lifetime."[21] Many "saltwater" Africans' vivid memories of their ancestral ways have been passed down to posterity.

The continuum of the legacies of the ancestors, in addition, influenced the consciousness of "free" blacks who, while constituting a different class from the enslaved, were surely of similar caste as the slaves in relation to whites. Manumitted blacks, such as Olaudah Equiano and Ottobah Cugoano, born in Africa, sold into slavery, and later Christianized, agitated for a return to black Africa, as did the North American Quaker Paul Cuffe.[22] A seminal ancestor of Pan-Africanism, Cuffe was born in the Americas. He was nonetheless probably aware of African values. Cuffe's father, for instance, in all likelihood from the Gold Coast, conceivably exposed Paul to the African values that influenced Paul's commitment to emigration.[23] Cuffe's proximity to slave culture undoubtedly heightened his awareness of the difference of African people from Euro-Americans and gave substance to his Pan-African sentiments.[24] African people of the Diaspora saw themselves as African people whose destiny was linked to the redemption of Africa.

From at least the seventeenth to the end of the nineteenth century, the oneness of African people in the West was expressed in terms of abolition, emigration, assimilation and Christianization. Those impulses toward assimilation, emigration, and Christianization, however, indicated a certain alienation from the African Heritage. As I will show later, evidence of this alienation is found in a relatively elite group of black clergy who embraced Africa in terms of Eurocentric mores that vitiated their pro-African theologies. Indeed, much of the history of Pan-Africanism reveals a perspective that gives little thought to the more liberating trajectory of popular culture, as found for instance in the thoughts of Paul Robeson and Amilcar Cabral.[25]

Preceded by notions of Pan-Negroism, which were influenced by pandemic European movements, the word "Pan-Africanism" appears to have been used for the first time in 1893 at the Chicago congress attended by clergy such as Alexander Crummell and Bishops Henry McNeal Turner and Alexander Walters.[26] Prior to the twentieth century, Pan-Africanism was expressed in theological terms, emphasizing Providence. After the deaths of clergy such as Blyden, Majola Agbebi, Henry McNeal Turner, and Alexander Walters, the theological expression of Pan-Africanism appears to have been significantly curtailed by secular expressions.

At the dawning of this century, Pan-African tradition was expressed in various publications, such as *The African Times* and *Orient Review* and represented by organizations, such as the Pan-African Association. Heavily represented by blacks from the United States and the West Indians living in London, Pan-Africanism focused on the mistreatment of Africans of the Diaspora and the problems of the colonization of Africa. A historic Pan-African Conference was convened in 1900 in London.[27] W.E.B. DuBois, who attended that conference with Sylvester Williams and Bishop Walters, was to become after World War I the driving force of four Pan-African Congresses.[28] During the periods between 1919 and 1945, London was a center of Pan-African organizations such as the West African Student Association, the League of Colored People and the Pan-African Federation. This period also saw the waxing and waning of the UNIA and the publication the *Negro World*, both of which were led by Marcus Garvey, whose Back to Africa Movement was preceded by that of Chief Albert Sam.[29] The Council on African Affairs, founded by Paul Robeson, also reveals the Pan-African consciousness of black North America.[30] In Paris, the *Négritude* movement of Maran, Césaire, and Senghor was represented by the publication of *La Race Nègre* and the organization *Ligue de Défense de la race Nègre.*[31] In Africa, Pan-Africanism was represented by the National Congress of British West Africa.[32] In 1945, the so-called Fifth Pan-African Congress was convened in

Manchester.[33] Although Dr. DuBois was present, the driving force behind the Fifth Congress was a group of militant blacks from the West Indies and Africa, especially the socialists George Padmore, C.L.R. James, and Kwame Nkrumah. The Fifth Congress marks the shift in leadership of Pan-Africanism from blacks of the Diaspora to black Africans, ushering in the burgeoning movement — centered in the Gold Coast and led by Kwame Nkrumah — which modified colonialism.

In 1957, with the independence of the Gold Coast, renamed Ghana, and most of black Africa's swift devolution to "independence" shortly thereafter, Pan-African traditions were represented by valences related to an alliance of African states or a union of African states.[34] Ideological conflicts, such as those embodied among the representatives of the Casablanca Declaration and the Monrovia Declaration, were subsumed, but not resolved, in the troubled Organization of African Unity (OAU) in 1963.[35]

Although with "independence" Pan-Africanism focused on issues related to Africa, the movement continued to have vitality in the Diaspora. Notable here are so-called neo-Pan-Africanists, such as Kwame Touré (Stokely Carmichael), who were in large measure products of the Civil Rights and Black Power movements and allegedly beset by a truncated vision of Pan-African theory.[36]

A Sixth Pan-African Congress was convened in Dar Es Salaam in 1974. According to one source, this Congress, unlike the one in 1945, was marked by ideological confusion. "There were Ghanaian nationalists and American integrationists, Euro-Africans, black capitalist and Marxist-Leninists, and neo-colonial compradors. The result of this was that instead of being a meeting of people sharing the same ideological orientation, the Congress turned out to be a confrontation between diverse ideological groups."[37]

Certainly, as I have noted, Pan-Africanism hardly means one thing. Even if one assumes an ideological consensus among revolutionary Pan-Africanists, nuances of meaning are bound to emerge. Nonetheless, the fact remains that Pan-Africanism has a long history and is part of the consciousness of African people. C.L.R. James put it this way:

> The history of the Negro in his relation to European civilization falls into two division, the Negro in Africa and the Negro in America and the West Indies. Up to the eighties of the last century, only one-tenth of Africa was in the hands of Europeans. Until that time, therefore, it is the attempt of the Negro in the Western world to free himself from his burdens which has political significance in Western history. In the last quarter of the nineteenth century European civilization turned again to Africa this time not for slaves to work the plantations of America, but for actual control of territory and population. Today, the positions of Africans in Africa is one of the major problems of contemporary politics.[38]

In the tradition of James, I understand Pan-Africanism to be a very rational, if diverse, response to white domination. The assertion of the German historian, Imanuel Geiss, that Pan-Africanism is basically an irrational constellation of ideas is false.[39]

Liberation and Pan-Africanization: Hermeneutical Leitmotifs of a Pan-African Theology

P. Olisanwuche Esedebe's definition of Pan-Africanism is relevant to formal thematic principles from which this theology takes its redemptive substance. According to Esedebe:

> Pan-Africanism is a political and cultural phenomenon which regards Africa, Africans and African descendants abroad as a unit. It seeks to regenerate and unify Africa and promote a feeling of oneness among the people of the African world. It glorifies the African past and inculcates pride in African values.[40]

I do not, however, glorify the African past. Glorification of a past is fraught with idolatrous implications. Esedebe, however, notes the critical *political* and *cultural* dimensions of the Pan-African theology I envision. Political and cultural dimensions signify the processes of *liberation* and *Pan-Africanization.* Both distinctly complementary terms will be consistently held together in order to employ hermeneutics of the Pan-African experience. Reference to liberation and Pan-Africanization will accent historical and political similarities as well as religio-cultural affinities among people of African descent, rooting this theology in Pan-African and Judeo-Christian traditions. Indeed, liberation and Pan-Africanization define, in terms of the interrelation of social and religio-cultural analyses and Afro-Christian exegesis, a hermeneutical cycle of living, dying and rebirth within the Pan-African experience. In order to avoid later misunderstanding as to what I mean by liberation and Pan-Africanization, I should now like to briefly discuss these processes.

Liberation signifies the participation of the oppressed in what they believe to be God's opposition to oppressive praxes. Liberation in this text refers to an option for the African-American underclass and the black African peasants. Mutually corrective interaction of theological reflection and radical activism can effect liberation, indicating a redemptive way of formulating theology. In praxis, Scripture and tradition are subjected to hermeneutics guided by an eschatology eschewing vulgar reform.

Emergent from a consciousness sensitive to the sin of deifying its worldview, the struggle for liberation does not just expose the systemic evil of Eurocentrism. Liberation means that Providence is inimical to all oppression, including the oppression perpetuated by blacks and Soviet expansionists.[41] Much of Pan-African theology, however, must focus on the problems of white supremacist capitalism, as the West is the dominant hegemonic force that continues to victimize the African people of the Americas and South Africa and subject the rest of black Africa to neocolonialism. Indeed, this problem is critical for obtaining historic insight into Pan-African perspectives. (My indictment of white supremacists does not of necessity implicate all whites. Nonetheless, if the majority of whites, either unconsciously or consciously, were not white supremacists, the problem would not be such a hegemonic, oppressive force.) The ugly problem of white supremacy is inextricably linked to an unscrupulous occupation with surplus, profit, and the disequilibrium of surplus value. Inasmuch as God stands against such exploitation, I must clearly state what God rejects and the plight of those whom God supports.

In focusing on liberation, I will attempt to draw out specific implications of the hermeneutical principle, *social analysis*.[42] Social analysis includes levels of examination of distinct contradictions of an unjust international matrix. Social analysis focuses on the contradictions of given contexts in order to demarcate theo-political options related to the liberation of the oppressed. Indeed, a liberation theology, writes Juan Luis Segundo,

> consciously and explicitly accepts its relationship with politics. First of all, it incorporates into its own methodology the task of ideological analysis...situated on the boundary...between sociology and politics. And insofar as direct politics is concerned, it is more concerned about avoiding the (false) impartiality of academic theology than it is about taking sides and consequently giving ammunition to those who accuse it of partisanship.[43]

Direct politics, that is partisanship, signifies here a *trans-contextual* perspective.

A transcontextual perspective focuses on diverse situations and seeks to transform them in a praxis that does not annul the distinctiveness of those situations. Pan-African theology seeks to join distinct options for the poor in order to see, through them, the benefits of black solidarity. A cardinal benefit is a dual, if ambivalent, resistance to structures responsible for the oppression of African people. Among African people a Pan-African praxis requires transcendence of indigenous contexts in order to forge a creative alliance against imperial forces. To the extent, then, that the black North American underclass and the African peasantry complement each other in the struggle for liberation, they constitute a "transcontext" that illuminates the Pan-African meaning of liberation. It bears repeating that the juxtaposition of these oppressed people does not obfuscate their disparate realities, though they are fairly equally victimized by the hegemonic West.

Liberation also signifies black nationalism.[44] Certain black nationalists, who are often Pan-Africanists, have refused to parrot assumptions of Eurocentric civilization. Those who try to totalize others in terms of Eurocentric thought too often obscure that, within the providence of God, civilization is composite. Civilization is not only "Euro," but unquestionably "Afro" as well.

For their refusal to acquiesce in Eurocentric hegemony, black nationalists have suffered from the inept charge of reverse racism. No truly freedom-loving person, however, should be put off by that charge. Black nationalism is not "tribalism," leading to xenophobia and hate-mongering.

Pan-Africanization means that blacks in quest of liberation must do theology by way of ancestral symbols that structure their essential humanity. Pan-Africanization embodies social analyses, but is defined by *religio-cultural* analyses that also reflect the relativity of the Pan-African experience.[45] Seeking to broach differences in a flexible consciousness receptive to the nuances of black existence, Pan-Africanization heightens appreciation of the religio-cultural affinities of Africans and African-Americans. I define Pan-Africanization broadly in order to bring out the many implications of a transcontextual consciousness. Thus, Pan-Africanization indicates the processes of Africanization and African-Americanization.

Africanization, also known as indigenization, refers, as I have noted, to a process entailing the absorption and the transformation of Christianity by religio-cultural modalities of Africa. I have also noted that the old guard defined their theologies in terms of indigenization rather than liberation. Basically, they interpreted elements of African traditional religion in terms of systematic theology in order to facilitate the Christianization of the grassroots of national culture and the neocolonial explication of the so-called African personality.[46] It bears reiteration that they did not clarify the distinction between acculturation (Africanization) and inculturation (Christianization). The distinction is more satisfactorily realized in the work of new guard theologians such as Mercy Oduyoye.

According to Mercy Oduyoye, acculturation refers "to the efforts of Africans to use things African in their practice of Christianity, inculturation [refers to] the manifestation of changes that have come into the African way of life as a result of the Christian faith."[47] An *African* Christianity, then, emerges from the acculturative power of ancestral legacies that resist alienating, Eurocentric values as significant themes of the Christian story modify, enrich and regenerate ancestral values.

I understand acculturation as the *spontaneous* force of traditional values that naturalizes missionary Christianity within the substratum of national culture. This grassroots process is observed within the African independent churches. Among Bakongo influenced regions of Zaire, for instance, "Kimbanguism" has represented an African Christianity precisely because of the preponderance of things African in its expression. Inculturation signifies the Christianization of traditional BaKongo religion, without obscuring the acculturative force of ancestral values.[48] Without inculturation, African *theology* is not Christian; without acculturation, Christian theology is not *African*.

African-Americanization must be understood in relation to the fact that blacks are so-called minorities in the United States. Indeed, acculturation in the United States seems to refer to the predominance of European elements — given the white majority — such as Euro-Christianity, the English language, dress, and harmony. Inculturation — divested for the moment of its Christian implications — seems to refer to the influence African elements have exerted upon Euro-American culture. It would appear, then, that Europeanization is to acculturation as African-Americanization is to inculturation. Yet such distinctions, between Afro-American and Euro-American cultures, are overly reductionistic and obfuscate the interrelation of the American masses. From at least the seventeenth century to the present, African, Amerindian and European elements have mutually conditioned one another. Black culture, for instance, is distinct from white and Amerindian cultures, but bears marks of their influence. The complexity of cultural nuances in North America frustrates assertions that there is in the black community a direct analogy to Africanization as there is no "pure" African culture. Nonetheless African-Americanization is at work.

Appreciation of the Africanity of American culture is heightened in appreciation of specific modalities — such as the Sanctified church and expressions of black music. Among the black underclass, polyrhythm, polyphony, a "blue" timbre, other poetic modes, patterns of community organization, patterns of speech — all indicate the dynamic persistence of the African heritage and condition and transform the meanings of popular Christianity within the black community. Popular Christianity, moreover, is part of a larger religious complex indicative of nuances of Afro-American culture, namely black religion. Black religion is the progeny of the slaves bearing cultural legacies of Africa. In its diverse expressions among the poor, black religion reveals an otherness distinct from Euro-Christianity.

African-Americanization neither implies that everything distinctive about African-American cultures is traceable to ancestral legacies nor that religio-cultural realities of Africa are relevant to African-Americans by the very nature of the case itself.

It is important to remember that Pan-Africanization signifies the critical juxtaposition of African-Americanization and Africanization. The juxtaposition constitutes a hermeneutic emergent from a religio-cultural analysis that is based on a transcontextual perspective. Frequent reference to elements gleaned from African traditional religion, African independent churches, black religion, and African-American music, especially jazz, will be conjoined to suit the purposes of this theology.

I turn now to Part one of this text, "Ancestor Theology: Legacies of Pan-African Theology" and begin with an analysis of the legacy of Alexander Crummell.

Part 2
Ancestor Theology: Legacies of a Pan-African Theology

2.

Alexander Crummell (1819-1898):

Two Warring Ideals in One Dark Body

After the Egyptian and Indian, the Greek and Roman, the Teuton and Mongolian, the Negro is a sort of seventh son, born with a veil, and gifted with second-sight in this American world, — a world which yields him no true self-consciousness, but only lets him see himself through the revelation of the other world. It is a peculiar sensation, this double-consciousness, this sense of always looking at one's self through the eyes of others, of measuring one's soul by the tape of a world that looks on in amused contempt and pity. One ever feels his twoness, — an American, a Negro; two souls, two thoughts, two unreconciled striving; two warring ideals in one dark body, whose dogged strength alone keeps it from being torn asunder.

— W.E.B. DuBois, *The Souls of Black Folk*

For I do not the good I want, but the evil I do not want I do.

— Romans, 7:19

W.E.B. DuBois reveals, in the epigraph above, an Afro-American neurosis applicable to Alexander Crummell, a great but misguided ancestor of Pan-African theology.[1]

More specifically, Professor DuBois, in his *Souls of Black Folk*, had this to say of Crummell:

> Tall, frail and black he stood, with simple dignity and an unmistakable air of good breeding. I spoke to him....eagerly, as I began to feel the fineness of his character — his calm courtesy, the sweetness of his strength, and his fair blending of the hope and truth of life. Instinctively I bowed before this man, as one bows before the prophets of the world. Some seer he seemed, that came not from the crimson past or the gray To-Come, but from the pulsing Now, that mocking world which seemed to me at once so light and dark, so splendid and sordid. Four score years had he wandered in this same world of mine, within the veil.[2]

No critical view of Crummell can diminish the radiance of his life of Christian service and his optimism for the future. Crummell "never faltered, he seldom complained; he simply worked, inspiring the young, rebuking the old, helping the weak, guiding the strong."[3]

Well known, though, is that Alexander Crummell's theology is too frequently unsatisfactory today for blacks with a correct image of Africa. Priested in the Anglican church in 1844, Crummell went to Cambridge, England to study at Queens College from which he graduated in 1853. That same year he emigrated to

Liberia. Living in Liberia for twenty years as an educator and missionary, Crummell was part of an oppressive settler regime founded in 1822 under the auspices of the American Colonization Society (ACS).[4] Disillusioned with the "'constant enmity and opposition' of mulattoes," Crummell left Liberia for good in 1873.[5] Serving as Rector of St. Luke's Church in Washington, D.C., and founding the American Negro Academy, he lived in the United States until his death. My exegesis of his thought, however, focuses on his Liberian years. Specifically I will examine his notion of Providence in terms of The Redemption of Africa; The Anglo-Saxon Tongue; African Traditional Religion, Slave Culture and the Missionaries; and African History.

The Redemption of Africa

"All human events," writes Crummell, "have their place in that grand moral economy of God."[6] Even evil, asserts Crummell, drawing upon the story of Joseph and his brothers, is used by God in the service of a benevolent purpose. The story of Joseph, Crummell writes, suggests "the forced and cruel migration of our race from [Africa], and the wondrous providence of God, by which the sons of Africa...trained, civilized, and enlightened, are coming hither again; bringing large gifts, for Christ and his church, and their heathen kin!"[7] Although slavery was an evil institution, God, asserts Crummell, intended that its end would result in Africa's redemption. For Crummell, God allowed Africans to be enslaved in the Americas as part of a providential plan to redeem "pagan" Africa with Christianity. Accepting Christianity, the Africans would become enlightened and refined.

According to Crummell,

> the children of Africa have been called, in the Divine Providence, to meet the demands of civilization, of commerce, and of nationality; and...to grapple with the problems which pertain to responsible manhood, to the great work of civilization, to the duties and requirements of national life, and the solemn responsibility of establishing the Christian faith amid the rude forms of paganism.[8]

Slavery, for Crummell, was the beginning phase of Africa's redemption.

Crummell supported his view of Providence by appealing to Exodus. In Exodus, enslavement is preparation for the redemptive practices of colonization and emigration, which were synonymous terms for Crummell.[9] Drawing on Deuteronomy, in addition, Crummell likens the "Jacobites'" uncertainty before they entered Canaan to African-Americans' apprehension prior to their emigration to Liberia. The successful conquest of Canaan, like the successful conquest of Liberia, reveals the meaning of Providence. Crummell claims that "the hand of God was upon the [Jacobites]; and when the hand of God is upon a people it is destiny, and they cannot resist it."[10] Similarly, he thought God's hand was upon the Americo-Liberian settlers.

Crummell also thought that Western support of African-American emigration would lead to the advancement of peace and justice. "The providences of God," he claims, "have placed the Negro race, before Europe and America, in the most commanding position."[11] By way of African people, God, he thought, would test the readiness of the leading European powers to join in the regeneration of Africa, which would advance the cause of "BROTHERHOOD AND HUMANITY."[12]

Crummell's vision of a "beloved community" is edifying. Tolerating the fact of pluralism and benefitting from the healthiness of relativity, Pan-African theology should advance the quest for a new humanity. I agree with Crummell that the "relations which nations bear to the whole family of man in the aggregate, attest this obligation, and press this duty."[13] Crummell is right: "there is a relation between individual, distinctive, nationalities, and the entire race."[14] He writes:

> The endless migrations, the strange wanderings, the multitudinous progenitures [sic], and the colonial formations which have originated the nations of the earth, eschew the idea of isolation, and show that all are but fragments, separate, broken, detached, from some large parent form, itself of like origin, which has spread itself out, on every side, the common mother of nations and races. For such is the light which shines even from the gloom of history:

> from one single pair and parentage — a race; from the dawn of time to the days of Noah.[15]

Crummell's biblical view of the common ancestry of humankind indicates the truthfulness of myth.[16] Indeed, Genesis is indispensable for a contemporary anthropology which seeks to define Covenant relationships within the providence of God.

Crummell's understanding of Providence, however, was taught to him by white men believing in a hierarchy of "races" rather than the oneness of the human race. Certain of these men founded the ACS, an organization whose motives were not substantially, if at all, benevolent.[17] The extent to which Crummell's image of Africa is unsatisfactory today is proportionate to the extent his thought is a product of white supremacist estimates of the value of African people.

For Crummell, nations "must have either a free system or a repressive one."[18] He writes:

> Behind our settlements, on the St. Paul, there is the most heterogeneous mixture conceivable, of divers tribes and families, who have thus sought the protection of our commonwealth. Numbers of the Bassas, Veys, Deys Golahs and especially the PESSAS, the hereditary slaves of the interior, have thus come to our immediate neighborhoods. Although I am doubtful of the moral effect of this movement on ourselves [the Americo-Liberians], yet I feel no little pride in the fact that this young nation should become, so early, a land of refuge, an asylum for the oppressed! And I regard it as a singular providence, that the very time our government was trumpeted abroad as implicated in the slave trade, our magistrates, in the upper counties, were adjudicating cases of runaway slaves, and declaring to interior slaveholders that, *on our soil*, they could not reclaim their fugitives.[19]

"I call that a free system," asserts Crummell, "which guarantees universal personal freedom [and]...allows no shackles to fetter the mind."[20] Unfortunately, Crummell's mind was fettered by a European notion of civilization. Crummell did not see how he oppressed those he would liberate in attempting to force alienating values on African cultures comprised of at least three language groups: (1) Mende speaking peoples, such as the Mandingo, Vai, Mende and Gbandi; (2) West Atlantic speaking peoples, such as Gola and Kissi; and (3) Kwa speaking peoples, such as the Bassa, Dey, Grebu, Kru and Belle.[21]

Colonization in Liberia, and in Sierra Leone, did indeed mitigate the slave trade.[22] It would appear that in Monrovia, the capital of Liberia, God was at work against slavery. But to claim without qualification that Liberia was an asylum of the oppressed is ahistorical — the views of Padmore and DuBois notwithstanding.[23] Critical study of the rule of the Americo-Liberians from 1822 to the rise of Colonel Doe in Liberia reveals that Americo-Liberian rule was oppressive.[24]

Indeed, in an address Crummell made to young men of Liberia in 1863, he glorifies the shameful confrontations between African-American colonists and Africans. "On the 1st December, 1822," Crummell writes, "a few brave colonists were beset by hosts of infuriate savages intent upon the complete destruction of the weak, sickly, and enfeebled settlement which was then encamped upon Fort Hill."[25] Crummell points out how the Africans were about to vanquish the colonists when:

> one of those events, as beautiful and poetic as it was decisive...secured the fortune of the day. A female colonist by the name of Mary [Matilda?] Newport, seeing the perilous position of the settlers, snatches a match and applies it to a cannon now held by the enemy and scatters death among hundreds of the native foe; courage fires in the bosom of the gallant colonists. Once more they pour united fire into the scattered ranks of their adversaries; they stagger in their course; they turn in despair from their aroused and valiant victims; they flee, broken and defeated, into the wilderness; and from that day supremacy and might have ever crowned the hill of Monrovia and sent their influence abroad along the whole line of our coast.[26]

Crummell claims that the violence of the settlers against the Africans, who justifiably sought to defend *their* land, was necessary to spread the Christian faith. "It was," he writes, "no less than to set up a civilized nationality...amid the relics of barbarism, and to extend the blessings of Christian enlightenment among these rude people, their, and our own kinsmen."[27]

Like white oppressors who partitioned Africa, Crummell argues "historic fact shows that force, that is authority, *must* be used in the guardianship over heathen tribes."[28] According to Crummell, such force is legitimate only if it is *"the forces of restoration and progress."*[29] For Crummell, legitimate force "anticipates the insensate ferocity of the pagan, by demonstrating the blessedness of permanent habitation and lasting peace; which forestalls a degrading ignorance and superstition, by the enlightenment of schools and training...which nullifies and uproots a gross heathen domesticity by elevating women and introducing the idea of family and home."[30]

Unable to appreciate the profound African sense of family and home, Crummell advocated destruction of values indispensable for African well-being. He really believed that his settler theology would in practice have avoided the wars with the Bassa in 1861 and 1866. Conflicts, however, between the settlers and African cultures would emerge precisely because of a Eurocentric notion of Providence. In his benevolent denigration of African traditional life, Crummell pitted one religion against another, one civilization against another. Tragically, he made no attempt to coexist with African traditional societies in a way continuous with the legacy of his African ancestors. To that extent, Crummell's theology serves the process that keeps Africa a slave to the West. His motives differ from those of European settlers — such as those in South Africa and Kenya. But, he operated with many of the same assumptions, including the view that the bloody wrenching of the land from those to whom it has belonged for centuries is the privilege of the Christian elect.[31]

Crummell staunchly supported settler efforts to push inland.[32] He claims Americo-Liberians should be vexed "that the wealth of... [their] Africa, should make *other* men [sic] wealthy and not [themselves]."[33] His statement is like that of British imperialists. Indeed, for Crummell, the colonization of Liberia was similar to the mission of the English in India.[34] His imbibition of certain Western values prevented him from soberly seeing how those values were oppressive. Crummell reveals the truth of the biblical idiom that is often the evil that we would not do that we do.

Crummell attempted to do good in advocating what he thought was best for the Africans. He holds that the Africans' assimilation of Western culture and Americo-Liberians' judicious use of African labor would make the Africans the equals of the settlers. Crummell even chastises the settlers, arguing that the disparity between the settlers and the Africans led the former to exaggerate their abilities, making them "oblivious of [their] own humbling antecedents."[35] He then criticizes Americo-Liberians for not more thoroughly undermining traditional African culture. "See," he writes, "how carelessly, thoughtlessly, we have ignored the *national* obligation to train, educate, civilize, and regulate the heathen tribes around us."[36] Crummell, revealing the influence of the British philosopher, John Stuart Mill, writes that Americo-Liberians have the "stern necessity of assuming...the childhood of the natives; and, consequently [Americo-Liberian] responsibility of guardianship over them."[37]

I have noted that Crummell's motives differ from the whites who colonized Africa. Indeed, Crummell was critical of white supremacy, even though aspects of his legacy evince its tragic ramifications. On the one hand, he upholds the cultural and political and religious superiority of Anglo-Saxons; on the other, he is critical of white supremacists' denigration of blacks. Slavery, for him, was not merely providential, but also very wicked. Speaking to an assembly of African-Americans, Crummell states:

> We are here a motley group, composed, without doubt, of persons of almost every tribe in West Africa, from Goree to the Congo. Here are descendants of Jalofs, Fulahs, Mandingoes, Sussus, Timmanees, Veys, Congos; with a large intermixture, everywhere, of Anglo-Saxon, Dutch, Irish, French and Spanish blood — a slight mingling of the Malayan, and a dash, every now and then, of American Indian.
>
> ...Our very speech is indicative of sorrowful history; the language we use tells of subjection and of conquest. No people lose their native tongue without the bitter trail of hopeless struggles, bloody strife, heart-breaking despair,

> agony, and death!...But this fact of humiliation seems to have been one of those ordinances of Providence, designed as a means for the introduction of new ideas into the language of a people; to serve, as the transitional step from low degradation to a higher and nobler civilization.[38]

Crummell was quick to defend his so-called Negro race, and would debate dilettantes dedicated to diatribes on black inferiority.

For Crummell, slavery, not the alleged inferiority of blacks, was a cause of black deprivation in the United States. According to Crummell, slavery never "raised up anywhere an intelligent, thrifty, productive peasantry! Never built up a single Negro institution of any value....Never produced a single scientific or scholarly or learned black man!"[39] Rather, claims Crummell, slavery has produced "darkness, degradation, semi-barbarism, immorality, agonies, and death!"[40] Although Crummell failed to see the redemptive meaning of slave culture, he surely does not always blame the victims for the dehumanization they suffered.[41] Thus, although Crummell embraced alienating values, he was essentially committed to the view that blacks are equal to whites in the eyes of God. Despite enslavement in the West, Crummell insists that the "negro race is a living, not a dead race — alive in the several respects of industry, acquisitiveness, education, and religious aspiration."[42] He attributes the remarkable resiliency of blacks to a savior, "who has wrought out a most gracious and saving Providence."[43]

That Crummell would defend African-Americans but seek to raze their African roots contradicts his assertion that blacks are a living "race." Blacks who depreciate their African ancestry desiccate their life-sustaining roots. Evident again is how Crummell unwittingly fights against himself, but without subscribing to notions of the genetic inferiority of blacks. I must stress that this deformed conception of Providence signifies Crummell's attempt to deal creatively with the problem of theodicy. Indeed, how does one reconcile faith in Providence within the oppressive milieu in which that faith is learned? The opacity of the problem of theodicy endures, and I appreciate Crummell's eschatological effort to make the benevolence of God transparently clear: "You meant it for evil but God meant it for good."

The Anglo-Saxon Tongue

Responding to a question as to the meaning of Providence, Crummell writes:

> The only way in which, in a fit manner, I can answer this question is, by inquiring into the respective values of our native and our acquired tongue. Such a contrast will set before us the problem of "Loss and Gain" which is involved therein. The worth of our father's language will, in this way, stand out in distinct comparison with the Anglo-Saxon tongue,our acquired speech.[44]

Crummell concludes with Dr. Leighton Wilson — a scholar of the nineteenth century whose archaic views on Africa represent bad scholarship — that West African languages "...[are] harsh, abrupt, energetic, indistinct in enunciation, meager in point of words, abound with inarticulate nasal and guttural sounds, possess but few inflections and grammatical forms, and are withal exceedingly difficult of acquisition."[45] "As the speech of rude barbarians," writes Crummell, "[West African languages] are marked by brutal and vindictive sentiments, and those principles which show a predominance of the animal propensities."[46] He presumes that African languages are base compared to Western chirographic languages. Indeed, Crummell thinks African languages are hardly able to express the truths of liberty. The English language, for Crummell, however, "is characteristically the language of freedom."[47]

He believes "love of liberty is inwrought in the very fibre and substance of the body and blood of all people; but the flames burn dimly in some races."[48] The flame, for Crummell, burns especially dimly in the Africans, but especially brightly in the Anglo-Saxons.[49] Crummell claims that the British are:

> scattered, in our own day, all over the globe, in the Great Republic, in numerous settlements, and great colonies, themselves the germs of mighty empires; see how they have carried with them everywhere, on earth, the same,

> high, masterful, majestic spirit of freedom...which makes them giants among whatever people they settle, whether in America, India, or Africa....[50]

The British passion for freedom, asserts Crummell, is so strong that it undermines their proclivities toward hatred of inferiority and tendencies to condone caste.[51] As examples of British magnanimity, Crummell cites the example of abolition in England, and in South Africa.[52]

Crummell, then, understood the redemption of Africa in Victorian terms, which he thought expressed the eternal reality of Freedom. For Crummell, Anglo-Saxon culture contained the memory of quintessential Ideas that Africans had to assimilate if they were to be liberated. He, in part, attributed the blessedness of Victorian culture to his perception of the Africans' identification of the English language with emancipation.[53] African resistances to Americo-Liberian rule, however, evince Crummell's view here is distorted. Guerrilla assaults of the Gola, Grebo and Kru peoples upon Americo-Liberian settlers exemplify historic resistances to the importation of an alien culture.[54]

Indeed, in his ode to the Anglo-Saxon tongue, Crummell condones cultural imperialism in a way that would be opposed to the Third World consciousness expressed today in the Ecumenical Association of Third World Theologians (EATWOT).[55] African languages are not less valuable than languages signifying different historical experiences. Which languages, tied to their matrices, are normative outside of their contexts, epistemologically, philosophically, theologically?[56]

In Anglophone territories of the twentieth century, it is true, the English language expressed the rhetoric of independence. That rhetoric formally expresses either a radical Marxist-Leninism or a bourgeois liberalism, which the upper echelons of national culture convey to the masses.[57] Varieties of democratic rhetoric, however, neither deprivilege nor devalue symbols of resistance among the African peasantry. Freedom languages are hardly adventitious to Africa. The freedom fighters of PAIGC and FRELIMO, for instance, speak the language of revolution in autochthonous dialects.[58] Their non-Western approach to freedom has yet to be sufficiently appreciated by captives of Eurocentric language. In their particular case, imported tongues, such as Portuguese, are not freedom languages. Crummell's legacy here is of no positive value to the political process that Cabral defines as "re-Africanization."[59]

I must continue to note Crummell's attempt to walk the tension between the evil of white supremacy and the Providence of God. He wishes to show that God produces good in human history despite human wickedness, but does not mitigate the outrage of that wickedness. He writes:

> No! I do not forget that to give our small fraction of the race the advantages I have alluded to, a whole continent has been brought to ruin; the ocean has been peopled with millions of victims; whole tribes of men destroyed; nations on the threshold of civilization reduced to barbarism; and generation upon generation of our sires brutalized![60]

Crummell fervently believed the English language and the culture it expressed would providentially facilitate the liberation of the oppressed. "Indeed," he writes, "it is only under the influence of Anglo-Saxon principles that the children of Africa, despite their wrongs and injuries, have been able to open their eyes to the full, clear, quiet, heavens of freedom, far distant, though at times they were!"[61]

African Traditional and Slave Religions and the Missionaries

African Traditional Religion

Crummell denigrated African traditional religion.[62] For Crummell, African traditional religion constitutes "wretched rites" and "miserable ceremonies which attend the passage of the dead from the hut to the grave."[63] In his alienation, Crummell thought reverence of the ancestors entails "absurd notions of an after-life." According to Crummell, "the exhibition of debasing superstitions over dead bodies and the open graves of the departed" is revolting. He thought this *rite de passage* was "the abject subjection of...poor creatures to the power of the devil, to whom they degrade themselves lower than the beasts of the field."[64] For him, those rites evinced that Africans, though not cursed, had fallen from grace. Crummell claims that traditional African spirituality represents the taint of sin rather than the impress of a varied, ubiquitous, general revelation.

Crummell writes:

> ...our forefathers, in remote generation, 'when they knew God, glorified him not as God' and 'did not like to retain Him in their knowledge,' and from age to age their sons, *our* ancestors, wandered off further from the true God and kept heaping abominations upon abominations through long centuries, until the divine patience was exhausted, and God withdrew from our sires and extinguished the 'forbearance and long suffering' of ages; which is the direst wrath![65]

Slavery, then, was providential punishment: "If you come to Africa, you find the fruitful source of her heterogeneous ills and sufferings is sin.[66]

Slave Religion

In assessing the significance of slavery, Crummell resorts to a truncated view of the Christianization of African-American slaves. He writes:

> mercy was mingled in with all this wrath. Their lot was caste [sic] in the lands of men where the cross shone from the temple-spires, and the Bible was read at their altars. Terrible as was the ordeal of slavery, yet God restrained the wrath of their oppressors; not seldom did He turn the hearts of Christian masters and mistresses to them and their children...until now, at the close of nigh three centuries, millions of the children of Africa, on the isles and continent of America, have been turned from the paganism of their fathers...[67]

That God restrained the wrath of the oppressors is, as C.L.R. James reveals in his exposé of the heinousness of Haitian slavery, a fallacy. Equally fallacious is Crummell's claim that African-Americans turned from the legacies of the ancestors.[68]

North American slaves often interpreted Christianity differently from the teachings of proselytizing slaveholders, regardless of their "benevolence" (as if there could be a kind master). White missionaries tended to proselytize without opposing Christianity to chattelization. A significant number of African-American slaves rejected that teaching. African values of the ancestors facilitated the African-Americanization of Christianity. For many slaves, Christianity, assimilated in ancestral modalities, was inimical to the religion of slaveholders and slavery's advocates.[69] Chattelization did not create in the minds of the slaves a *tabula rasa*, as Crummell would have us believe. Slaves remembered their African heritage and fitted it to American realities; if they had not, they would not have had the wherewithal to resist their oppression.

The Missionaries

Crummell advocated sending New World blacks and Westernized Africans into the hinterland in order to propagate Christianity and develop trade. According to Crummell, "Christianity never secures thorough entrance and complete authority in any land, save by the use of men and minds somewhat native to the very soil."[70] Crummell's view here resembles the Yoruba bishop, James Holy Johnson's. Unlike Johnson, however, Crummell did not advocate the Christianization of elements of African traditional religion.[71]

Johnson, a Pan-Africanist, thought elements of christology were "embedded in...[African] religious system."[72] E.A. Ayandele explains that Johnson thought that Christianity "was a culturally neutral ideology which was capable of growing in different cultures and environments without losing its sublimity or compromising its tenets."[73] According to Johnson:

> Christianity is a Religion intended for and is suitable for every Race and Tribe of people on the face of the Globe. Acceptance of it was never intended by its Founder to denationalise any people and it is indeed its glory that every race of people may profess and practice it and imprint upon it its own native characteristics, giving it a

> peculiar type among themselves without losing anything of its virtue. And why should not there be an African Christianity as there has been a European and Asiatic Christianity?[74]

Johnson conservatively sought continuities between African traditional religion and Christianity.

Crummell, however, saw African traditional religion as a debased sinfulness to be unconditionally purged.[75] "Be tender and pitiful and earnest to the heathen around you," writes Crummell, "for their souls' sake, and for Christ." But, he continues, "resist steadfastly for your children's sake, their vicious habits and their corrupting influences."[76]

African History

According to Crummell, black Africans are progeny of Cush, one of the four sons of Ham. For Crummell, Ethiopia:

> ...is in the original Cush. This Cush was one of four sons of Ham. His descendants, in part, settled in Asia between the Euphrates and the Tigris, and there first distinguished themselves. There Nimrod, his son, laid the first foundations of empire of which we have any record, and founded Ninevah. Subsequently, the Cushites spread themselves abroad through Arabia, from the Persian Gulf to the Red Sea. By and by...a portion of them crossed the Red Sea and settled in Africa.[77]

Crummell distinguishes the Cushites from both the progeny of Phut (northwestern part of Africa) and Mizraim (Egypt). Descendants of Phut and Mizraim, asserts Crummell, have become mixed with Mediterranean whites. According to Crummell, the Cushites, the blacks, cut off by the desert and hemmed in by the ocean, had little contact with Europeans until the slave trade.[78]

Crummell claims that black Africans migrated from Asia into Africa.[79] Africa, however, is the original home of the blacks. Current evidence, moreover, indicates that humankind developed from the soil of Africa.[80] The differentiation of homo sapiens into "races," is in part a product of migration of early human types from the continent.

Although it is difficult to pinpoint the emergence of blacks as a distinct people, it is clear that black Africans existed side by side with other stone age hominids.[81] As early as the middle stone period, Mediterranean types and "Negroid" types had social intercourse in the verdant Sahara region. Around the third millennium, cultures had begun to settle in the alluvial richness of the Nile delta further east. Well-respected scholars of the black community marshal impressive evidence indicating the first Pharaohs were blacks whose origins lie above the sixth cataract (or first cataract depending on your perspective).[82] It is plausible that other black stone age cultures lay in other parts of the continent as a result of migrations set off by the Sahara's desiccation.[83]

Although Crummell is incorrect about the birthplace of humanity, he challenged the argument that the black "race" is under a curse. For Crummell, Scripture reveals that only Canaan and his progeny are cursed. It is clear for Crummell that "Africa was...settled by the descendants of Ham, *excepting his son Canaan.*"[84] (His sense that Canaan rather than Cush was cursed cast aspersion on the nonblack people of "Palestine, Phoenicia, Carthage.") [85]

According to Crummell:

> It cannot be proved that *all* the sons of Ham were included in the curse pronounced upon Canaan. Ham had four sons... 'Cush, and Mizraim, and Phut, and Canaan'...Canaan, it is evident, was the *youngest* of these sons, and Cush the *eldest.*[86]

Crummell, in the tradition of the African abolitionist, Ottobah Cugoano, argues that blacks would have been cursed if Canaan had been the eldest.[87] He writes, "the common rule among men is that 'THE GREATER INCLUDES THE LESS.'"[88] For Crummell, a curse extends from the top down, not the bottom up. According to Crummell,

> if Ham himself had been the person designated by Noah, then all disputation on this matter would be, at once, at an end; for then the inference would be natural, legitimate, and indisputable, that *all* his posterity were impli-

> cated in the curse which fell upon himself. But this...is nowhere stated in Scripture.[89]

Crummell's argument serves to undermine the "pro-slavery theology pressing [blacks] to the earth, as well as the all-grasping cupidity of man."[90] For Crummell, whites have no biblical evidence for the claim that the chattelization of African people fulfills a divine curse.

Crummell nonetheless continues to reveal an alienation from his ancestry — he was allegedly a descendent of West African royalty.[91]

He writes:

> So far as *Western* Africa is concerned, there is no history. The long centuries of human existence, there, give us no intelligent disclosures. "Darkness covered the land, and gross darkness the people."[92]

Although Crummell here attributes this "backwardness" to isolation, rather than to innate inferiority, he ignores the impressive Islamicized states of the Western Sudan and the eastern, coastal, Islamicized areas. Indeed the history of the Western Sudan stretches back at least to the dawn of the iron age.

During the Medieval period, impressive grassland African kingdoms near the trade routes south of the Sahara waxed and waned over a period of over six hundred years. Equipped with powerful armies and cavalries, well-endowed in gold, ivory, kola nuts and slaves, Islamicized kingdoms such as Ghana, Mali, Songhai, Kanem-Bornu, and the Hausa states were well-respected powers in the trans-Saharan trade. "Further south were non-Muslim states such as the Mossi who organized themselves into a federation of five states in the Upper Volta region."[93] In the Guinea, the Akan traded in gold. The Yoruba kingdoms and the kingdoms of Dahomey and Benin were remarkable civilizations. The list of African civilizations is impressively augmented by the great Bantu realms of Central and Southern Africa, such as those of the BaKongo, that of Great Zimbabwe, and those of the regents Shaka and Moshoeshoe.[94]

Crummell's ignorance of African history is peculiar as his

contemporaries, such as Martin Delany and Edward Blyden, were quite aware of the history of Africa. Crummell and Delany were acquaintances. Indeed, during Delany's journey toward the Niger, he was Crummell's guest during his stay in Liberia.[95] Delany's legacy reveals that Crummell's Eurocentrism was not totally due to the times in which he lived. Although Delany shared aspects of Crummell's view of Providence, he, more satisfactorily than Crummell, did not see Africa through the eyes of whites, whose invested interest lay in African underdevelopment.

Delany claimed that ancient Egypt was essentially a black civilization, and that the black Egyptians "were the greatest [people] of ancient times."[96] Delany reveals that the European conspiracy against Africa is evinced not only in the facts of slavery and the incipiency of colonialism but in the deliberate effort to rob blacks of their historical achievements. Delany cast doubt on the view that any semblance of civilization in Africa was due to external influence. For Delany, Levantine and Southern European cultures owed much to Black Africa. According to Cyril Griffith, Delany held that: "the idea that kings were the human embodiment of God was an African concept which evolved in ancient times...Delany claimed that when the Jewish people were held as bondsmen by Africans, they acquired some of the latter's political and religious symbols and later used them in their anthropomorphic expressions of God."[97] Indeed many of Delany's views resurface in the thought of Pan-Africanist such as Maulana Karenga, Yosef Ben-Jochannan, Cheik Anta Diop, Chancellor Williams, John Jackson and George James.

Unlike Crummell, Delany reveals a continuity with the legacies of the ancestors. His positive regard for Africa is an important value indispensable for Pan-African theology today. Delany, for instance, writes:

> ...I cannot see the utility of the custom on the part of Missionaries in *changing* the names of native children, and even adults, so soon as they go into their families to live, as though their own were not good enough for them. These native names are generally much more significant, and euphonious than the Saxon, Gaelic, or Celtic. Thus, Adenigi means, "Crowns have their

> shadow"...It is to be hoped that this custom among Missionaries and other Christian settlers, of changing names of the natives will be stopped, thereby relieving them of the impression, that to embrace the Christian faith, implies a loss of name, and so far a loss of identity.[98]

Delany's remarks are quite profound, for the retention of persons' *African name* is the posterity contiguous with the legacy of their ancestors.

The way in which Crummell reveals an African-American ambivalence toward Africa is seen further in his discussion of the explorations of European explorers such as Mungo Park, and David Livingstone. Crummell claims that in opening up the hinterland, the explorers

> have modified the degrading prejudices concerning the negro, by contrasting him as free, dignified, powerful and ingenious, in his native superiority with the miserable caricature of him, shorn of his manhood, ludicrous, and benighted, in chains and slavery; and have led to the discovery of superior peoples, mighty nations, vast kingdoms, and populous cities...subject to manufactures, agriculture and extensive commerce.[99]

How could Crummell be unaware of the contradiction between his estimates of Western Africa and the Africa the Britons "found"? Still, though Crummell appreciates those interior kingdoms, those too pale for him beside the brilliance of European culture.[100] It bears repeating that the tragedy of his thought is that, though he espoused a Pan-African theology, Crummell did not liberate it from the alienating values of white supremacists. Infected by those values, he spread the virus of oppression in the land of his ancestors.

His paradoxical opposition to white supremacy is the positive aspect of his legacy.

He writes:

> There seems to me to be a natural call upon the children of Africa in foreign lands to come and participate in the opening treasures of the land of their fathers. Though

> these treasures are the manifest gift of God to the negro race, yet that race reaps but the most partial measure of their good and advantage. It has always been thus in the past and now as the extent of *our* interest therein is becoming more diminutive...the negro, on his native soil, is but "a hewer of wood and drawer of water"; and the sons of Africa in foreign lands suffer the adventurous foreigner, with greed and glut, to jostle them aside, and to seize with skill and effect upon their own rightful inheritance.[101]

Aside from the capitalist and imperialist implications, Crummell's words here are useful for Pan-African theologians today. Providence does call the Diaspora to support the struggle to protect African resources from exhaustion by oppressive regimes. Indeed, "the resources of Africa are being more and more developed," but not indigenously. The black continent is still subservient to the West as "hewers of wood and drawers of water." Africans do indeed yet suffer "the adventurous foreigner, with greed and glut, to jostle them aside, and to seize with skill and effect upon their rightful inheritance." The West, which enslaved and colonized Africa's children, has still the balance of technological power, with which it extracts the wealth from the African soil, processes it abroad in metropolitan industries, leaving the peasants and the workers with nothing but the problem of staggering debt, famine, and poverty.

Indeed, Crummell was aware of the avariciousness of Europeans and, given his focus on emigration, was Afrocentric, though in a vitiated sense. He writes of those resistant to emigration to Africa:

> Alas for us, as a race! So deeply harmed have we been by oppression that we have lost the force of strong, native principles and prime natural affections. Because exaggerated contempt has been poured upon us, we too become apt pupils in the school of scorn and contumely. Because repudiation of the black man has been for centuries the wont of civilized nations, black men themselves get shame at their origin and shrink from the terms which indicate it.[102]

Still, how does one castigate traditional Africa for its alleged backwardness and reproach others for pouring contumely upon black people?

What do we learn from Crummell's blindness to the way he implicates himself in his criticism of antiemigrationists? To answer that Crummell was completely against black liberation defined in Pan-African terms would make a mockery of his memory and be a travesty of interpretation. Crummell was a talented, bright gentleman of great integrity and sincerity. He envisioned that Africa would be free from the neocolonialism currently stifling Africa in a violent structure of dependency. Crummell, then, can hardly unequivocally be said to be an oppressor like the Europeans whose values he espoused. He took great pride in his blackness, believing that races, "like families, are the organisms and the ordinances of God; and race feeling, like the family feeling, is of divine origin."[103]

He was completely outraged by the mistreatment of blacks during slavery and was quick to oppose leading white supremacists. His acceptance of white supremacists' values is undoubtedly due in part to the historic nature of his socialization. Yet, as I have shown, to attribute the contradiction of his thought entirely to his historical context would obscure the fact that other African-Americans of his age had views more acceptable to a contemporary Pan-African theology. Attention to Delany — as well as Johnson — should counter views that I unfairly criticize a revered African-American.

My analysis of Crummell, and reference to his peers, leads me to conclude that if the histories of African people throughout their stone and iron age histories are devalued, African civilization will be exclusively evaluated in terms of the histories of Europe. This hegemonic perspective will equate Providence with imperialism, and Christianity with the Eurocentric mediums that obscure the relativity of Christianity in modalities of its indigenizations.

Alexander Crummell is an ancestor whose life "behind the veil" caused him to advocate a demonic notion — in the Tillichian sense — of Providence. He sought the liberation of blacks and yet saw black liberation in terms of whites for whom he had too much admiration. He rightly implies that whites will generally accept blacks only in proportion to the extent that blacks approximate Eurocentric culture. He wrongly concludes that blacks' assimilation of that culture will redeem the African and African-American masses "peripheralized" by the center.

Pan-African theologians today must overcome the terrible "twoness" that blinded Crummell to the redemptive ways of the ancestors: a second sight achieved in the removal of the alienation responsible for the veiling of the integrity of the ancestors. Their integrity is the a priori of the pretext of enslavement and colonization, a pretext which dissimulates itself in equating oppression with Providence.

In the providence of God, redemption is coming to Africa. God, having pressed the *imago dei* first on the dark ancestors, is incarnate today in Africa, which is in quest of a new humanity. Today, Africans will teach African-Americans, so that the latter may divest themselves of the "Prometheus syndrome" and understand more of the precious ancestral spirituality edifying for a Pan-African theology. An ancestor who recognized this more clearly than Crummell was Edward Wilmot Blyden.

3.

Edward Blyden
(1832 - 1912):

Blameless Ethiopian

He came not in thunder, or with sound, but in the garb of humble teacher, a John the Baptist among his brethren preaching rational and national salvation. From land to land and shore to shore his message was the self-same one, which, interpreted in the language of Christ was: "what shall it profit a race it is shall gain the whole world and lose its soul?"

— Casely Hayford (regarding Blyden)

Princes shall come forth from Egypt;
Ethiopia stretches forth her hand to God.

— Psalms 68:31

Hollis Lynch, an authority on Blyden, asserts that "Blyden's Pan-Negro ideology was undoubtedly the most important progenitor of Pan-Africanism."[1] Indeed, P. Olisanwuche Esedebe refers to Blyden, a Presbyterian minister, as the "Father of Pan-Africanism," a title usually reserved for W.E.B. DuBois.[2]

I focus on Blyden's understanding of Providence under five headings: Westernization and Redemption; Racism: The Progeny of the Oppressor; Providence and Religion; Providence and Socialism; Providence and Liberal Education; and Africa's Redemption and Colonialism.

Westernization and Redemption

Blyden arrived in Liberia in 1851, having left his native St. Thomas and finding North American colleges closed to blacks.[3] He became an advocate of an Americo-Liberian talented tenth. Seeking the patronage of outstanding European intellectuals, Blyden proclaimed: "This little Republic...is no doubt destined...to revolutionize for good this whole part of Africa. But we need, in order to carry out the great work...men of enlightened minds, of enlarged views, of high-toned character."[4]

Like Crummell, he was, at first, an elitist insensitive to the dominated Africans. Blyden "unquestionably accepted the...view that Africa was the 'dark continent' and that a new and progressive civilization would be created through the influence of Westernized Negroes."[5] He thought that "liberation"of the "aborigines" would set in motion a providential juggernaut that would crush the "heathenisms" of the powerful Ashanti and Dahomean kingdoms.

To Blyden's credit, however, his encounter with the Vai — a people in possession of a script thought to be traceable to Pharonic Egypt — began to modify significantly his Eurocentric worldview.[6] Although his settler theology was evident in the 1853 campaign against King Boombo of the Vai, his encounter with them increased his respect for traditional African people. "He found King Boombo's town 'remarkably fortified'...and proof of 'the unfairness of those who represent the native Africans as naturally indolent and living in a state of ease and supineness.'"[7] Blyden would then criticize Americo-Liberians for their disdain of the autochthones whom he sought to include in the affairs of the Republic. After the Vai encounter, Blyden argued "that all assertions of Negro inferiority were...unfounded propaganda by Anglo-Saxons to justify their atrocities against Negroes."[8]

He evinced a salvific, Afrocentric love for black people. Within matrices of Westernization, a black consciousness like Blyden's surfaces from a redemptive awareness of the integrity of the African heritage. It is true that Blyden's Pan-Africanism was formally influenced by the Pan-Slavism of Russians like Dostoyevsky who "had, in their reaction to European technological and cultural superiority, idealized the rural Slav as 'perfect man' and had prognosticated that Russia would be the 'founder of a new civilization and the bearer of universal salvation.'"[9] According to Lynch, moreover,

> Blyden seemed...to have been profoundly influenced by the writings of such European philosophers and naturalists as Herder, Fichte, Hegel, and Mazzini, who advocated racial and national unity and averred that every people had its special mission to fulfill. Ideologically Blyden seemed to have been influenced most of all by Herder. If we substitute Herder's nationality for Blyden's 'Race', we find a striking similarity in their ideas. Theirs was a humanitarian nationalism which disavowed conquest or domination of other people...They both believed that the ultimate goal of a nation or race was to serve humanity at large, and that the individual could fulfill himself best through unselfish, dedicated service to nation or race.[10]

Nonetheless, Blyden's independent valuation of the integrity of African cultures is indispensable for an appreciation of his vindicationist position.

Blyden sought to explode the myth of the Negro past long before, but in a way distinct from, Melville Herskovits. Blyden, like Delany, was fascinated with ancient Egypt and the seminal contribution of blacks to its civilization.[11] Blyden especially took exception to the views of the Euro-American A.H. Foote, who argued that if everything blacks

> have ever done were to be obliterated from recollection forever, the whole world would lose no great truth, no profitable arts, no exemplary form of life. The loss of all that is African would offer no memorable deduction from anything but the black catalogue of crime.[12]

To refute Foote, Blyden, having mastered Hebrew and Greek, relied upon the Hebrew version of the Old Testament, focusing on the tenth chapter of Genesis. He also relied upon evidence provided by Herodotus and Homer.[13] Blyden argued that blacks "had been partly responsible for 'the germs of all the arts and sciences.'"[14] Subscribing to the diffusionist theory, Blyden claimed the ancestors of the Western Sudanese Kingdoms were progeny of the ancient, black Egyptians whose ancestral home was above the sixth cataract.

Whereas Crummell sought to discard African traditional culture, Blyden envisioned the retention of traditional African values in an African civilization critical of the Enlightenment. Resisting certain modernizing forces, Blyden appreciated how African traditional values could benefit blacks in the postmodern age. If Crummell thought modern science should immediately replace "heathen superstition," Blyden had a more critical view of Western science.

Indeed, Blyden in his criticism of Western science, reminds me of the contemporary Asian theologian, Aloysius Pieris.[15] Blyden thought: "Science for all the really higher purposes of humanity is a dead organism of latent forces unless it is taken up by the moral nature, unless it is animated by earnest purpose and inspired by a great spiritual idea."[16] For Blyden the greatest spiritual idea was Christian, the antithesis of "dehumanized technocracy" (Pieris). As if he could foresee the horror of Hiroshima and Nagasaki, Blyden wrote:

> Science is not the last word for humanity. It cannot be. It is continually threatening the existence of the mighty offspring to which it gives birth. It keeps itself armed to the teeth against its neighbor. Its most popular and lucrative inventions are machinery for the destructions of life. It multiplies its armies and increases its navies; and men wonder when all this would end and where it will lead.[17]

According to Blyden, Western technology threatened the unique development of African civilization. Blyden in part attributed this threat to the narcissism of Eurocentrism. According to Blyden:

> From the lesson he everyday receives, the Negro unconsciously imbibes the conviction that to be a great man, he must be like the white man. He is not brought up — however he may desire it — to be the companion, the equal, the comrade of the white man, but his imitator, his ape, his parasite. To be himself in a country where everything ridicules him is to be nothing. To be as like the white man as possible — to copy his outward appearance, his peculiarities, his manners, the arrangement of his toilet, that is the aim of the Christian Negro — this is his inspiration. The only virtues which under such circumstances he develops are, of course, parasitical ones.[18]

Blyden saw clearly that blacks' imbibition of white supremacist values came by way of Euro-Christianity.[19] The anecdote to that poison, for Blyden, entails African people's realization that they bear the image of God naturally, and need not aspire to the hubristic mores of the whites who dominate them. For Blyden there is perhaps

> no people in whom the religious instinct is deeper and more universal than among Africans. And in view of the materializing tendencies of the age, it may yet come to pass that when, in Europe, God has gone out of

> date...then earnest inquirers after truth leaving the seats of science and the "highest civilization" will take themselves to Africa to learn lessons of faith and piety; for "Ethiopia shall stretch forth her hands unto God."[20]

According to Blyden:

> Africa's lot resembles Him also who made Himself of no reputation, but took upon Himself the form of a servant, and, having been made perfect through suffering, became the 'Captain of our salvation.' And if the principle laid down by Christ is that by which things are decided above...that he who would be chief must become servant of all, then we see the position which Africa and the Africans must ultimately occupy.[21]

Blyden's concept of the way in which blacks bore the image of God is related to his notion of the African personality. Antedating the thoughts of Aimé Césaire and Leopold Senghor, Blyden claimed the African was naturally cheerful, sympathetic and service orientated.[22] Reminiscent of Diop's two cradle theory, Blyden argued that the African was less coldly aggressive than the European.[23] Anathema to him were the "harsh, individualistic, competitive and combative" mores of Nordic races.[24] Blyden claimed agricultural enterprise fitted the alleged irenic temperament of blacks. According to Blyden, the African is closer to nature than the European. The African, writes Blyden, "in the simplicity and purity of rural enterprises, will be able to cultivate those spiritual elements which are suppressed, silent and inactive under the pressure and exigencies of material progress."[25] He speculated that blacks as inhabitants of the spiritual "'conservatory of the world'...would act as peace-makers among the ever-warring European nations, and as 'consoler' when the destructive scientific inventions of white men led to a crisis in their civilization."[26] "The African," writes Blyden, "is the feminine; and we must not suppose that this is of least importance in the ultimate development of humanity."[27]

Unfortunately Blyden internalized European liberal values in his defense of the African "race."

As Robert July explains, Blyden knew that theories of Black inferiority

> were nonsense, but European ideas and ways of thinking had long since become an integral part of his mental and psychological apparatus so that when he sought to refute these racist doctrines, it did not occur to him to scrap the whole structure with its network of unconscious assumptions which so completely prejudiced the case. In effect a psychological Eurafrican, Blyden began by accepting the racial theories of European anthropologists with their divisions of the world's races according to cultural and physiological characteristics, and then proceeded with great skill to present theological, historical, anthropological and sociological arguments to show that the conclusions of a European racial superiority were simply not tenable.[28]

That Blyden did so is seen throughout his *Christianity, Islam and the Negro Race*. Blyden approvingly quotes whites who claim that blacks are more spiritual than whites. Some of these views are quite outrageous: "There is more of the child, of the unsophisticated nature, in the Negro race than in the European."[29]

Nothing is wrong in celebrating the virtues of women and children, but there is little virtue in parroting white liberal paternalism. Despite Blyden's singular genius, his inheritance of European dilettantism has lain a problematic foundation of *négritude*. Indeed, Blyden's "natural African" is like Rousseau's noble savage. Progressive African theologians today realize the *négritude* movement is alienated from the masses.[30]

Blyden, moreover, as an agent of the American Colonization Society (ACS), subscribed to values destined to invest in the continent at the expense of human beings. Blyden thought Africans should concentrate upon agriculture, allowing whites to expand in industrialization and technology. Blind to the incipient wickedness of olden colonialism, Blyden thought agriculture fitted the alleged "feminine" temperament of blacks. Indeed, myopic concentration on agriculture impedes the industrialization of Africa, facilitating colonial expropriation of African labor. Nonetheless, Blyden writes:

> Europe is overflowing with the material productions of its own genius. Important foreign markets, which formerly consumed these productions, are now closing against them. Africa seems to furnish the only large outlet...So that Africa...will have again to come to the rescue and contribute to the needs of Europe.[31]

Blyden did not see that the extension of European capital into Africa was a continuum of the slave trade, the ramifications of which still bring to blacks a profound misery.

Racism: The Progeny of the Oppressor

Blyden, nonetheless, held a vision of Africa's redemption. His vision, however, excluded mulattoes, whom he despised, though he married a mulatto woman. His contempt for mulattoes was related to his realization of the problem of caste among African-Americans and his concept of race purity. More decisive for determining black identity, however, is not "race" but socialization in the cultural and socioeconomic realities of people of African descent. Blacks, phenotypically similar to their European progenitors, may indeed define themselves as African-Americans.

For Blyden, "mulatto values" signified white supremacists' mores and alienated one from the liberation struggle of the African people. Unquestionably, Blyden recognized the relation between mulatto identity and socioeconomic advantage in the United States and Liberia. "Indeed," writes Robert July, "the Liberian settlers, many of whom were mulattoes in any case, hardly regarded themselves as Negro by comparison with the indigenous people surrounding them, while the latter invariably referred to the settlers as white men."[32]

Blyden thought only unbigoted blacks could serve the world, but he failed to wrestle with his own bigotry. Of mulattoes, he writes:

> The European side of his nature appears in his social affectation. I found generally...that Negroes were indifferent to mixed school and some opposed to it, but the mulatto thought it was a natural and inalienable right

> for which he was bound to contend: and so he confuses the instincts of his black brother[,] who while anxious to stand upon his race individuality and independence, is harassed by the mulatto who is always restless and dissatisfied.[33]

Blyden's hatred of mulattoes drove him to seek the support of whites such as William Coppinger, a friend of Blyden's and an official of the ACS. The ACS was capable of exploiting divisions within the black community. Blyden sought to control the influx of mulattoes into Liberia, by opposing, through the ACS, the Liberia Exodus company run by blacks. He thought the company would increase the number of mulattoes in Liberia. In opposing the Liberia Exodus Company, Blyden, unwittingly I assume, opposed Martin Delany, who was not a mulatto, and Henry McNeal Turner, a mulatto of whom Blyden approved.[34] Indeed the AME Bishop, Henry McNeal Turner, is a seminal ancestor who knew the depth of the evil white supremacy and fought it vociferously until his death.[35] The failure of the Company is regrettable because it could have been a significant model of Pan-African praxis. Yet Blyden was relieved at its failure. He claimed the failure of the company was "a blessing to Liberia; the Republic wanted to rubbish."[36]

"Mulatto values," however, are present even among blacks with no European ancestry. Abandonment of "mulatto values" is indispensable for the liberation of black minds as these values alienate them from their African ancestors. Dispensable, though, is indiscriminate dislike of mulattoes or light-skinned blacks whose European ancestry is indelible. Blyden's hatred of mulattoes exposes the fascistic danger of racism. Dislike of mulattoes impoverishes Pan-African community in setting blacks against themselves.

In fighting against the Liberia Exodus Company Blyden contradicted one of his most excellent insights. He writes:

> ...among the phenomena in the relation of the white man to the Negro in the house of bondage none has been more curious than this: that the white man, under a keen sense of wrong done to the Negro, will work for

> him, will suffer for him, will fight for him, will even die for him, but he cannot get rid of a secret contempt for him.[37]

Few knew this better than Delany and Turner. Indirectly, but no less tragically, Blyden worked against his siblings also in quest of Pan-African liberation.

Providence and Religion

Islam and Christianity

According to Blyden, Islam, as a non-European religion, was more adaptable to the African context than Euro-Christianity. Whereas Euro-Christianity had promoted a literacy inhibiting the "African personality," Islam had providentially nurtured a literacy which allowed the greatness of kingdoms such as Mali and Songhay to be recorded.

Whereas Christianity, especially after the Berlin Conference, had aided the partition of Africa, Islam, according to Blyden, fostered the unification of the Western Sudan during the Sokoto Jihads. Whereas Christianity tended to legitimate the status of blacks as pariahs, Muslim conquerors, claimed Blyden uncritically, were more sensitive to the humanity of blacks. Blacks, argued Blyden correctly, were first largely Christianized as chattel or protocolonial subjects. White Christians, Blyden asserts, taught blacks "lessons of utter and permanent inferiority."[38]

According to Blyden, Islamized blacks, on the other hand, were in fraternal relations with their Semitic proselytizers. Blyden noted well that Islam has a long history in Africa — spreading literacy, fusing with African values, and becoming significantly indigenous to Africa. To a degree, Blyden's position is consistent with the assertion of the Black Muslims of the Pan-African community today. The black Muslims of Elijah Muhammad and Louis Farrakhan, indigenous to North America, and black orthodox Muslims claim Islam is more a black person's religion than Christianity. Blyden's claim, however, that Islam has been less oppressive of Africans than Christianity is problematic.[39] Pan-African scholars such as Chancellor Williams show clearly the destruction wrought in Africa by Islam, which I do not distinguish from the Arab invaders.[40]

As part of his notion of Providence, Blyden thought that Islamized Africans and Christianized African-American emigrants were providential agents indispensable for Africa's redemption. He writes:

> [Islam] — by its simple, rigid forms of worship, by its literature, its politics, its organized society, its industrial and commercial activities — is rapidly superseding a hoary and pernicious Paganism. The exiled Negro in the Western hemisphere, on the other hand, in spite of slavery, in spite of the bitter prejudices, the dark passions of which he has been the victim, has come under influences which have given him the elements of a nobler civilization. The seed of a spiritual, intellectual, industrial life has been planted in his bosom, which, when it is transferred to the land of his fathers, will grow up into beauty, expand into flower, and develop into fruit which the world will be glad to welcome.[41]

Despite Blyden's assessment of Islam, he believed Christianity, once stripped of its Eurocentrism and integrated into the African personality, would redeem Africa. Islam was to be the fertilizer for Christianity.[42] Blyden, however, was mistaken in his view that Islam would fade in the light of Christianity. Islam has not been replaced by Christianity, nor should it be. The expectation today in Pan-African theology is not that Christianity will render Islam obsolete, but that Muslims and Christians will complement one another in praxes of liberation.

African Traditional and Slave Religions

In his *Christianity, Islam and the Negro Race*, a compilation of essays published in 1887, Blyden tended to denigrate African traditional religion. He writes:

> It is evident that, whatever may be said of the Koran, as long as it is in advance of the Shamanism or Fetichism of the African tribes who accept it — and no one will doubt that Islam as a creed is an enormous advance not only

> on all idolatries, but on all systems of purely human origins — those tribes must advance beyond their primitive condition.[43]

Aside from the fact that all religions are, to a degree, human creations, Blyden's views here represent a Eurocentric definition of "primitive." Like Crummell, Blyden here reveals the tragedy of alienation. That Christianity and Islam are better religions than African traditional religions is a view that undermines continuity with the legacies of the ancestors. Indeed, Blyden's admiration of Islam and Christianity tended to undermine his positive view of the way African people bear the image of God.

Blyden's early misunderstanding of African traditional religion led to his distortion of slave religion. He believed that "Africans who were carried to the Western world were, as a general rule, of the lowest of the people in their own country [who] did not fairly represent the qualities and endowments of the race."[44] According to Blyden, those dregs of the African people made a mockery of already inferior African traditional religions: "and so the elements of civilization and barbarism — of Christianity and Heathenism — ...were inlaid...into each other, in a sort of inharmonious mosaic all over the western hemisphere."[45] Blyden would have blacks emigrate to Liberia, but they were to be Protestants of the "orthodox stamp," purged of the heathenism of slave religion.[46] Blyden would have blacks as agents of redemption, who would ironically be alienated from the most *African*-American bearers of redemptive culture.

Blyden also thought that slave religion was but a reflection of the corrupt Christianity of the slavers. Blyden claims that the slavers deprived slaves of the true "religion of Christ."[47] "As a rule," claimed Blyden, "the Christianity of the Negroes is just such a grotesque and misshapen thing as the system under which they were trained is calculated to produce."[48] Slaves' assimilation of Christianity, however — it bears repeating — was not the inept mimicking of the idolatry of slavers. Indeed, much of slave "Christianity" was redemptive precisely because slaves rejected, in memories of their ancestors, the deformed Christianity of slavers.

Despite the presence of heathenism and the corrupt

Christianity of the slaves, Blyden thought Providence was at work in slave religion. Reminiscent of Crummell, Blyden thought, "There streamed into the darkness of their surroundings a light from the cross of Christ." This, he claimed, accounted for the otherworldly characteristic of slave religion and the haunting pathos of the spirituals.[49]

Blyden would later correct his view of African traditional religion. Indeed, in *African Life and Customs*, Blyden shows, more so than in *Christianity, Islam and the Negro Race*, a sensitivity to the values suited to the exigencies of black Africa. According to Blyden, *"you may change the Theology of a people, but you cannot change their Religion* [emphasis added]."[50]

Suggesting the positive meaning of the legacies of the ancestors, Blyden writes:

> Owing to the intense and increasing materialism of Europe, especially Anglo-Saxondom, the people have lost touch with the spirit world. This is no reason why Africans should forget the privileges enjoyed by their fathers. The inter-communion between the people of the earth and those in the spiritual sphere is a cardinal belief of the African and will never be uprooted. Death is simply a door through which men enter the life to come or the Hereafter.[51]

Blyden recognizes that the religion of the ancestors, while subject to change, is fundamental to the humanity of the masses. According to Blyden, eugenics; secret societies training adolescents for adulthood and enshrining the roles of parents and elders; polygamy, exogamous marriages, prearranged marriages; the magico-religious taxonomy of fauna and flora; and corporate ethics are all dimensions of a traditional life imbued with sacred values necessary for a posterity rooted in ancestral legacies.[52] To lose touch with the progressive values of that religion is to lose touch with the uniqueness of black humanity. Hindsight reveals that a liberating Christianity has spread in Africa among people profoundly in touch with the acculturative power of ancestral worldviews.[53]

Blyden anticipates the issue of inculturation in his recognition of the difference between a "pure" Christian doctrine — whatever that is — and doctrines vitiated by white supremacist values:

> There is...only one Prophet for all times and for all nations — the immaculate Son of God; and the teachings which he inculcated contain the only principles that will regenerate humanity of all races, climes and countries. But the Gospel, though it has been promulgated for eighteen hundred years, has, as yet, taken extensive root only among one race — the Indo-European.[54]

In his mature judgment, Blyden asserts that Europeans misrepresented the legacy of Jesus. According to Blyden,

> [the gospel] was travestied and diluted before it came to...to suit the "peculiar institution" by which millions of human beings were converted into "chattels"...upholding a system which every Negro felt was wrong.[55]

For Blyden, moreover,

> [religion] binds us to a higher power, and is practiced by men of all climes and countries. Theology is our conception of and our attempt to describe the Being worshiped, Who has no name. What He is to one race, He is not in every respect to another...Religion is the ocean, theology the river. All rivers flow into the ocean, but the ocean is not the river, and the river is not the ocean. The African does not attempt to formulate a Theology.[56]

(Blyden's position reminds me of the historian of religion, Charles Long, who raises the important issue of the inappropriateness of imposing Eurocentric theology on African traditional religions.)[57]

For the mature Blyden, Africa did not need

> the theological interference of Europe, for the Theology of Europe is derived from the conceptions of Roman, Celt and Teuton, which have modified the Semitic ideas promulgated in the Bible. European Christianity is Western Christianity — that is to say, Christianity as

> taught...on the mount of Beatitudes, modified to suit the European mind or idiosyncrasies.[58]

European Missionaries

According to Blyden, missionaries came to the coast "imbued with the notions they have derived from books, of the 'sanguinary customs' and 'malignant superstitions' of the natives."[59] For Blyden, however, "The Negro of the ordinary traveler or missionary...is a purely fictitious being, constructed out of the traditions of slave-traders and slave-holders...who were taught to regard the Negro as a legitimate object of traffic."[60] Blyden insightfully notes that missionaries "under the influence of their malarious surroundings...gain more in irritability of temper than in liberality of view, often acquiring greater ignorance of the people then they had before they came."[61]

Blyden has little use for a missiology that

> preaches a crusade against the harmless customs and prejudices of the people — superseding many customs and habits necessary and useful in the climate and for the people by practices which, however useful they might be in Europe, become, when introduced indiscriminately into Africa, artificial, ineffective and absurd. The "thin varnish of European civilization," which the native thus receives, is mistaken for a genuine mental metamorphosis, when as a rule, owing to the imprudent hurry by which the convert's reformation has been brought about, his Christianity, instead of being pure is superstitious, instead of being genuine is only nominal, instead of being deep is utterly superficial, and, not having fairly taken root, it cannot flourish and become reproductive.[62]

Indeed, the distinguished African theologian Eboussi Boulaga today makes a similar point:

> ...those who have been subjected to Christianity's assaults on their own traditions will never be content with half-measures and half-truths. Christianity will never recover its credibility, at least in the eyes of some. It will suffer from inadaptation to an Africa on the move

> until such time as the deepest, most radical questions are no longer handled by preterition and evasion.[63]

In the tradition of Blyden, new guard theologians are more radically interpreting what it means to be an African Christian. Blyden, though, does not overcome his ambivalence toward Europe. Despite his appreciation of African cultures, Blyden unprovidentially cooperated with European imperialist — a contradiction I will explore later in this chapter.

Providence and Liberal Education

Blyden claims in *Christianity, Islam and the Negro Race* that the African people must be independent of Eurocentric epistemologies.[64] Blacks, however, must go farther than Blyden in terms of being independent of Eurocentric pedagogy. "Law and philosophy," writes Blyden, "we may get from the Romans and the Greeks, religion from the Hebrews."[65] Hellenistic civilization should not — indeed can not — be ignored. Uncritical reverence, however, of the Hellenism that Blyden commended will — at American universities for instance — support detractors of African-American studies.

George James's view that Greco-Roman civilization is a legacy stolen from black Egyptians, is plausible, to say the least.[66] I have noted that Blyden knew Egypt was a black civilization, and that the Greeks looked to Egypt "to gaze upon its wonders and gather inspiration from its arts and sciences."[67] Unlike James, however, Blyden did not religiously relate Greek achievement to Egyptian civilization in order to undermine white supremacists who attribute the roots of civilization solely to Aryans.[68]

If Blyden uncritically commended the study of Hellenism, the "roots of Western civilization," other aspects of his pedagogy are more edifying for Pan-African theology today. Blyden served as President of Liberia College from 1880 to 1884. "Ultimately," explains Lynch, "the role of Liberia College was to counteract the evil influences which European ideas and teaching had on the Negro, to correct European misrepresentation of Africa and the Negro, and to play the leading role in interpreting Africa to the rest of the world."[69]

Blyden wished to curtail the teaching of the intellectual history of the Enlightenment. According to Blyden, it was during the modern period that "the transatlantic slave trade arose and those theories — logical, social and political — were invented for the degradation and proscription of the Negro."[70] Blyden, proficient in classical languages, thought the

> study of the Greek and Latin languages and literature was permissible because there were in them "not a sentence, a word, or a syllable disparaging to the Negro." They could give the Negro mental discipline without "injecting him with race poison."[71]

Hellenism, however, undergirded the "scientific theories" of black inferiority, which developed during the Enlightenment.

Intrinsic to Blyden's pedagogy was creative assimilation of the legacies of the ancestors. He writes: "We must study our brethren in the interior who knows [sic] more than we do the *Laws of the growth for the race* [emphasis added]."[72] Although Blyden's presidency at Liberia College failed, his vision of new pedagogical "forms representing the African idea...African literature with the smell of Africa upon it...African freedom, African thought and African theology" signifies an understanding of Providence upon which I will build.[73] Indeed, according to Lynch, Blyden asserts that Americo-Liberians should "'amalgamate with [their] aboriginal [siblings]' and carefully study [their] 'social organization, [their] religion, [their] politics' which, though they might be modified somewhat, must form the basis of a distinctive African culture."[74]

Blyden's quest for cultural and epistemological self-definition is similar to what progressive African theologians, such as Éla, assert today in terms of the African independent churches.[75] In the struggle to liberate black Africa from foreign domination, African theologians and the African masses bearing traditional values must complement one another.

Moreover, according to Blyden, African people must remember that

> the part of the oppressor is not less to be despised than the part of the oppressed — that the part of the man-stealer and man-seller is far more contemptible than the part of the men stolen and sold...The brilliancy of the universal and prolonged success which has given the European the idea that he has a right to despise others, and to proclaim the fact — the glories which have followed in the wake of his progress and conquests — are getting sadly dimmed in the light of a fuller understanding of the Gospel of Christ.[76]

Again, Blyden's view are providentially instructive for a Pan-African theology looking toward the twenty-first century. In terms of a transcontextual christology, the forging of new cultural and political realities of African-Americans and Africans will be facilitated in defining the common oppressor. When blacks are no longer ambivalent toward Europe and themselves, they will have greater incentive to work for black liberation. On both sides of the Atlantic, their understanding of Christ will be expressed through the redemptive legacies of the ancestors, legacies already hinted at by the African-American theologian James Cone.[77] Indeed, in the task to clarify Pan-African hermeneutics, far more study of the African heritage, transformed across time and space, is imperative.

Providence and Socialism

Earlier in this chapter I critiqued Blyden's captivity to Western definitions of civilization. By 1908, however, with the publication of *African Life and Customs*, Blyden was more critical of that civilization, though his views were vitiated by a strange optimism in relation to the Berlin Conference. According to Blyden:

> Civilization as it exists in practice is quite contrary — really antagonistic — to the original and radical idea of the word...Its modern tendency is to beget classes and masses — to emphasize the *I*, and suppress the *We*, to create the capitalist and the proletariat; and is a constant struggle between the "top and the bottom dog."[78]

Erudite scholar that he was, Blyden was probably aware of Marx's and Engel's position on alienated labor and exchange value. Blyden writes:

> The production of wealth in Europe is communistic in the highest degree; but the distribution is individualistic in its most intense form, hence the social unrest and discontent. The proletariat are ever on strikes — men and women not only clamoring for higher wages but for a more equitable division of the results of the communistic labor; that is the results which capital and labour together have produced. All combination for Industrial [sic] purposes is co-operative, but the difficulty in Europe — we should perhaps say the impossibility — is to get an equitable share of the proceeds for each party who contributes to the result.[79]

Blyden argues that the modern contradictions of political economy corrupt because European mores are flawed. Blyden thought Africans should resist the decadence of the capitalist order, which produces "Poverty, Criminality, Insanity — people who live in whorehouses, prisons, and lunatic asylums."[80] He thought that African values were better suited than European values for the advancement of socialism. For Blyden, "under the African system of communal property and cooperative effort every member of a community has a home and a sufficiency of food and clothing and other necessaries of life and for life."[81] What is more, claims Blyden,

> Africans living under native laws and Institutions would never co-operate with any man or company to the end that one man or company should appropriate to his or their own use and benefit the whole of the surplus wealth resulting from their joint efforts. The whole of the surplus wealth accumulated under our Native System by co-operative labour is regularly divided and in a most orderly manner sub-divided among all the people co-operating, "Unto each according to his several ability." The internal wars of the African have been largely in defence of his Social Institutions, resisting men of his own tribe anxious to aggrandize themselves at the expense of the people...wars against Europeans have also been in defence of...Institutions [regarded] as sacred.[82]

His view of African values, however, though very important, and true in part, reflects a picture of precolonial Africa that is too idyllic. While many precolonial societies, unlike relatively centralized kingdoms such as Dahomey and Buganda were, indeed, communal, feudal societies, such as the Tutsi of Rwanda and Burundi, reveal that the notion of African socialism is ahistorical with respect to parts of Africa.

In *African Life and Customs* Blyden, nonetheless, reveals his progressive intuitions. Although Blyden obfuscates the contradictions of the African past, his valorization of African values is edifying for a Pan-African theology today. Blyden's sense of the relation of African culture to models of socialism is an enduring legacy for radical theologians who refuse to parrot Eurocentric Marxists.

Africa's Redemption and Colonialism

Blyden's good intentions were neutralized by serious errors in political assessment and historical judgment. Despite, for instance, his condemnation of the expropriation of labor in Great Britain, he supported British imperialism in the wake of the partition of Africa.[83] Indeed, Blyden goes overboard in his confidence in the providential role of the British in Africa. Despite his early criticism of Anglo-Saxon propaganda, Blyden, like Crummell, was inordinately enamored of what he perceived to be British virtues.[84]

Like James A. B. Horton of the seminal Fanti Federation, Blyden thought that European rule would lay the foundation for the infrastructure of a United West Africa. So zealous was Blyden to use the British to effect Pan-African unity, that he advised the British to cultivate amiable relations with the powerful Asante, supporting the merits of so-called indirect rule. According to Lynch, Blyden thought that "'the fundamental error' of the British" was that they developed trade with "the 'feeble and demoralised natives on the coast in hostility to the more industrious, more intelligent and better organized races of the interior.'"[85]

Blyden thought that European powers in Africa would gradually repair "the waste places and [teach] the natives to make the best possible use of their own country, by fitting it for exiles in distant lands who may desire to return to the ancestral home."[86] "All that Europe can do," he writes, "is keep the peace among the tribes, giving them the order and security necessary to progress; while the emissaries of religion, industry and trade teach lessons of spiritual and secular life."[87]

Blyden believed Providence decreed that the climate would soon force Europeans to surrender their empires to blacks allegedly resistant to endemic diseases.[88] European medical advances, however, mitigated the threat of those diseases. Nonetheless, Blyden was so convinced of the imminency of European withdrawal, that he worked out a plan for devolution.[89]

Despite Blyden's *naïveté,* Richard Sklar, a professor at the University of California, praises Blyden's cooperation with the imperialists. According to Sklar, Blyden's thought "anticipated the comprehensive impact of cultural domination and charted a course of resistance to cultural imperialism together with a tentative program for principled interaction with colonial institution."[90]

Sklar writes:

> Blyden was not attracted to lost causes; nor was he disposed to utter lamentations. He understood that no force on earth could prevent the colonial occupation of Africa and did not regret the tide of history. On the contrary, he viewed political imperialism with favor as a necessary stage of historical development which could, if wisely conducted, have highly beneficial effects for the people of Africa. In that regard he shared the proto-imperialist sentiments of most progressive and worldly intellectuals of his time, including Marx, Engels, and the younger Lenin.[91]

Sklar thinks that Blyden's legacy represents "the 'epochal' roles of heretofore underappreciated African builders of durable institutions under colonialism."[92] African scholars, then, who study Blyden should

> refocus the study of Africa on Africa itself, on African initiatives and responsibilities, achievements and failures, rather than African responses to external initiative or

> African grievances against olden or neocolonialism. An Afrocentric political science would be neither anti-colonial nor, reflexively and as a matter of convention, anti-imperialist, regardless of the relevance or irrelevance of that posture to the problems of African development.[93]

Sklar's hegemonic perspective presents colonialism as if it were a neutral thing that could be manipulated from an Afrocentric perspective. Like olden colonialism, however, neo-colonialism perpetuates the disequilibrium between center and periphery. Neocolonialism forbids a truly Afrocentric perspective of the revolutionary poor. "Neutral" acceptance of colonialism enhances precisely the underdevelopment that exacerbates human misery among the African poor.

Blyden's cooperation with colonial powers was not progressive, but retrogressive. Certainly, Blyden knew that Africa, weakened by the slave trade, was no match for the war technology of industrial Europe. Surely Blyden could not have prevented colonialism, but it would have been better for posterity if his legacy reflected a more perceptive consciousness of the satanic significance of colonialism.

Blyden wrongly asserted that Africa

> has been partitioned in the order...of Providence, by the European powers, and...in spite of what has happened or is now happening or may yet happen, this partition has been permitted for the ultimate good of the people, and for the benefit of humanity.[94]

Hindsight reveals that only the imperial bourgeoisie and the black elite parasitic on the black oppressed have benefited from the legacy of partition. The oppression of the African masses can hardly be called providential. The "red rubber" of Leopold's Belgium, whom Blyden supported; the padlocked lips of dissident Angolans; the forced industrial labor in which millions of Africans died as outrageously as did the enslaved blacks of the Americas; the prevailing victimization of the starving African peasants; the plunder of African resources; the heinousness of apartheid; the death by millions of diarrhea-stricken, malnourished infants — all evince that the African people have given too much to the West. To the African people, the West continues to give nothing — death and desiccation.

Blyden was not correct in his understanding of Providence in relation to the tragedy of partition; but he correctly valorized African culture. His appreciation of the redemptive values of African culture is indeed a providential legacy. Blyden's words still have great significance for posterity:

> Your first duty is to be *yourselves*...You need to be told constantly that you are Africans, not Europeans — black men not white men — that you were created with the physical qualities which distinguish you for the glory of the Creator, and for the happiness and perfection of humanity; and that in your endeavors to make yourselves something else, you are not only spoiling your nature and turning aside from your destiny, but you are robbing humanity of the part you ought to contribute to its complete development and welfare, and you become as salt which has lost its savor — good for nothing — but to be cast out and trodden down by others.[95]

If God is Creator, if bearing the image of God signifies the equality of diverse human beings — so-called "races" — then values traceable to the cultures of the ancestors signify no ontological privation.

Blyden's legacy conveys the redemptive sense that any theology that places blacks

> out of sympathy with [their] people is a curse to...them...the religion which separates [blacks] from [their] people and makes [them] stand off from them in contemptuous scorn, is a religion not from God but from the devil.[96]

Indeed, to insist that theology must be dictated in terms of European civilization serves not God but a satanic white supremacy that advanced the cultural aggression of too many Eurocentric missionaries in Africa and the Americas. (My criticism of "Euro"-missionaries cannot apply to the just martyrs of Central America, such as the Maryknoll missionaries, Maura Clarke, and Ita Ford, who opted for the *campesinos* of El Salvador.)

Conclusion of Part 2

I have criticized Crummell and Blyden only to advance a theology of liberation and Pan-Africanization, which is in touch with the pain of the black poor (and the black middleclass). Blyden's and Crummell's views of Providence reveal the problem of alienation and the positiveness of continuity. Blyden's legacy is more positive than Crummell's. Both ancestors, however, missed the mark in not recognizing that Providence is meaningful primarily in terms of an intense, Afrocentric identification with the socioeconomic struggles and the religio-cultural innovations of the black poor.

My critique in no way diminishes my respect for the two clergymen. Indeed, their legacies help me to understand, in a positive and negative sense, that Providence yields the recreative presence of God in the political cultures of the black poor who may participate in a redemptive transformation despite the sin and death of oppression. In order to draw out current implications of this view I turn now to Part 3 of this text, which begins with a chapter focusing on social analysis.

Part 3
The Visible and the Invisible: The Providence of God

4.

Social Analysis: at the Crossroads of the Hermeneutical Circle of the Pan-African Experience

The continuous growth and confinement of a permanent underclass within the community signals the depth of the socioeconomic crisis faced by Blacks....Inattention to the underclass represents the single greatest danger to maintaining a healthy cohesive Black community.

— Douglas G. Glasgow *The Black Underclass*

The babies are quiet with hunger; the hunger had allowed colds and diarrhea to take hold. Noses and eyes streamed with mucus; the mucus attracted flies, which crawled across open eyes. Mothers breasts were flat, empty. Many mothers were trying to care for both their children and their own parents, men and women probably no more than 40 years old but as decrepit as I remember my own 95 year-old great-grandmother. Women were pre-chewing food for their parents. Men had all their possessions in small sacks, and no seeds for the future. The camp "hospital" had all the luxury of a tin roof and the smells that only hundreds of cases of diarrhea in a closed room can cause. Corpses were left in place for a long time, because it was so hard to tell the dead from the merely exhausted.

— Lloyd Timberlake *Africa in Crisis*

I seek to build upon the legacies of Blyden and Crummell but in terms of an epistemological break expedited by social analysis. To facilitate this paradigm shift, I reiterate that I will assimilate a methodology of the South, the "underside of history," as expressed by the Ecumenical Association of Third World Theologians (EATWOT), as well as *L'association oecuménique des théologiens africains* (L' AOTA).[1] While Crummell's and Blyden's theologies where conditioned by political issues of Africa and North America, they were too alienated from the masses. Indeed they are not to be held responsible for knowing a theological method that has come to the fore after their deaths. Nonetheless, social analysis is indispensable for theological reflection on a praxis of liberation. In this chapter, then, I will first explain the place of social analysis within a hermeneutical paradigm of the "underside of history." Second, I will briefly analyze socioeconomic problems of the black North American underclass and the African peasants. I do not propose a blueprint for a transcontextual praxis, but diagnose the oppression of the poor in terms of certain ideological positions.

For liberation theologians, theology emerges from critical theory tested in political struggle. Thus, orthopraxis, the balancing of theory and practice, produces correct hermeneutics in opposition to the structural violence of oppressive societies. Orthopraxis is dependent upon a radical socioeconomic analysis of the contradictions between the oppressed and the oppressor. Orthopraxis is fructified in political actions necessary for societal transformation. Indeed, according to Juan Luis Segundo, "a theology worthy of the attention of the whole human being is not the outcome of abstract scientific or academic interest. It stems from a pretheological human commitment to change and improve the world."[2] Theology is the second step, it comes after opposition to social inequity.[3] The wretched of the earth — and the theologians edified by them — first resist their "thingification," a process whereby the oppressed are heinously dehumanized.

Thingification is described by Frantz Fanon in his discussion of the colonial experience of Africa's poor:

> Hostile nature, obstinate and fundamentally rebellious, is in fact represented in the colonies by the bush, by mosquitoes, natives, and fever, and colonization is a success when all this indocile nature has finally been tamed. Railways across the bush, the draining of swamps and a native population which is non-existent politically and economically are in fact one and the same thing.[4]

In the United States thingification is evident as the black underclass are "incarcerated" within the boundaries drawn by urban planners and threatened by the "sanitizing" process of gentrification.

Douglas Glasgow describes gentrification as follows:

> For over a decade after the [riots], the ghettos were allowed to lie dormant in decay; now, however the city has become a prime area for relocating whites. The influx of younger generation whites in search of metropolitan conveniences has heralded the return of small businesses, the flow of monies from banks to areas previously redlined (systematically denied bank loans), the rise in the cost and value of housing, and the increased reclamation of dwellings by absentee owners for private use or for resale. The housing problems of the poor have become critical as more and more are being pushed out of their traditional multidwelling inner-city rental units without either practical means for relocating or housing programs that meet their needs.[5]

Among the black oppressed, resistance to thingification is related to the recognition of material contradictions. The contradiction between the oppressed's and oppressor's experiences of reality forces the radicalized oppressed to oppose the hegemony of the status quo — the capitalist West. Because radical blacks on both sides of the Atlantic oppose this oppression, resistance to thingification refers to the transcontextual consciousness I defined in chapter 1. Indeed, the complementarity of resistances is indispensable for a transcontextual method that emerges from the struggle for liberation. This struggle seeks an equilibrium — itself necessary for Pan-African consciousness — between Africa and Diaspora.

Equilibrium in the struggle for liberation is maintained in a posture radically critical of Eurocentric hegemony. According to Fanon:

> We need a model, and...we want blueprints and examples. For many among us the European model is the most inspiring. We have...seen...what mortifying setbacks such an imitation has led us. European achievements, European techniques, and the European style ought no longer to tempt us to throw us off our balance.[6]

Equilibrium in Pan-African theology is maintained only as blacks trust their orientation in theory and practice. Equilibrium here does not refer to the bourgeois theory of August Comte, which dissimulates social-economic contradictions in the valorization of the status quo.[7]

Equilibrium in Pan-African theology, in addition to its relation to social analysis, refers to two other elements I have noted — religio-cultural analysis and interpretation of Scripture. These three interconnected elements mutually condition one another and shift in significance according to the realities of specific contexts. Social and religio-cultural analyses together produce liberating meaning from both the Pan-African experience and selected elements of Scripture and Christian tradition. Liberating meaning is not produced if religio-cultural and social analyses do not structure the rereading of Scripture. These three elements, moreover, constantly revolving around one another in contexts of political struggle, constitute an interpretative dynamism similar to Segundo's liberation of Bultmann's hermeneutic circle.

According to Segundo: "A hermeneutic circle always presupposes a profound human commitment, a *partiality* that is consciously accepted — not on the basis of theological criteria, of course, but on the basis of human criteria."[8] Human criteria here are commitments to a Pan-Africanism based upon appreciations of the distinctions of the socioeconomic realities of African people. Orbiting within this circle, social analysis focuses on the general similarity of black experiences, and studies the distinct orthopraxes of the poor that irrupt in resistance to "thingification."

Unemployed, homeless, suffering from drug abuse, suffering disproportionately from diseases that plague America — especially AIDS — the black underclass in North America are concerned with survival in a white supremacist context. And so are the African peasants assaulted by a barrage of problems such as desertification, pauperization, starvation and AIDS — all of which are related to neocolonialism.

Yet I am uncertain of the extent to which the masses of people, in both places, are committed to Pan-Africanism. The black underclass and the African peasantry have shown no sustained interest in each other. Nonetheless, in Africa, the continuing appeal of the thoughts of Kwame Nkrumah, Amilcar Cabral, and Nelson Mandela suggest that Pan-Africanism is not so alienated from the African masses as to be irrelevant to a praxis against neocolonialism. The historic mass appeal of Pan-Africanists such as Marcus Garvey and Malcolm X, and the African-American outrage at the Italo-Ethiopian War and apartheid, as well as the popular support of Afrocentric symbols, suggest that black North American masses have been receptive to Pan-African discourse. Pan-African consciousness — on which it is hard to place a statistical value — still inspires the liberation struggles of oppressed blacks.[9] Indeed, the black oppressed are integral to the definition of a Pan-African theology. This chapter seeks to deepen an awareness of this Pan-African consciousness in terms of social analysis, which"is not the answer to social problems, but a tool for dealing with them."[10]

The Black North American Context

The black underclass have inherited the wretchedness of their slave ancestors. Although the conditions of today's black underclass and the slaves of yesterday are not identical, the ghetto and the slave quarters are historically connected. Failure to see the connection of the ancestors to the present indicates a blindness to the prevailing victimization of black folk trapped in poverty, illiteracy, and disease. For nearly four hundred years, black misery has proliferated in a context that teaches contempt of blacks.[11]

The underclass are trapped in the same neighborhoods as their progenitors.[12] Excluded from unions that give institutional strength to European emigrants; weakened by low tax bases and inferior and exorbitantly priced housing; forced to attend inferior schools; disproportionately unemployed and incarcerated; dispossessed of the means to control the economies of their communities; suffering from inadequate public services, inadequate health care, rampant drug addiction, internecine violence, and high infant mortality — the black underclass show clearly that black North Americans are pariahs like other people of the Third World.[13]

The proliferation of the black underclass is related to what Martin Luther King, Jr. called the white backlash.[14] This backlash — the ascendancy of neoconservative politics in the United States — is proportionate to the dismantling of the Civil Rights and Black Power movements and the censuring of the radical legacies of Martin Luther King and Malcolm X.[15] Indeed, the white supremacist infrastructure has made it difficult for blacks to inch forward in the United States.

It is well known that the Civil Rights movement did not significantly benefit the black underclass. Rather, the movement benefited the black middleclass — a pseudo bourgeoisie. Alienated in many ways from the underclass, the middleclass in general has not been able to determine what will move the black masses to action.[16] Often unaware of the meaning of black suffering at its root, unconscious of the continuum of African-American values emergent from the ancestral legacies of the slave era, and too comfortable with material gains, the "Crummell-like" middleclass, for the most part, is ill-equipped to make an unambivalent political commitment to the black underclass. As Cedric Robinson explains in terms of Richard Wright, too few of the middleclass see "the necessity of a critical commitment, the sort of commitment which achieves its purpose by extraction from the historical legacy: the consciousness capable of recreating meaning."[17] This commitment gave birth, in fact, to the Civil Rights movement and could significantly improve the lot of the black underclass. Integrationists must see that white America's fundamental contempt for blacks disallows blacks' participation in white institutions in a way commensurate with the ratio of blacks to whites.

Black nationalists, particularly those who work among the underclass, are acutely aware of the ugly contempt whites have for them and realize that white supremacy is fought through institutions unambivalently dedicated to black liberation. It bears reiteration that integration means at best a margin of visibility and a modicum of power in predominately white contexts. Black nationalists, however, have tended to be more critical of those structures. Black nationalists, such as Malcolm X, have realized that white America is fundamentally committed to a pragmatism disturbingly akin to fascism.[18] As the black underclass continue to proliferate, integration, in the view of black nationalists, is a misnomer.

Although critics attempt to pigeonhole black nationalism, black nationalism has many implications.[19] These emerge from blacks' consciousness of their essential *difference* from white Americans — a difference that is due to the historical and socioeconomic realities of the black experience. This difference makes the strengthening of autonomous institutions necessary given the virulence of white supremacy.

Black nationalism represents neither a retreat from the problem of white supremacy nor a return to the vulgar segregation of Jim Crow. Rather, black nationalism signifies a pragmatism, a *proyeto* that which will succeed only to the degree political energies are charged in the black masses.

The African-American pragmatism to which I refer here was expressed by Malcolm X as follows:

> America's problem is us. We're her problem. The only reason she has a problem is she doesn't want us here. And every time you look at yourself...a so-called Negro, you represent a person who poses such a serious problem for America because you're not wanted. Once you face this fact, then you can start plotting a course that will make you appear intelligent, instead of unintelligent.[20]

Indeed, intelligence is related to the recognition that blacks are, unwillingly, a "nation" pushed out of a nation.

Although blacks are not formally a nation, they are disinherited Americans and their deprivation makes them, when compared to whites, people of *another country*. Were this not so, there would be neither a "dark ghetto" nor an underclass nor the problem of white supremacy. Although black labor was the foundation of the primitive accumulation of capital and though blacks gave — and still give — their lives in the armed forces and pay taxes, they continue to be excluded from full participation in the dominant nation of the whites.[21] It is true that whites are comprised of diverse groups that are often bigoted toward one another. Still, white supremacy signifies the transcendence of those old world bigotries. Diverse white ethnic groups achieve unanimity in their racism against blacks.

In the words of Malcolm X, blacks are the "victims of [that] Americanism."[22] And blacks must deal pragmatically with their victimization, ground themselves in the struggles of the black underclass, and divest themselves of the illusion of integration.

Above all, black Americans must come to grips with their alienation from one another before they can embrace their African cousins in revolutionary struggle. Indeed, black nationalist values are prerequisites for the development of transcontextual praxis.[23] If capitalism in the United States is but the domestic side of imperialism abroad — and if white America's contempt of Africa is but an extension of its hostility toward its black counterpart — then blacks of the United States must gain the relative institutional autonomy to resist racist capitalism at home, a resistance bound to support the struggles of the African poor.

Black Africa

Africa, making up the majority of the poorest nations of the world, suffers from the highest infant mortality rate and the lowest per capita income in the world. The great suffering of Africa's poor is related to the political instability of a continent subjected to successive coups that have empowered fascist military governments such as those of Amin, Doe, Mobutu. Indeed, the most heinous human rights violations occur in Africa.[24] Thousands of people are murdered in Africa by fascist regimes instituted by the West, which profits immensely from its presence in contexts of incredible cruelty. Indeed, to quote Jean-Marc Éla, "The torture that rages in the African regimes would seem to be nothing but a creation of the imperialism operating through the mediation of the artificial elite it has fashioned for itself in order to insure the total dependence of the African economies on the metropolitan center."[25]

According to Julius Nyerere, former President of Tanzania, "Africa's debt burden is intolerable. [Africans] cannot pay. You know it and all our creditors know it. It is not a rhetorical question when I ask, should we really let our people starve so that we can pay our debts?"[26]

Tendencies to blame starvation on desertification, drought and misuse of soils obscure the facts that drought and traditional agriculture are hardly the causes of famine.[27] Rather, famine is due to gross mismanagement and improper priorities related to the machinations of imperialists whose exported capital is of little use to the masses.[28] The development of the African people is rarely a priority. Africa's illiteracy rate, for instance, is over 75 percent. According to one source, "if Africa's population doubles by the year 2000, as expected, 60 percent of the continent will be illiterate. It will be the highest concentration of illiterate people in the world."[29] At the dawning of independence Africa produced most of its own food. Now, with the exception of South Africa, the continent imports its food.[30]

Much of the misery of the peasants has been due to the African policy of the rival superpowers. The United States and the Soviet Union have attempted to outmaneuver one another in order to control strategic space and raw material.[31] Indeed, the export of oppressive, self-serving values — both ideological and material — impedes the liberation of the peasants, who are subjected to what Engelbert Mveng calls a *pauvreté anthropologique*.[32] "In...post-colonial societies, peasants find themselves at the bottom of stratified societies because their occupations have been accorded the least value and they have not been given any training to upgrade their positions in society."[33]

Oppression of the peasants is also due to precolonial stratifications, seen historically, for instance, in feudal relations among the Fulani and the Hausa of Nigeria, the Tutsi and the Hutu of Burundi, and the Buganda and the Ankole of Uganda. As Jean-Marc Éla has pointed out, the idyllic notion of a communitarian Africa of yesterday masks the economic and social conflicts among the ancestors.[34]

Metropolitan powers used the iniquity of indigenous contradictions to further exploit the peasantry.[35] The exploitation of such a peasantry was seen, for example, in Ghana. Feudal structures were further assimilated in the "Africanization" of the colonial infrastructure.[36]

According to Éla, the peasants of the Sahel, oppressed by neocolonial contradictions, are made to uproot life-giving millet in order to plant cotton for export. The peasants, he writes,

> have to devote the best land, rented each year from their traditional superiors, to a crop that they are told will bring in foreign currency. But the illiterate farmers watch the machinery roll by every year with pangs of anguish, for they can be sure that they will be robbed of what they sow. After the multiple claims of a series of intermediaries have been satisfied, the peasants, who labor extraordinarily hard though they live and work in deplorable conditions, find themselves once more in the ever-recurring cycle of cotton, taxes and debts.[37]

The peasants become politicized as they resist the expropriation of subsistence modes of production. Subsistence modes of production, bearing ancestral values, cut famine and yield a surplus that mitigates policies of crop-liening. Another factor leading to the politicization of the peasantry is the legacy of settler regimes. "European [and Americo-Liberian] settlers expropriated the Africans' land and forced [them] to operate both as tenant farmers and grossly exploited rural proletariats."[38] Here the oppression of the peasants reveals another dimension of the problem of caste. According to Ebitini Chikwendu, a lecturer in political science at the University of Nigeria, the "response of the national peasantry in Mozambique and Angola was to develop a tradition of resistance, right from the earliest times of colonialism, which culminated in the peasant-based nation-wide revolution leading to victory and independence of these countries."[39]

The oppression of the peasants, then, makes them revolutionary catalysts. Thus Fanon writes:

> The peasantry is systematically disregarded for the most part by the propaganda put out by the nationalist parties. And it is clear that in the colonial countries the peasants alone are revolutionary, for they have nothing to lose and everything to gain. The starving peasant outside the class system, is the first among the exploited to discover that only violence pays. For him [sic] there is no compromise, no coming to terms; colonization and decolonization are simply a matter of relative strength.[40]

Today Fanon's view has been criticized by Soviet Marxist, Yuri Smertin, as a form of "socio-psychological thinking" of "non-proletarian revolutionaries" who believe that "revolution hinges on volitional factors" rather than scientific factors.[41] According to Smertin, who has recently written a book on Kwame Nkrumah, "The objective prerequisites for direct struggle, not to mention armed struggle, and for the socialist reconstruction of society, do not, as yet, exist in Africa. The struggle to bring about political and socioeconomic change that will eliminate backwardness and pave the way for socialism is the order of the day."[42] That Marxist view assumes "that the social and historical processes which matter, which are determinative, are European."[43] Such a perspective claims to be free of racial chauvinism, but is — as a form of "prolet-ayranism" — blind to its embodiment of the ethnocentrism that set Europe against itself.[44]

The peasant cannot wait for a liberation beholden to dogmatic Marxist theorists. In Pan-African theology, the Marxist imperative, fraught with racism, can only further alienate the masses starving in the exigencies created by "fortress Europe," the Russians and the United States. As African theologian Jean-Marc Éla reveals in his liberation theology of the peasantry: "It is illusory to believe that the development of the human being in Africa will consist of moving from the magico-religious mentality to a scientific, technological mentality. Indeed, this view of the problematic is ideological rather than scientific."[45] Contrary to the Marxist view, I agree with Éla, "the major need of the dominated human being is not his or her deprimitivization or the attainment of a certain level of 'civilization' in order to enter into a phase of development, but an escape from all manner of alienation by world imperialism."[46]

In Pan-African theology, social analysis cannot rely on the export of ideology, but must rely on *African* assimilations of radical thought — assimilations related to the African theologian's, Barthélemy Adoukonou's, reappropriation of *l'Africanisme du dedans*. Here, radical African thought negates alien assessments of Africa. According to Adoukonou, these foreign assessments "have consisted of a sterile and alienating repetition of the problems and solutions of the West. To take refuge in them as a new sholasticism would be to give in to the pretensions of cultural imperialism that subtlety transforms problems related to culture into a single problem true for all of humanity [my translation]."[47]

Adoukonou's sense of *l'Africanisme du dedans* is implicit in Éla's elaboration of his view of African traditions.

Éla writes:

> The African traditions may seem to act as a brake on social changes, but in reality it is in an awareness of their identity that black peasants find their reasons for rejecting a developmental model that generates an economic surplus to be divided up by foreign capitalist and local bureaucracies. Their religious life has ever enabled African peoples to fight foreign economic, political, and cultural domination. In colonialism, the religion of the subjugated peoples does not tend to become what Marx calls the opium of the people.[48]

In Africa, in places such as Mozambique, revolution, anchored in the sensibilities of the peasants, "is informed by political, moral and ideological presumptions with priorities which *precede* their envelopment into the modern world system [emphasis added]."[49] In identifying the particularity of peasant revolt, in terms of material contradictions, one sees the dynamism of the foundations of national cultures to which socialist theory must adapt itself.

Conclusion

Theologians must have the courage and creativity to shepherd their churches beyond theory to a liberating practice dictated by the black poor. *L'association oecuménique des théologiens africains*, including African-American theologians, for instance, might embark upon ecclesial experiments that seek to test the unifying power of the oppressed across contexts. The distinct praxes of Africa and the United States will be strengthened in a Pan-African commitment that is transcontextual.

In this process of forging a transcontextual praxis of liberation, African people might define a matrix of accountability. The single most important criterion would be whether political policies of the Pan-African community oppress the poor across contexts. If, for instance, an African-American organization supports a fascist regime like Amin's Uganda, as CORE did in 1973, that organization must be criticized as an obstruction to the struggle for the liberation of the Pan-African community.[50]

I forge ahead now to theological reflection. The remaining chapters seek to explore religio-cultural, biblical, and theological elements.

5.

The Religio-Cultural Circle of the Transatlantic World

...in spite of the onslaughts of Christianity, African spirituality abides, as human beings' conscientization of their position in the world through the cycle of tasks and seasons and ages of life and social roles, through the bond among the generations, through healing and festival. It abides as the permanent, regulatory metaphor of the structures and the basic activities of existence, by which are accomplished the genesis of human beings, the conditions of their being, and the access to their humanity until death comes and is accepted as necessary to the truth of life, and as a source of solidarity communication, and reciprocity among the living. African spirituality is a spirituality in which the afterlife is in the hands of others. My survival is other people's problem, not mine. The important thing is to exist really, without ever seeming to have discharged one's obligations towards other's, living or dead. True life is never absent.

— F. Eboussi Boulaga

The oppressive element in the religions of the oppressed is the negation of the image of the oppressor and the discovery of the first creation. It is thus the negation that is found in community and seeks its expression in more authentic forms of community....based upon the first creation, the original authenticity of all persons which precedes the master-slave dichotomy. There is thus a primordial structure to this consciousness, for in seeking a new beginning in the future, it must perforce imagine an original beginning.

— Charles Long

We must unlearn our slavery to the conceptualization of words and begin to see the black manifestation of truth in the rhythm of black life.

— James Cone

Neither Crummell's nor Blyden's notions of Providence entailed a religio-cultural dimension adequate for a contemporary Pan-African theology. In this chapter, then, I will discuss religio-cultural dimensions that I think are adequate. In carrying this out, I will first discuss my understanding of African traditional religion, the parent, so to speak, of the black religion emergent from the struggles of black North Americans. Second, I will discuss black religion and thereafter discuss black religion in terms of a cultural modality that facilitates Pan-Africanization.

African Traditional Religion

Although I have discussed African traditional religion elsewhere, it must be discussed here as a foundation of Pan-African theology.[1] African traditional religion suggests sources of values of Pan-African theology and facilitates critical evaluation of these values. I discuss African traditional religion in order to note certain similarities and dissimilarities between Africans and African-Americans. Discernment of the extent to which values of the Diaspora find their prototypes in Africa requires a comparison between traditions of ancestors and descendants, Africans and African-Americans. My goals are to specify how elemental themes of African traditional religion are used idiomatically in a Pan-African theology and to draw conclusions, clarifying what is meant by Pan-Africanization. My discussion of African traditional religion focuses on the ancestral religion of the BaKongo whose rarified legacies are found in black North America. My discussion also reflects an appreciation of the legacies of the Yoruba, Fon, Igbo, Akan, Dogon, and Fang.[2]

Much of the ethnographic and survey literature on African traditional religion tends to obscure the social and socioeconomic significance of specific African societies.[3] Flawed by Christian bias in terms of a proselytizing methodology that blurs distinctions between chirographic and mnemonic cultures, much of the discourse reflects symbols and values of Western civilization.[4] African traditional religions, however, are independent entities and require interpretation within their ambits. African traditional religion is a varied phenomenon best understood regionally in terms of distinct taxonomies.[5] "No definite results can be expected from studies of the variation and diffusion of reified complexes such as 'twinship' if structural matrices in which they are studied are neglected."[6] One must, to some degree, be initiated into the meanings of the living contexts of popular cultures. Éla puts it this way:

> The problem for African peasants is not that of a return to the sources. African peasants have never lost their living culture. Yet the liberation of the masses is a basic problem — and offers a point of departure from which popular culture may become a truly vital culture, with its own place in contemporary history. The rural populations are now the source of African culture.[7]

Fanon's dictum, "...culture has never the translucidity of custom," is true.[8] African traditional religion lives as it reflects the dynamic religio-cultural realities of the African poor. African traditional religion, positively bearing ancestral legacies, changes in response to the historic exigencies of its environments. "We are not piecing together a fossil," explains Eboussi Boulaga,"we are dealing with something living, something that reacts, mobilizes, and creates antibodies to resist aggression from without."[9] Stellar examples of this dynamism are independent churches.[10]

Sky, Earth and All Those Things

African traditional religion signifies the visible and invisible — the sky, the earth, and all these things. By the visible, I mean human beings, flora, fauna and the artifacts, insignia and mnemonic utterances that signify the metaphoric and metonymic values of a localized cosmos.[11] The visible is the natural and cultural environment, of which humans, always in the process of transformation, are at the center.[12]

The perpetual process of death and rebirth, which entail the reciprocity of the living and the dead, signify *rites de passage.*[13] For BaKongo, human life has no end. Life constitutes a cycle in which death is a transition to another mode of being.[14] Life's cycle is seen in the newly born, and coded in the ancestors, in pools and stones of spiritual entities, and at the crossroads of the forest and the cemetery. Among other ethnic groups, life's cycle is seen in the possession-trance of anthropomorphic beings who regulate social life.[15] According to Boulaga, "all life has its roots in death and feeds on death. All 'coming alive,' all creation, and all passage to another order are obtained only at the price of death and demise. Hence the set of schemata, images, and archetypes whose actualization and effectuation integrate existence into being, by submitting the human being to the latter's laws."[16]

The laws of existence, taught by the ancestors, signify the invisible. By the invisible I mean especially the ancestors of certain Niger-Congo societies such as the BaKongo. Among the Bakongo, the ancestors "as they formerly existed in the different regions of Kongo show a close association with various forms of chieftainship and therefore with the corporate organization of Kongo society and government."[17] Essentially linking a people to their archetypical origins and life-sustaining rituals, the ancestors (*bakulu*) are cherished for purposes of sagacity and fecundity, equilibrium and fertility.[18] By the invisible I also mean the Ultimate Being, but especially the spirits, divinities, and witches whose presences are decoded by religious specialists who know the "signifiers and indices" of the visible.[19]

The coexistence of the invisible and the visible is honed and renewed through rituals expressed by way of symbolic colors, dances, rhythms, artifacts, and all those things that humans fashion and do in order to survive and thrive, often in hostile environments.

The invisible and the visible signify bipolarities that structure traditional society. The traditional Kongo universe, for instance, is

> divided into two parts such that, in different aspects, the relations between the two are relations of time, space and cause. The people themselves speak of the two parts most often as "this world" (*nza yayi*) and "the land of the dead" (*nsi a bafwa*). The worlds are separated by a body of water, traditionally called Kalunga but most often referred to as *nlangu*, "water," *m'bu*, "ocean," or *nzadi*, "great river" or by various other ordinary words for water, pools, and rivers.[20]

The ancestral BaKongo world is divided by two mountains, the mountain of the living (*ntoto*) and the mountain of the dead (*mpemba*). These mountains would be joined at their bases were they not separated by water.[21] Traditionally, the BaKongo have signified their world in a cosmogram in which the vertical pole of a cross, essentially unrelated to the Christian cross, is like an axis mundi. The horizontal pole of the BaKongo cross is the watery boundary separating the mountains of the living and dead. The four points of the cross signify the *trajectory* of the rising and setting sun and the reciprocating universe of the living and the dead. The ambivalence of the cosmos enhances communication between bipolarites such as the mountains of the living and the dead. The greater the distance among polarities, the greater their need of communication in terms of their complementarity and integration.[22]

While I am aware of the shortcomings of a structuralist's approach to African traditional religion,[23] certain African traditional religions might be conceived heuristically as follows:

sky	earth
divinity	humanity
dead	living
white	black
male	female
north	south
east	west
village	forest
culture	nature

Bipolarites imply one another in terms of myth (time) and ritual (the practice and extension of mythic time in space). Thus the distinction between culture and nature imply other complementary elements of a localized cosmos, such as male and female, north and south, village and forest. These elements are the "grammar" of existence that imbues the human body and soul with religious meaning.

In BaKongo thought, writes Wyatt MacGaffey,

> the path of the sun and of the soul are analogous; both describe the periphery of a divided universe. Included in the analogical structure are the points of transition between the visible and the invisible worlds:
>
> | | | |
> |---|---|---|
> | day | sunrise, sunset | night |
> | the living | birth, death | the dead |
> | land | water | land[24] |

At dawn and dusk the living and the dead exchange day and night. Dusk signifies death, and dawn, rebirth.[25] The deceased have been "buried with their heads toward the rising sun so that on rising the deceased might [continue to] journey in the counter-clockwise direction.[26]

Bipolarites valorize complementarity and opposition, separation and integration. These cosmological valences tend to signify the quest for equilibrium. "Kongo religious activities," writes MacGaffey, "can be seen as so many efforts to ameliorate and stabilize daily life by linking it with permanent factors."[27] The sky, the earth, and all these things, must be kept in their place in order to be brought together for the harmonious maintenance of the cosmos — its fecundity, fertility, cyclical regeneration and the waning spiral stretching back towards the sacred time of ancestral homelands.[28] In the words of Boulaga, African traditional spirituality entails:

> correct insertion and reciprocity, in respect for and obligation toward what is "ourselves otherwise." We must leave everything in its place. There is a time for each thing. We must repair every breach of harmony, every wound and lesion.[29]

The autochthonous quest for equilibrium, for healing and wholeness, is the spirituality of the masses. African traditional religion presents the most authentic idioms necessary for the synthesis of political and cultural concerns.

African Traditional and Slave Religions and Pan-Africanization

Although black American theologians study what African theologians are doing, they cannot simply follow examples of their African cousins and Africanize black theology in modalities of African traditional religion. The differences among contexts make black theologians' appeal to African traditional religion problematic. In Africa, Christianity is indigenized in religions of specific ethnic groups. North American blacks are hardly, if at all, ethnic in that sense. Although descended from Niger-Congo groups such as the BaKongo, they barely represent continuities of those groups. The black underclass have not defined themselves as a people in terms of neolithic archetypes or according to rituals that strengthen life from the clan to the kingdom. The black underclass have not been tied to their dead and other anthropomorphic beings in a way characteristic of the African peasantry.

What, then, is the relation of African traditional religion to black North American realities, especially in relation to black religion? Although I noted that "legacies of the ancestors" is symbolic, the idiom would be too reified if it did not participate in historical reality.

The bridge between black and African traditional religions is the sacred time of the slave era. This fact facilitates a Pan-Africanization of theology based on the transcontextual symbol of the ancestors.

Sterling Stuckey, in the tradition of DuBois, Melville Herskovits, Zora Neal Hurston, and Blyden, reveals that African traditional religion was the essential foundation of slave culture.[30] According to Stuckey, records of slave culture, such as the story of "King Buzzard," the pathetic lament of the "Slave Barn" and the "carnival-like" John Kunering pageant, reveal an African spirituality decisive for an appreciation of slave religion.[31] Essential to slave religion were the counterclockwise movement of the ringshout and the spirituals. Featured prominently in this circle of culture, Stuckey claims, was the legacy of the BaKongo people, who, captured in large numbers, greatly influenced black North American culture.[32] Stuckey, in fact, lends credibility to Herskovits's discredited view of the African-American sense of Christian baptism. According to Herskovits, slaves assimilated the rite of baptism in terms of their memory of "the association of water with African ritual."[33] Indeed, it is plausible that the reciprocating cosmos of the BaKongo, signified by the BaKongo cross, influenced slave religion.[34] The spiritual "Wade in the Water" may indeed express an ancestral legacy in which the watery boundary separating the living from the dead symbolizes regeneration.[35]

Stuckey claims, in addition, that cosmological similarities among African slaves facilitated their convergence in the ringshout — the circumference of the liminal ground of slave religion.[36] The slaves circled together, anchored in the depths of ancestral legacies. The birthplace, says Stuckey, of this rhythmically sophisticated ritual was the graveyard.[37] If, as Albert Raboteau claims, the gods died — the vodu, orisha, and abascom — the ancestors did not.[38] According to Stuckey, the tale of the Redhill Churchyard, featuring the mediating trickster, Brer Rabbit, strongly suggests that the cemetery was the threshold from which African-Americans communicated with the numinous departed — the ancestors.[39] As in traditional African religions of West and Central Africa, the ancestors in slave religion were the integrating focus of the disparate cosmos.

Specific identities of ancestors fade as successive generations no longer remember them by name. Yet, argues Stuckey convincingly, the transformation of ancestral legacies in the Americas is decisive for an appreciation of the uniqueness of African-American people. One might think of these legacies as invisible. Stuckey puts it this way:

> When one bears in mind that slave folklore was not created to be transcribed or even to be heard by whites, one must conclude that what was eventually transcribed is just a small portion of that which dies on the night air or continues to live, undetected by scholars, in the folk memory.[40]

If the folk memory suggests the invisibility of the legacies of African traditional religion, the visibility of its legacies is clearly heard and seen in dimensions of black religion and black music.

The relation of African traditional religion to the folk memory leads me to conclude that African traditional religion is a philosophical element, a creative component of a theological enterprise. It marks an aspect of the development of historic religio-cultural categories of Africa and Diaspora. I am not claiming African traditional religion is a philosophical element like philosophies traceable to the Greeks and the ancient Egyptians before them. My meaning is apologetic, threefold and more basic. I refer to:

(1) an attitude formed for the goals of a very specific perspective — namely Pan-Africanization;

(2) an account of the rationale for premises essential to this perspective — namely the link between black and African traditional religions;

(3) an establishment of the transcontextual symbols of Pan-African theology.

Elements of African traditional religion are distilled through an Afrocentric theological imagination and emerge, in relation to black religion, as motifs of Pan-Africanization. Fundamental is the symbol of the ancestors, the leitmotif of this book.

Black Religion

Black religion, anchored in slave religion, signifies varieties of African-American expressions such as Vodun, Santeria, "Hoodoo," the Moorish Science Temple, the Black Jews, the Nation of Islam, the Shrine of the Black Madonna, Kwanza, as well as the black church.[41]

I will first discuss what I perceive to be the epistemological problem of black religion which has been spun out from the circle of slave religion. Second, I will look at three perspectives on black religion: those of Charles Long, James Cone and Theo Witvliet. These perspectives will serve as the background for my sense of a mode of Pan-Africanization that heightens appreciation of black religion in relation to African traditional religion.

What distinguishes black religion from other North American religions? The views of both Charles Long and James Cone, whom I discuss more substantially later, along with others, help provide answers to this question. James Cone claims that black theology is closest to the religious orientation of the black masses of the United States.[42] According to Long, though, Cone's *theological* understanding of black religion is, in the final analysis, too Eurocentric. For Charles Long, a Eurocentric discipline cannot deal with the opacity of black religion. By opacity Long means "the specific meaning and value of [an-other] culture and/or language."[43] Theological elements of Europe, according to Long, distort the structures of black religiousness and confuse its opaque distinctiveness with "transparent" modalities of a Euro-American consciousness.[44]

Certainly, black religion is related to Christianity, i.e., Cone's black theology. But, as Long explains, "not all the religious meanings of the black communities were encompassed by the Christian form of religion." For Long, the cutting edge of the hermeneutical task is isolation of the distinctiveness of black religion. Long questions the meaning of this distinctiveness, this orientation: "that is, how one comes to terms with the ultimate significance of one's place in the world."[45] According to Long, Christian values are penetrated by or exist along side of other forms of African-American "orientation" that "have had great critical and creative power. They have often touched deeper religious issues than those of the church leaders of their time."[46]

In the sanctified church, for instance, many "saints" do not claim that their religion has a "surplus of meaning" and a surfeit of power unrelated to a Protestant understanding of the Bible. Yet, "saints" "filled by the holy ghost" yield a behavior traceable to the mnemonic power of African spirit possession.[47] Their music, in addition, reveals African values — cymbals, drums, tambourines, saxophones, bass guitars, hands and feet produce very rhythmically sophisticated sound. Also indicative of an African poetics (Mveng) are the tonality and timbre of these churches. The shrieks and screams — "Sprung from the African forests, where its counterpart can still be heard,"[48] — that punctuate gospels and spirituals with a polyrhythmic and polyphonic *blueness* are the essences of great black music. Thus within black churches a non-Christian element remembers a structure resistant to European hermeneutics. Not unlike the independent churches of the African masses today, African-American churches have transformed Christianity in a way that is indeed opaque (Long) to European theological paradigms. This cultural reality, insinuates a self-sufficiency of insight (Lincoln) that unveils religio-cultural dimensions anchored in slave religion.

Cone agrees with much of Long's view. The problem for Cone, however, has been "not at the point of the sources of Black theology," in terms of religio-cultural analysis, "but in its norm."[49] According to Cone, black scholars who seek to "de-theologize" an interpretation of black religion fail to pin down the meaning of the African heritage in a way that is normative. In his *God Of The Oppressed*, Cone asserts that the norm is christological.

If Sterling Stuckey is correct, the "norm" of slave religion was not Jesus Christ, but "the ancestors and elders."[50] Indeed, Jesus himself tended to be interpreted in terms of the religiosity of ancestors.[51] Thus, the "Christian faith answered to African religious imperatives."[52] Drawing together the visible and the invisible — the seen and unseen matrices of the sky, earth and all these things — the hermeneutical center is an "Africanness," from which the matrix of black religion is diffused in time and space. According to Stuckey:

> The two visions of religion...the traditional African and the Christian were complementary and explainable in relation to the African view of religious experience, which does not function from a single set of principles but deals with life at different levels of being. The African spiritual vision of the universe is synthetic, does not claim that everything can be deduced from a single principle — that is to say, the center of the African's morality is the life process and the sacredness of those who brought him [sic] into existence.[53]

That Jesus Christ has been central to expressions of black religion cannot be denied. But whether Jesus Christ is as normative for popular culture as he is for a *christology* derived as much from Europe as from "a black church tradition" is a critical issue.

A clue to this ambiguity is provided in Dr. C. Eric Lincoln's definition of black religion:

> Black religion derives, in the first instance, from that aspect of the Black experience that made it difficult to resolve the apparent incongruities between Christianity and Black slavery. It was not only a repudiation of the concept that slavery was acceptable to God, but has always been a critical medium through which the Black community has institutionalized its efforts to effect Black liberation. Inevitably this has meant a certain estrangement of the Black church from Christian "orthodoxy" as understood and practiced by the white church. Hence the salient tradition of the Black religion has always been the sufficiency of its own insight.[54]

Indeed, appreciation of the heterodoxy of black religion is critical for development of the hermeneutical principle of self-sufficiency *qua* Pan-Africanization. At work here is not only an interpretation of Scripture and tradition in terms of "Christianity," but also an interpretation of an "Africanness."

Dr. Lincoln's definition also heightens an appreciation of the *political* significance of black religion. As Stuckey reveals, the roots of black nationalism are in slave religion. Indeed the seminal nationalism was that of the slaves. Their nationalism was essentially African nationalism, spiraling from ancestral values intransigent to the dehumanization of slavery. As I noted in Chapter 1, the slaves were compelled to transcend ethnic conflict as they became an African-American people. Their formation into a New World people was essentially a Pan-African creation that sought to repel the cruel, avaricious whites who surrounded them.

It bears reiteration that slave culture contains the "archaism" providing clues to the meanings of a black religion true to its African heritage, a heritage moving in the recesses of the folk memory. Long puts it this way:

> historical memory is aided by a hermeneutic...of the archaic [which] raises the problem of the constitution of the subject in the process of knowing. If it is the aim of

> historical knowledge to understand behavior and objects as well as ideas, the interpreting subject must be pushed back to a level of consciousness commensurate with the forms that the subject wishes to understand. This is the radical empirical level of meaning which is expressed in the forms of history.[55]

The "radical empirical level of meaning" indicates the historic autonomy of black American consciousness of Africa — a *Pan-African consciousness.*

The autonomy of a Pan-African consciousness is related to Gayraud Wilmore's sense that black religion is emergent from an African *substratum.*[56] The question is *how* this substratum became the basis of the various forms of the black religion. Charles Long, a historian of religion, explains this substratum, in terms of (1) the religious image and historical reality of Africa; (2) the "involuntary presence" of blacks in North America; and (3) the Deity: the "experience and symbol of God in the religious experience of blacks."[57]

The historical reality and religious image of Africa persist, according to Long, in "soft culture," that is in "a characteristic mode of orientating and perceiving reality," which is the legacy of the ancestors.[58] According to Long, in addition, the phenotypic distinctiveness of blacks in North America heightened the "relationship between their physical being and their origins."[59] Thus, even in cases where blacks, such as Crummell, were alienated from the legacies of the ancestors, the image of Africa took on profound religious significance.[60] The image of Africa, writes Long, "has been one of the primordial religious images of great significance."[61] For Long, the image of Africa constitutes "the religious revalorization of the land [of the ancestors], a place where the natural and ordinary gestures of blacks were and could be authenticated."[62] The image of Africa in African-American consciousness is unique, asserts Long, for African-Americans are ostensibly a landless people. Thus the image of Africa "points to the religious meaning of land even in the absence of these forms of authentication. It thus emerges as an image that is always invested with historical and religious possibilities."[63]

The involuntary presence of blacks in North America reveals their centuries-long mistreatment. For Long, white supremacy set the wider context for a black spiritual resistance, which Long defines as *oppugnancy*. In order to create meaning despite the absurdity of white supremacist America, the slaves, claims Long, had "to come to terms with the opaqueness of their condition and at the same time oppose it. They had to experience the truth of their negativity and at the same time transform and create another reality."[64] Thus the involuntary presence of African-Americans in a land ineffably hostile to them gave critical impetus to the "self-sufficiency of insight" from which black religion emerges in the fight against oppression.

The experience and symbol of God in black religious experience is for Long rooted in the archaism — the soft culture — of the folk memory. This memory, according to Long, reveals "a range of religious material extending from trickster-transformer hero to High God."[65] According to Long, "biblical imagery was used because it was at hand; it was adapted to and invested with the experience of the slave."[66] The juxtaposition of African and Christian elements structured perceptions of the deity. According to Long, this structure "is not merely a case of God acting in history, for the historical events are not the locus of activity but then neither do we have a complete lack of concern for historical events in favor of a mystification of consciousness."[67] According to Long, "the presence of the deity has enabled blacks to affirm the historical mode by seeing it more in terms of an initiatory structure than in terms of a progressive or evolutionary understanding of temporality."[68]

Long's synchronic view of a black consciousness of God deprivileges a dogmatic, eschatological view, thus liberating God-the Symbol (Tillich) from the structures ill-equipped to appreciate the deep feeling of black religion. For Long, moreover, history of religion facilitates this break from systematic theology and the appropriation of "modes of experience and expression that formed [oppressed] communities in their inner and intimate lives."[69]

Methodological issues Long raises edify an analysis of black religion. Well aware of the whence of this religion, Long's vision of its whither is intriguing. For Long, analysis of black religion will lead to an epistemological break from Eurocentric paradigms, especially Continental theology. Yet, Dr. Long's view renders not only the heretofore dogmatic approach of Professor Cone problematic, but also Long's own epistemology rooted in the Eurocentric paradigms of Husserl, Otto, Wach, Eliade, and Van der Leuw. Is one assimilation of European consciousness better suited than another for an analysis of a religion opaque to European consciousness in any case? Given the relation of oppression to literacy, perhaps so.[70] Nonetheless, perhaps in the debate between Cone and Long we observe blacks' assimilation of epistemological battles fought in Europe over the meaning of religion. What is at stake, however, is not the valorization of history of religion over theology, but the liberation of the black oppressed. Black theologians and black historians of religion, especially those who are not Eurocentric in intention, should seek to complement one another in a praxis of liberation.

The black theologian James Cone considers the "substratum," particularly in terms of liberation and Christian ethics. In fact, he wants to know the extent to which black "survival today depend[s] upon...recognition of the *essential* African structure of our lives and the building of the liberation program upon that structure [emphasis added]."[71] In *God of the Oppressed,* Cone refuses to change his kerygmatic point of departure merely because of "the *intellectual* persuasion of a few black theologians who know more about Africa than the masses of black people."[72] According to James Cone, the "black theologian cannot claim to know what the people *ought* to believe or claim to have a 'secret' knowledge that transcends the faith of the community."[73]

Thus, explains Cone,

> what I write as Black Theology is what I believe to be the faith of the black church community which claims my allegiance. This means that I am persuaded that Black Theology is *Church* theology. It is this community about whom it seeks to speak.[74]

Can an *African*-American structure rest on the ecclesial foundation that Cone erects, though he wisely links it to the sacred time of slavery? Indeed, if Cone still claims his theology is a continuum of the spirituals, his theology may be alienated from their inner meaning.[75] Stuckey writes:

> Too often the spirituals are studied apart from their natural ceremonial context. The tendency has been to treat them as a musical form unrelated to particular configurations of dance and dance rhythm. Abstracted from slave ritual performance, including burial ceremonies, they appear to be under Christian influence to a disproportionate extent. Though the impact of Christianity on them is obvious and considerable, the spirituals take on an altogether new coloration when one looks at slave religion on the plantations where most slaves were found and where African religion, contrary to the accepted scholarly wisdom, was practiced. Because that was true, principles guiding African culture were found there, none in greater force than the practice of one determination or form leading to and containing vital elements of another. This is seen when one adds to the words of the spirituals the African rhythms that regulate all movement as worshipers circle counterclockwise in the shout.[76]

Principles guiding the spirituals appear to have been significantly unrelated to a church theology of seminal clergy and laity of African Methodist Episcopal churches, such as Richard Allen, James Varick and Daniel Alexander Payne. Cone says that he takes his stand with Richard Allen and James Varick. According to Cone: "Their faith is my faith, and that is why I cannot exclude Jesus Christ and his witness in the scripture, although I insist that Jesus' person must be defined by the oppressed of the land."[77] To be sure, Cone's ingenious definition of the political and social dimensions of a black christology is not the issue. Today, moreover, Cone is critical of the Eurocentric theology of the black church.[78] Nonetheless, if there is a tension *which presupposes a cultural continuity* between the slaves of Allen's day and the black underclass today, the faith of Allen may be distinct from the religion of the masses — then and now.

Theo Witvliet (see below) discusses the continuity between slave religion and contemporary black religion as a

> spiritual reservoir on which the black community, and especially its lowest layers, have constantly drawn in order to be able to survive in times of bitter need and repression. This popular religious feeling is certainly to be found in the black churches, but not only there: it *lives* and flourishes in the charismatic movements, in the countless sects and cults, and in the various expressions of black nationalism. Therefore the locus of black theology *cannot just be the black church*. Black theology has to do with the life of the black community as a whole, and above all with its *lowest strata* [emphasis added].[79]

Ancestors such as Richard Allen take us away, in a certain sense, from the religion of the "lowest strata." Like Crummell, AME clergy such as Daniel Alexander Payne devalued the religion of slaves whose Christianity was quite different from that of AME clergy. Although Allen had been a slave undoubtedly in touch with the spirituality of "less fortunate" slaves, he, like Crummell, went in the wrong direction in his understanding of Providence, thus heightening his alienation from the masses who shuffled counterclockwise in ringshouts.[80] The ecclesiology of Allen, though opposed to slavery and reflecting the African heritage, is rooted in Great Britain rather than the African-American masses. Allen was a Methodist in the tradition of John Wesley. Ordained deacon by Francis Asbury in 1799, he subscribed to "rules and discipline" definitive of Methodist doctrine.[81] In order to recover redemptive dimensions of black religion, a Pan-African theology must go in a direction of the black masses.

The Way of the Black Messiah, written by a European theologian, Theo Witvliet, is an excellent paradigm of a white theologian who takes black theology and the study of black religion very seriously. According to the black historian-theologian, Gayraud Wilmore, Witvliet "writes like a black theologian...By being so open he gets in touch with the power of *metanoia* in the black religious experience."[82]

For Witvliet, black theology, in order to be a liberation theology, must meet epistemological criteria defined by Latin American theology. He concludes that black theology is in fact a liberation theology that must be appreciated in terms of the North American context. Witvliet then substantially discusses the genealogy of black theology. According to Witvliet, "no dogmatic conversation with black theology is possible without a thorough knowledge of the history of black slavery and the opposition to it."[83]

Witvliet then attempts to answer the question,

> How can black theology be a theology of liberation if black history and experience shows nothing of this reality of liberation? This question is focused on the historical question whether black religion has a liberating or an oppressive character. Investigation in terms of the history of religion shows that black religion is a phenomenon in which elements from African religion and revivalist Protestantism from the South of the United States have become fused in a unique way. How was the relationship established between the black religious experience and the biblical witness? Can black religion be interpreted in christological terms?[84]

In answering these questions, Witvliet attempts to Christianize black religion. He in fact throws away his erudite analysis of black religion in his valorization of the Council of Constantinople (381) and the Athanasian Creed.

According to Witvliet,

> the hermeneutical foundation of the relationship between the biblical witness and black experience must be sought in pneumatology; the hermeneutical, methodological process that connects the liberating praxis of Jesus of Nazareth with black history and culture is therefore a pneumatological obligation.[85]

Thus Witvliet critiques Cone for his neglect of the third article of faith.[86]

Cone is on more solid ground as he seeks to place black theology within his own church tradition and in dialogue with other theologies of the Third World.[87] Witvliet would impose his pneumatology on those who are not Christian, even on Malcolm X![88] In fairness to Witvliet, he admits that his thesis is "valid only within the framework of a hermeneutical process in which Bible-reading and black experience mutually clarify one another."[89] But even here there is no necessary "pneumatological obligation."

During Malcolm's ministry in the Nation of Islam, for instance, he often reread the Bible in order to clarify the meaning of the black experience (qua the lost-found tribe of Shabazz).[90] As a Black Muslim, Malcolm would have been highly offended were one to suggest that his use of the Bible was the work of the Holy Spirit — the Yakub spook god — and not the black, flesh and blood God of the Original People.[91] Later, as a Sunni Muslim, Malcolm saw his spiritual vocation in terms of the Koran.

Devotees of the Kemetic tradition, moreover, the Black Jews of Moses Israel, the Black Moors, the Five Percent Nation, the American Muslim Mission, and the followers of Louis Farrakhan all tend to read the Bible in clarifying what they believe to be the shortcomings of a dogmatic pneumatology.

Although Witvliet has good intentions, he does not break epistemologically with the dogmatic theologies of Europe. He recognizes the uniqueness of the African-American spirituality in black religion, but is not open in his conclusions to the opacity significantly unrelated to an evangelical theology emergent from Germany.

A Metonym for Varieties of Black Religion: Polyphony,Polyrhythm and Dissonance

I should now like to explore my vision of the whence and whither of black religion. Focus is on how my perception is related to Pan-Africanization and to a theological perspective that does not attempt to Christianize religious dimensions that are independent of dogmatic categories.

The relation of black religion to African traditional religion is seen in a life-style that also audibly reveals an aesthetic of the African heritage. The value of aesthetics was brought home to me as I read Eboussi Boulaga's *Christianity without Fetishes* that reminded me that I am "one three centuries *removed* from the scenes [my] fathers loved" (Cullen). I, nonetheless, seek to transcend that distance through an imagination dependent on African values defined in part by Boulaga.

According to Boulaga:

One of the great events of our experience, and perhaps of our age is the advent of esthetic human beings. Their fashion of attaching to the past, to traditions, is neither dogmatic nor rationalistic. They have no intention of worshipping what their fathers venerated nor of burning it at the stake either. They are not concerned about a choice between the thesis of the unsurpassable wisdom of the ancients and the Ancestor, and the antithesis of the antiquated imbecility of these same ancients or Ancestor. Their minds are elsewhere. For them, traditions are treasures of forms and models, and the most durable of them are styles that cannot be reproduced without fakery, but which ever inspire and enchant, which lend more zest to the present, our present, and more assurance to our own quest for the beauty that abides. For these styles procure for us the necessary space and distance to play our own game, ephemeral but unique. They refer us to the irreducibility of sensation, of the sense of situation. This sense is the presence of the human beings to the simultaneous totality, momentary and epochal, of things and beings — a totality that is the explosion of the origin, revealing human beings to themselves as a total part of the world. The esthetic human being endeavors to be equal to the new currency of totality, where the past appears only in fusion with the vivacity of the present, in the instant being lived by living human beings, sons and daughters of their times.[92]

Boulaga's words refer me to Duke Ellington's description of his poignant "tone parallel to the history of the American Negro": Black and Brown and Beige.

A deeply religious and ingenious composer, Ellington said of his plans to compose the work:

If only I can write it down as I *feel* it. I have gone back to the history of my race and tried to express it in rhythm. We used to have, in Africa, a "something" we have lost. One day we shall get it again. I am expressing in sound the old days in the jungle, the cruel journey across the sea and the despair of the landing. And then the days of slavery. I trace the growth of a new *spiritual* quality and then the days in Harlem and the cities of the States. Then I try to go forward a thousand years. I seek to express the future when, emancipated and transformed,

> the Negro takes his [sic] place, a free being, among the peoples of the world [emphasis added].[93]

Ellington reveals that in the United States, as in Africa, aesthetics signify reappropriations of African values profoundly expressed in black music.

As Long suggests, moreover, black music offers relatively unexplored expressions of black religion, which intensify conceptions of "certain creative possibilities" within the religious existence of the Pan-African community.[94] Indeed, analysis of black music promises perspectival advances in Pan-Africanization.

Jazz: Inseminating Spirits of Meaning and Power

"Jazz" — a word which Ellington disliked intensely — of all expressions of black music, most fully conceives a black spirit that blows where it will, sanctifying varieties of black religion without losing its center — a rhythmic, "metronome sense" that is Africa's gift to the new world.[95]

In suggesting that jazz is black religion in a transferred sense, I make a phenomenological observation based on the views of seminal musicians such as Duke Ellington, Mary Lou Williams, Dizzy Gillespie, and John Coltrane — innovators and geniuses of the music.

My notion that jazz is a hermeneutical key that opens up religio-cultural dimensions of Pan-African theology may seem scandalous. This is because interpretations of the music have suffered from racist values that depreciate the integrity of a black aesthetic. Blacks have been taught to associate the music with anything but the holy, from which the music emerges. (Indeed, the African theologian, Barthélemy Adoukonou, argues that the music is derived from Vodun and is an essential element of a Pan-African spirituality. What is more, Mahalia Jackson herself called Duke Ellington's band "a sacred institution.")[96]

According to Stuckey: "The ring shout, prominent in Louisiana...helped form the context in which jazz music was created."[97] For Stuckey, "jazz was sacred in funeral ceremonies" and defined and sustained by "African secret societies."[98] The sacred rhythms of the ringshout and the shrieks and moans of the spirituals insufflated jazz with a holiness characteristic of the ancestral music mediating communication between the living and the dead. This circle of spirituality, Stuckey implies, was partly immersed in the primal waters of BaKongo values.

The word, "jazz," may indeed be derived from a BaKongo word. According to Robert Farris Thompson, a specialist in the history of African art, "The word jazz is probably creolized Ki-Kongo: it is similar in sound and original meaning to 'jizz,' the American vernacular for semen. And 'jizz,' suggestive of vitality, appears to derive from the Ki-Kongo word dinza."[99] "Dinza" indeed means to ejaculate, but not in a vulgar sense. It signifies the sacred release of a life-force, it is a metonym of continuity and the reciprocity of the living and the dead. It signifies the legacies of the ancestors.

The late Mary Lou Williams, a fine progressive musician anchored in the blues, asserts that, "Jazz — this derogatory title has been given to a great *spiritual* music — [is] a music that is healing to the soul [emphasis added]."[100] Describing the preciousness of this form of black religion, Williams, reminiscent of Ellington, explains that the music,

> came out of the suffering of an entire race of people — not of just one person or one artist — making it a special music — the only true art in the world. Through the suffering and experiences of the early black slaves...this music was born. This beautiful music has special *healing* power — because of the nature of its origin and contents — for those who listen with the ears of the heart. The healing power comes from the deep feeling that is in jazz — the feeling of the blues which is characteristic of all good jazz no matter what form it takes.[101]

James Cone has already drawn out the theological implications of blues, showing the way they have a sacred origin from spirituals, which emerge from the legacy of the slaves who danced religion in the old African way, passing down this providential legacy.[102]

Dr. Martin Luther King, Jr. has drawn out the theological meaning of jazz:

> God has wrought many things out of oppression. He has his creatures with the capacity to create, and from this capacity have flowed the sweet songs of sorrow and of joy that have allowed man to cope with his environment in many situations. Jazz speaks of life...When life itself offers no order and meaning, the musician creates an order and meaning from the sounds of earth which flow through his instrument. It is no wonder that so much of the search for identity among American Negroes was championed by jazz musicians. Long before the modern essayists and scholars wrote of "racial identity" musicians were returning to their roots to affirm that which was stirring within their souls. Much of the power of our Freedom Movement in the United States has come from this music. It has strengthened us with its powerful rhythms when courage began to fail.[103]

Through jazz, legacies of the ancestors live, move and have their being in the consciousness of the black masses.[104]

As Billy Harper, whose avant-garde music reveals the seminal influence of the spirituals, put it: "That thing about 'jazz is dead' is ridiculous. That really takes me out when someone says that because jazz is the musician himself [sic]. When they say 'jazz is on the way out,' isn't that like saying the black man [sic] is on the way out?"[105]

Harper's words are reminiscent of Long's. According to Long, "the religious consciousness of the blacks in America...is the repository of who they are, where they have been, and where they are going."[106] What is more:

> The religion of any people is more than a structure of thought; it is experience, expression, motivations, intentions, behaviors, styles, and rhythms. Its first and fundamental expression is not on the level of thought. It gives rise to thought, but a form of thought that embodies the precision and nuances of its source. This is especially true of Afro-American religion.[107]

Jazz is surely emblematic of the distinctive source of black religion.

The closeness of jazz to the source of black religion is seen further in certain musicians' relation to the Sanctified church that reveals the legacy of slave religion. Many artists, such as the avant-garde saxophonists, Albert Ayler and David Murray, were reared in or essentially influenced by the Sanctified church. Edified by its rich melismatic tones and vibrato, several seminal musicians learned "the crucial importance of an underlying beat sufficiently tight to allow all kinds of rhythmic flexibility on top."[108] In the words of Charlie Mingus, a master bassist influenced by the Sanctified church: "People went into trances and the congregation's response was wilder and more uninhibited than in the [AME church]."[109] "The blues," observes Mingus, "was in the Holiness churches — moaning and riffs and that sort of thing between the audience and the preacher."[110]

Dizzy Gillespie, a great elder of the rhythmically perspicacious Be-bop, put it this way:

> Like most black musicians, much of my early inspiration, especially with rhythms and harmonies, came from the church. Not my church though. In the Methodist church there wasn't too much happening musically — mostly hymns. But the Sanctified church had a deep significance for me, musically. I first *learned the meaning of rhythm there and all about how music could transport people spiritually* [emphasis added].[111]

Dizzy Gillespie explains that the Sanctified church was put down by certain blacks. This reveals their alienation from the legacies of the ancestors. According to Dizzy, "everyone knew...the whole congregation shouted. That was the lowest you could go because they practiced spirit possession and speaking in tongues, which was considered too much akin to African [traditional] religion."[112] Yet Dizzy Gillespie, a legend in jazz, asserts that he received his "first experience with rhythm and spiritual transport going down there to the well every Sunday, and I've just followed every since."[113]

One of the more intriguing observations of Arthur Paris is the similarity between the dynamics of the worship of the Sanctified church and the jazz band. According to Paris:

> If the rhythmic patterns and vocal styles of Africa have reemerged in Afro-America religious guise, despite separation by an ocean and a few centuries, it would seem likely that the striving for transcendent experience and collective creation central to the Afro-American religious tradition would be a key source for jazz's fundamental character as music of collective creation and improvisation and for the jazzman's [sic] concern to continually transcend the limits of form and enter more privileged realms.[114]

Indeed, for Albert Ayler, jazz musicians played "in a spiritual dimension." According to Ayler: "We can get a divine harmony or a divine rhythm that would be beyond what they used to call harmony."[115]

John Coltrane, another pioneer who pushed beyond harmonic structure, was the grandson of an AME minister.[116] Coltrane's departure from harmonic structure for the sake of modality was a way of returning to his spiritual roots.[117] Coltrane sought new forms of musical expression, as if each experiment were a liminal mode of religious perception. Coltrane's artistry reminds me of Long's view that religious orientation "is predicated on some new form of reality." To quote Long: "This manifestation has a double meaning; it makes itself known through some concrete form of cultural life, and its showing testifies to the reality of a mode of being that is prior to and different from the ordinary cultural categories."[118]

Coltrane's religion defied sectarianism. His attitude is reminiscent of Long's notion of the deity.[119] Each passionate, shriek of his horn, not unlike DuBois' definition of the "Frenzy" in the souls of black folk, was his prayer.[120] Coltrane writes on the liner notes of his album, *A Love Supreme*:

> I will do all I can to be worthy of Thee, O Lord....
> I thank you, God....
> Words, sounds, speech, men —
> Memory, thoughts, fear and emotions, time — all related
> They all go back to God...[121]

Indeed, Coltrane's music "shows itself [as] the sacred...a quality that permeates the object through which it is apprehended. The quality of sacredness may be described as those of power and ultimacy."[122] Certainly the incredible pyrotechnical power of Coltrane's artistry communicated his grounding in what he perceived to be the ultimate.

Coltrane was quick to note the African heritage of his music in relation to the black church. Particularly edifying in this regard for him was African music. One writer, Bill Cole, even asserts that Coltrane must be understood completely in terms of African traditional religion.[123] Although I have problems with his argument, he correctly asserts that Coltrane was "possessed by music — and more specifically, by the music of African-American people — and the spirit communicated through his music is rooted in the traditional black experience of religion."[124] Indeed, when hearing Coltrane's "Meditations" and "Cosmic Music" and seeing pictures of him in performance, I am reminded of possession trance.

Although jazz is not very popular in most of Africa, with the exception of South Africa, the music is a fitting paradigm of Pan-Africanization. It conveys an aesthetic that links African-Americans to Africa. Indeed, several of the great innovators of the music reveal a Pan-African consciousness.[125] Jazz also conveys the dissonance of black religion, while maintaining a *substratum* of the African heritage. The music reveals the persistence of the African heritage and challenges Eurocentric conceptions of the ultimate.

Jazz music is related to Long's view that the

> hegemony of Western Christian categories and thought models has come to an end. Notice that I did not say that they were invalid or useless; I am here making the relativity argument. I am saying that the kind of provincialism stemming from the aforementioned hegemony might be overcome if we take seriously the *otherness* manifested through and in the visibility of the black community. The visibility of the black community is our opening to a wider humanity, historically and contemporaneously.[126]

The otherness of a wider humanity, surely of Providence, brings me to a consideration of the relevance of revelation and Scripture to a Pan-African theology.

6.

Sky and Earth: Revelation and the Word of God

No need for me to understand what the animist [sic] or the Hindu or the Christian ultimately mean when they voice their respective worldviews. We may somewhat enjoy the beauty of...inexplicable concord out of so many dissenting voices. Pluralism tells us here that one should not assume for oneself (person or culture) the role of being the conductor of the human and much less the cosmic orchestra. It is enough with the music (the divine), the musician (the human), and their instruments (the cosmos). Let us play by ear.

— Raymundo Panikkar

We shall escape the fetishism of revelation only if we admit, *with all its theoretical and practical consequences, the metaphorical character of the notion of expression of "revelation."*

— Eboussi Boulaga

According to black theology, the idea of general revelation is primarily applicable to oppressed peoples. To the extent that we are creatures who rebel against ungodly treatment, God's self-revelation is granted. All human acts against alienating powers of enslavements are acts of God. We do not need to read the Bible to know that human enslavement is ungodly, and that slaves will do everything possible to break their chains. God has created all persons in such a way that none will coop-erate contentedly in their own oppression. We are not creatures who can be domesticated. In this sense, whether all persons know what some Christians call special revelation, they nevertheless know God — that is, it is their identity with the divine that makes all slaves rebel against their masters.

— James Cone

In this chapter, I will first discuss the significance of revelation within the context of the oppressed. Surely a Pan-African *theology* must give an account of God's self-disclosure, otherwise the theology will signify an apotheosis of the Pan-African experience. Second, I will discuss Scripture in order to demonstrate this theology's relations to Jesus and his ancestors.

Revelation

Revelation signifies God's gift of a righteous spirituality that sustains the liberation struggles of African people. Providentially, this spirituality, this revelation, is mediated through ancestral legacies. Without the medium of the African heritage, revelation would be alien to the Pan-African experience. Without the dynamism of ancestral legacies, doctrines of revelation become petrified relics irrelevant to the dynamic spirituality of the African peoples' struggle. Indeed, the Pan-African community receives no "revelation" outside of its ancestral values.

God is present in an African otherness that partially unveils the humanity of God. While God is essentially independent of humankind bearing the *imago dei* in astonishing diversity, the unveiling of God in this diversity makes humanity a vessel of God's ubiquity.[1] Humanity, as a vessel of God's ubiquity, is the genus of species of revelations through which Christianity partakes of a diversity that screams with the dissonance of creation, revealing God, who is all in all, even penultimately. God is revealed in the dissonance of life — the sacred drums of Africa, the shrieking saxes of black North America. Revelation of the plurality of human existence, moreover, heightens an appreciation of the anthropological moorings of theology.

Finite consciousness of God is never value-free and always relative to its context. Conceptions of revelation — no matter how beautiful and shattering, as in the image of a crucified God — must not totalize humanity from the perspective of its own tradition.[2] Indeed, consciousness of the relativity of revelation is necessary for a Pan-African theology that valorizes plurality in making no pretense to universalism.[3] Respect for the polyvalence of religious consciousness sensitizes one to the evil of absolutizing a human conception.

General and Special Revelations

In dogmatic Christian terms, the autonomy of revelation involves distinctions between general and special revelations. General revelation signifies recognition of the reality of God as mediated through nature and "the background of the various religions."[4] Special revelation, for Christians, signifies the direct unveiling of God in history through elect, often prophetic, persons. Special revelation is known quintessentially in Christ who cannot be mediated exclusively through a European self-understanding. Indeed, no human self-understanding is by itself able to convey God's redemptive purpose as it is revealed anew in each historical moment.

As Boulaga explains:

> How Jesus gathers all things in himself will be manifest only on the "last day." Meanwhile there is life's polyphony, and it may not be refused. The orders of truth are multiple, and the manners of being human irreducible one to another.[5]

In proclaiming the gospel, however, the oppressor has attempted to obliterate polyphony. The oppressors' proclamation of the good news of Jesus Christ is an oxymoron because their proclamation has been inextricable from their praxis of enslavement, partition and underdevelopment. An alienating doctrine of revelation, then, has been forced on the African people.[6] Black people have been made to believe dogma in an *unnatural* manner. The propagation of dogma has been the projection of the European psyche upon the world of color.

Christ, special revelation, is redemptive as he liberates the oppressed from the Eurocentric religion that has sought exclusively to define him. The special revelation enriching the legacies of the ancestors complements the general revelation of varieties of religious experiences of the Pan-African community. The dynamic complementarity of special and general revelations, related to acculturation and inculturation, is particularly observed in Africa. Indeed, the African context challenges African-Americans to be more radically receptive to the redemptive process of de-Europeanization. Concern, however, for transcontextualization guards against assumptions that African advances in the conception of revelation are relevant to African-Americans *ipso facto*. Nonetheless, on-going collaboration of African-American and African theologians promises that African paradigms will substantially influence the development of Pan-African theology. In Africa, contact between Christianity and African traditional spirituality is often creative because the self-giving of Christ on the Cross complements autochthonous modalities of sacrifice.[7]

Africans have given themselves away in sacrifice to promote fullness of life. Sacrifice serves to rid a community of the consequences of infractions that throw the community into chaos. The gift of expiatory victims symbolizes "the gift of self" which "is the means which allows" persons to better realize themselves. "The [African] dies," both by way of sacrifice and possession trance, "in order to relive. Death becomes a position of retreat which allows one to better conquer life."[8] Surely much of the Christianity of the African independent churches is predicated on a traditional sense of sacrifice that assimilates the crucifixion.

The redemptive implications of these churches is observed in the Kimbanguist church, despite Éla's correct criticism of this church.[9] Simon Kimbangu is revered as a black messiah in a way indicative of BaKongo values. In the Kimbanguist church one observes the convergence of special and general revelations: the Bakongo *ngunza*, a prophet who practices healing and divination, complements the gospel depiction of Jesus as a healer and the resurrected one who comes from God, dies and returns with special potency and power.[10] Here we have a concretization of the notion of God-given gifts that are not reified in alienating dogma. God is revealed in structures that differ from categories of European consciousness. The significance of Christ is discerned by way of hermeneutics emergent from the union of species of revelations which presuppose one Spirit — the Ultimate Being.

Special revelation in Pan-African theology signifies a conception of Christian faith embodied in ancestral legacies that indicate general revelation.

Scripture

The Bible is a form of special revelation that poses the problem of the relativity of hermeneutics. Boulaga puts it this way:

> All knowledge...snatched from scripture is artificial. The "biblical concepts" of this or that are those of nobody; they are robot photos made by a great number of individuals scattered over the centuries, of every age of life and both sexes. The unity of the Bible is mainly that of an encyclopedia, which gathers between the same two covers a great number of disparate compositions...Any coherence or semblance of objective unity is obtained at the price of violence to the real, and of falsification: for what is sought and found here has not hitherto existed, because it is the solution to be discovered in response to the events in function of the circumstances of a new, fresh age, of irreversible moments.[11]

To assert the primacy of the Bible without acknowledging the relativity of hermeneutics is to reify the Scriptures and obscure the dynamism of Christian tradition(s). Indeed, the fact of human plurality helps one appreciate the multiplicity of ecclesial traditions and the diversity of theological discourse.

Lest hermeneutics be no more than apotheoses of ideological convictions, penultimate expression must be distinguished from Ultimate truth — "for now we see in a mirror darkly, but then fact to face." Ultimately Scripture signifies a transhistorical reality of

God, who is independent of humans' quest for the meaning of their existence.

What of the Word of God?

The black South African Itumeleng J. Mosala reveals the importance of the issue of the relativity of hermeneutics. Like Boulaga, Mosala views the Bible as a compilation of many traditions revelatory of societal contradictions, particularly glaring during the period of the monarchy. Influenced by the work of N.K. Gottwald and committed to a Marxist view of history, Mosala argues that "the Bible is a product and record of class struggles."[12] For Mosala, theologians interpret the contradictions of biblical texts in terms of the ideologies revelatory of their political commitments. Mosala, then, calls for a "materialist biblical hermeneutics of liberation" which uncovers: the social contradictions of the biblical texts; the ideological tensions of the text that reflect the contradictions of the political economy; the caste and class of the readers and their concomitant ideologies.[13] Anathema to Mosala is a contemporary *Word of God* theology, which, emergent from a Eurocentric, bourgeois consciousness, obfuscates the postmodern conflict among classes. For Mosala, moreover, black theologians asserting that the word of God is the norm for theology inescapably adopt that oppressive, bourgeois paradigm.[14]

Mosala asserts that the claim that the Word of God "transcends boundaries of culture, class, race" undermines black theology. Indeed, according to Mosala, the Word of God is too broad in its ramifications to be relevant to black theologies of South Africa and the United States. If Blacks, moreover, are correct that Jesus is on their side, "how," asks Mosala, "can the same Jesus remain the supreme *universal* disclosure of the "'*Word of God*'?"[15]

Jesus would remain the same word of God for the oppressed and the oppressor if the *oppressed* agree — by God's grace — that *their* word signifies God's mercy to the oppressed and wrath towards the oppressor. James Cone put it this way: "The wrath of God is the love of God in regard to the forces against...liberation of the oppressed."[16] It is important to add, for methodological clarification, that Cone does not start with a reified concept of the

Word of God. Rather his interpretation of the Word emerges from a critical consciousness of historical and social forces that oppress the black poor. He writes:

> There is no "abstract" revelation, independent of human experiences, to which theologians can appeal for evidence of what they say about the gospel. God meets us in the human situation, not as an idea or concept that is self-evidently true. God encounters us in the human condition as the liberator of the poor and the weak, empowering them to fight for freedom because they were made for it. Revelation as the Word of God, witnessed in scripture and defined by the creeds and dogmas of western Christianity, is too limiting to serve as an adequate way of doing theology today. Theology, as Latin American liberation theologians have stressed, is the second step, a reflective action taken in response to the first act of a practical commitment in behalf of the poor.[17]

While I agree with Mosala regarding the illusion of a single Word of God, which obfuscates political struggle, I would hope that blacks drawn to Pan-Africanism can reach unanimity about their word of God. From a Pan-African perspective, the word of God is the actual presence of Jesus Christ in the struggles of the black oppressed. Indeed, Christ as the Oppressed One (Cone) would then transcend "boundaries of culture, class, and race." Blacks of the United States and Africa are oppressed regardless of their caste or class; and among other Third World people, oppression certainly transcends cultures and so-called races. What is more, if the struggle for liberation had no global dimension, the quest for creative alliance among Third World theologians would be impossible. Indeed, I am edified by Jean-Marc Éla's African understanding of Jesus Christ, an understanding he links to the Cross:

> If we view the Cross of Jesus Christ as the cross of the Third World, the very existence of the Third World shows us what sin is and how it is structured in history. The Third World carries within itself the hidden Christ. It is the historic body of Jesus Christ today.[18]

The "Word of God," understood here as the Cross, need not be discarded in hermeneutics of the black oppressed. The word of God — once demythologized Afrocentrically — has profound symbolic power. Were God not beyond, though revealed in, the material contradictions producing hermeneutics of the oppressed, Pan-African theology would be no more than a fetish. That God is on the side of the oppressed, however, is the good news of the ubiquity of God. The Bible yields the liberating message of the God of the oppressed.

Toward a Pan-African Understanding of Scripture

Pan-African hermeneutics require the de-Europeanization of interpretations of Scripture. De-Europeanization takes place in a hermeneutic that seeks equilibrium between biblical elements and spiritualities of African people. The two together nurture a political commitment that seeks to transform oppressive contexts into liberating ones through praxes of revolutionary humaneness.

I discuss Scripture as religious symbol. Scripture as symbol best allows for the complementarity of religio-cultural and social analyses in terms of hermeneutics of the oppressed of the Pan-African experience. Scripture as religious symbol conveys the sense in which "a symbolic expression...is negated by that to which it points."[19] Although Scripture conditions a Christian understanding of God, the eschatological activity of God is not circumscribed by the words of the Bible. Nonetheless, Scripture conveys the sense of God's identification with the oppressed. The difference between God and a community's self-understanding of God, however, forces interpretations of Scripture to acquiesce in their finite condition.

Serverino Croatto draws out the symbolic meaning of Scripture in his *Biblical Hermeneutics: Toward a Theory of Reading as the Production of Meaning*.[20] I agree with him that "isolating the objective, historical sense of a biblical text is illusory."[21] Scripture, by virtue of its semiotic structure, is polysemous.[22] The multiple implications of Scripture facilitate rereadings of the text coincident with the realities of the interpreters.[23] "The canon," writes Croatto, "has not closed everything."[24] It may be fixed but its mine of meaning is not exhausted. Each re-reading of Scripture opens the "closure of meaning that is the historical option of a community, an option seen as dictated by God."[25]

My rereading of Scripture reflects Pan-African values and is an element of what Croatto calls the "forward" of a text, which"makes it impossible for its past meaning to be eternalized."[26] The Bible has value for the oppressed of the Pan-African community, because the community is able to produce meaning from the Bible, which is relevant to the times in which they live. Indeed, Croatto writes:

> Creative rereading of the Bible is already being done from within the popular church, out of pioneer historical processes, out of cultural and religious contexts different from those of the Semitic or Western worlds, by theologians who are listening to, if not (more likely) immersed in the life of the people.[27]

"The hermeneutic enterprise," argues Croatto, moreover, "does not consist in listing relevant *themes*....but in the *structuration* of these themes in the total work that is the Bible."[28] The structuration at work in this Pan-African theology may be conceived as an eschatology which points to the God who creates, liberates, suffers in and transforms the world. Biblical elements that reveal this God and complement religio-cultural and social dimensions of African people are: themes from Genesis and Exodus, which reveal God the Creator-Liberator, and themes from the Gospel and Revelation, which reveal God the Incarnate Sufferer and Revolutionary.

I am not suggesting that these are the only elements relevant to Pan-African theology. But I find that they signify an eschatological perspective that links my view of Providence to Scripture. I examine Genesis first, Exodus second, the Gospel third, and Revelation fourth. In each case I will explain how these scriptural elements are relevant to many of the elements of Pan-African theology that I have discussed.

These elements include: the symbol of the ancestors, the dialectic of alienation and continuity, the processes of liberation and Pan-Africanization and the hermeneutical reciprocity between social and religio-cultural analyses. Focus will be on the hermeneutical insights of African theologians.

Genesis: God the Creator

I interpret Genesis, chapters one and two, in a way consistent with primal, African myths of the beginning. I do not analyze the relation of several African myths to Genesis.[29] I relate Genesis to the African values that have served as leitmotifs of this book. The first two chapters of Genesis assert that God created *homo sapiens*, whose first home appears to be Africa, with the intention that they live in harmony with one another and the flora and fauna of the cosmos. Indeed, Mercy Oduyoye writes: "I do not know of any primal worldview of Africa that leaves our existence to chance. God is at work making a new thing out of the chaotic world."[30] Appealing to an Akan cosmogony, Oduyoye shows the African sense of God's providential governing of the world, which brings about the equilibrium of the sky, the earth and all these things.[31] Respecting the unknown void before birth and in the wake of death, humankind here conceives their beginning as a creation of God, who established equilibrium among the sky, the earth and the genera and species of existence. Any human practice violating this equilibrium disrupts the human community.

Genesis is a paradigm for Pan-African theology as it commends a return to the source of equilibrium — the ancestral legacies inextricable from the orders of preservation that God has provided for the Pan-African community. God has provided for the Pan-African community in a way that compels it to seek its own good — liberation. The transcontextual implications of liberation are effected as each black community, overcoming alienation from ancestral legacies, stretches out its arms to its sibling community across the Atlantic. Pan-African concern for the oppressed entails the memory of the genesis of values signifying oneness in God in community.

Black people are in the God of Genesis to the extent that they appreciate their African heritage. Defining dimensions of this heritage, Boulaga writes:

> What is important is the reestablishment of community, the reestablishment of the circulation of life, so that life can go on transcending itself, go on bursting the barriers, or the intervals, of nothingness, go on being superabundant.[32]

Boulaga's conception of an ancestral sense of the reciprocity of the living and the dead signifies the primal spirituality of black existence. He indicates the genealogy of African values noted by African-Americans such as Sterling Stuckey and Cedric Robinson.

The internalization of the sin of oppression among the black underclass has produced climates where the communal values of the slave period are forgotten. The old are treated with obscene disrespect; the children are bastardized; the unborn are conceived without the sacredness conducive to prenatal care. Nonetheless, Boulaga's insights valorize ancestral values which, redefined in the light of present experience, determine a hermeneutic of Genesis efficacious for a praxis that seeks the reversal of the fallenness of black humanity. Indeed, the transcontextual struggle for liberation produces a meaning from Genesis that commends a praxis for self-love — "the reestablishment of community, the reestablishment of the circulation of life."

Genesis refers to a love, rather than a shame, of primordial images of ancestors who display a continuity with the lithic imagination of Africa. The image of God, intrinsic to Genesis, is God's gift of ancestral awareness — a point obfuscated in the legacy of Alexander Crummell.

Genesis, in addition, reveals the way in which a spiritual return to the source is the foundation of a certain eschatological awareness. God's image is recreated in the spiritual gift of a praxis participating in God's emancipating future. In the words of Jean-Marc Éla:

> The one God who calls men and women into existence by the power of the word is the same God who will "make all things new," as in a new exodus manifesting the might of the divine love. Creation is at once an anticipation and a prophecy of the liberation to come. Thus, the creation account is not a commemoration of the past, but a prefiguration of the future. Creation is

> ordered to the promise of salvation; Genesis turns our hope toward the future glory of the cosmos.[33]

Africa is the sacred place emblematic of God's creation. Black people have come from this God who will liberate them from both the chaos of self-hate, taught to them by oppressors, and the pain of wretchedness, perpetuated by oppressors.

Exodus: God the Liberator

If a rereading of Genesis valorizes the gift of blackness, then a rereading of Exodus heightens a determination to preserve that gift in the struggle for liberation. The view that God is the liberator of the oppressed has been central to this theology. Indeed, the story of Exodus is the definitive biblical paradigm indicating God's presence in history on behalf of the oppressed. The Exodus, writes Oduyoye, "has ceased to be the exclusive story of the descendants of the *Hapiru* and has become universally applicable to all peoples who believe in God the Creator, who saves from chaos."[34] Chaos signifies not only the violence perpetuated by the oppressor, but also the confusion of blacks alienated from the positive values of the ancestors.

"Saving us from ourselves," Oduyoye asserts, "God effects our exodus, thus beginning our re-creation."[35] In liberating African people from their alienation, an alienation revealing the chaotic state of self-hatred, in restoring them to their ancestors, God re-creates, "re-Africanizes," them. In re-Africanization, blacks perfect the struggle for liberation by way of a praxis that emerges from the gift of love.

Exodus signifies the path of God, who regenerates earthly life in bestowing consciousness of the equilibrium of the primal conditions upset by satanic forces. I do not envision an exodus from modernity and a return to neolithic modes of production and patterns of societal organization. Neither do I hold that Africa was a paradise. Indeed, exodus signifies a liberation from archaic custom opposed to the living dynamism of redemptive, popular culture bearing ancestral legacies.

As Oduyoye explains, the traditional

> ordering of society placed its own burdens on the African people. So African theologians do not see the problem as one of captivity only to foreign nations. The task is not to retain and uphold tradition until the exile is over and a return and rebuilding can take place. In relation to traditional society one can still see the exodus as a paradigm, a departure from inflexibly ascribed positions whose hierarchical ordering was accepted as "natural" and permanent. Notwithstanding the fact that almost everybody cooperated and deviants were punished, it was an oppressive system to the extent that to opt out was to be cast out.[36]

Still, Oduyoye values the religious base of African people. She writes: "The religious base of life in Africa enables us to read our history as 'sacred' history. *Gye Nyame*, 'Except God,' is one of the pillars of the primal religion of the Ghanaian, for without God nothing holds together."[37] Liberation, then, necessitates preservation of positive values symbolizing the reality of God to a people. Exodus signifies going forward to freedom in the Providence of the Creator of the ancestors.

Exodus witnesses to the God who leads humankind from the oppressive conditions inimical to the fecundating orders of preservation. Liberation is impossible if the Pan-African community is not insufflated by positive legacies which exorcise the alienation that prevents fullness of life for black humanity. African people cannot cross the seas of oppression leaving their essential, life-giving identities behind.

Indeed, the miracle of Providence at work among blacks of the New World has been blacks' determination to preserve the memory of traditional values in their resistance of the oppressors. Their ringshouts and spirituals and jazz reveal that the God of Exodus pressed a distinctive image on them. This image is the gift of the legacies of the ancestors. Éla puts it this way: "Ever since the slavery period, in Africa as in America, the religions of the blacks have always functioned as anything but obstacles to their struggles. They have been the cultural glue, they have been the weapons, in these struggles against oppression."[38] Here, Éla is referring to the religion of the masses who bear the legacies of the ancestors.

Exodus means that Providence has decreed that the oppressed will resist those whose history is a monument to the creed of Mammon: "and you will be like God." Exodus reveals the God who, in defeating Mammon, takes on the full humanity of the oppressed.

The Gospel: God the Incarnate Sufferer

The Gospel reveals God, who becomes one of the oppressed without losing the aseity of Divine identity. God is the Incarnate Sufferer, who assumes a true humanity within the legacies of an enslaved people. An interpretation of God as the Incarnate Sufferer emerges here from hermeneutics in which the African heritage complements the Gospel.

An element of this heritage is revealed in the spirituals of the African-American slaves. In certain spirituals, enslaved ancestors reveal their perception of the proximity of their suffering to Jesus:

> Oh, nobody knows the trouble I've seen,
> Nobody knows but Jesus.

As Sterling Stuckey has argued, the spirituals were wed to the ringshout. Theoretically, the ringshout allowed the ancestors to transcend spatio-temporal limitations. Lawrence Levine speculates that, "The shout often became a medium through which the ecstatic dancers were transformed into actual participants in [biblical events]."[39] Much in the same way that their sense of "sacred time and space" allowed the slaves to "fly home" to Africa in the ringshout, the slaves were able to place themselves at the foot of the Cross. James Cone explains that "slaves knew the significance of the pain and shame of Jesus' death on the cross [and] they found themselves by his side."[40] There they described the lynching of a fellow sufferer ("a nigger in pain"): "Dey pierced Him in the side...Dey nail Him to de cross...Dey rivet his feet...Dey hanged him high...Dey stretch Him wide."[41] For the ancestors, Jesus was their own, whose flesh was broken and whose blood was shed by oppressors.

It is plausible to me, moreover, that Stuckey is correct that the Cross of Jesus was interpreted in terms of BaKongo values during the slavery period.[42] According to Stuckey, the display of the cross in the form of a staff during baptism dissimulated the way in which the symbol revealed an African worldview.

Stuckey explains that Christian symbols

> provided a protective exterior beneath which more complex, less familiar (to outsiders) religious principles and practices were operative. The very features of Christianity peculiar to slaves were often outward manifestations of deeper African religious concerns, products of a religious outlook toward which the master class might be hostile. By operating under cover of Christianity, vital aspects of Africanity, which some considered eccentric in movement, sound, and symbolism, could more easily be practiced openly.[43]

It is also plausible, then, that the resurrection was interpreted in terms of the BaKongo sense of the reciprocity of death and imminent rebirth. Stuckey writes that when the staff was brandished during the rite of baptism,

> it was as if the sun in its orbit was suddenly mirrored, revealing the fullness of BaKongo religion. And since those who lived a good life might experience rebirth in generations of grandchildren, the cycle of death and rebirth could hardly have been more suggestive than through the staff-cross — a symbol of communal renewal.[44]

What is more, as Long suggests — and in this he is supported to a degree by Levine — the resurrection could have been interpreted in terms of an ancestral legacy related to "trickster-transformer heroes" or the conquering hero, High John, the Conqueror.[45]

In Pan-African theology, the incarnation and the resurrection are interpreted in terms of a spirituality that miraculously protects the life-sustaining identity of the black oppressed. Providentially, the communion of God and the African heritage is revealed in the Incarnate Sufferer, actually present — not dogmatically present — in the liberation struggles of the Pan-African community. James

Cone puts it this way: "Christ really enters into our world, where the poor, the despised and the black are, disclosing that he is with them, enduring their humiliation and pain and transforming oppressed slaves into liberated servants.[46]

Revelation: God The Revolutionary

The Book of Revelation signifies the recreation of the world at some point between its genesis and its resolution. At that sacred time, the Incarnate Sufferer, in flesh and blood, joins the oppressed, consummating their struggle, with the Spirit of transformation. Here, the Incarnate Sufferer is the Revolutionary who ultimately overcomes radical evil. The book of Revelation indicates that evil must be resisted in radical praxes that anticipate the ultimate end of evil.

Beastly as the Antichrist, evil civilizations dare to oppress in God's name. In the apocalyptic vision of John, "the beast was captured, and with it the false prophet who in its presence had worked the signs by which he deceived those who had worshipped its image" (Rev. 19:22). The Book of Revelation symbolizes the defeat of evil represented by a corrupt Babylon — an avaricious civilization. Christ defeats the beast. Christ is depicted as the ultimate revolutionary, wielding a double-edged Word of justice and retribution: justice, for the oppressed, retribution for the oppressor. The Book of Revelation evinces that God and the devil cannot be served simultaneously.

James Cone is correct: "Theology is always a word about the liberation of the oppressed and the humiliated. It is a word of judgment for the oppressors and the rulers. Whenever theologians fail to make this point unmistakably clear, they are...doing...the theology of the Antichrist."[47] In contexts such as Soweto and Harlem, words that judge the oppressor demand an activism that seeks radical transformation of wicked contexts. It is believed that the Spirit of God the Revolutionary produces among the oppressed a commitment to a new humanity for the sake of peace and love and justice. The will to resist is a spiritual gift of liberation that raises, from the underside of history, struggles for material transformation. The specific form of transformation is dictated by the contexts that have produced them. The apocalyptic struggle for material transformation, however, entails distinguishing redemption from salvation, the penultimate from the ultimate. Redemption concerns time and space. Salvation concerns the invisible, the eternal. "Salvation," writes Boulaga, "promises endless happiness after death, when there shall be no more tears, or needs, or sin. Redemption knows only healing...the rare joy of [siblings] dwelling together in unity...having...overcome fear and suffering in the name of justice."[48]

In the words of Boulaga, redemption, in this sense,

> forms part of penultimate realities, the ones we can see, those that make it possible to "verify" the ultimate, invisible ones, and to anticipate to them in hope. Redemption is to salvation what love of neighbor is to love of God. God, no one has ever seen — and those who pretend to love him [sic] while not loving their own brothers and sisters are living an illusion, lying to self. In like manner we have never seen a saved human being. We do not know what salvation is. We can only believe in it and hope for it.[49]

Valorization of the penultimate conditions a hermeneutic of Revelation, which can not be separated from transforming praxes that distinguish material transformation from the Kingdom of God.

Redemption signifies God's love of the Pan-African community, a love made visible in a transcontextual spirituality that participates in God's transformation of creation. Pan-African praxis is the penultimate activity revealing the community's love of God. Love of black Africa and Diaspora, moreover, anticipates the ultimate realization of Beloved Community.

Revelation complements an interpretation of Genesis which teaches self-love in the collective form of the Pan-African community. The book of Revelation illuminates the meaning of an invisible creative Source of a dynamic, this worldly, visible regeneration. The invisible God of all creation has been revealed in the exodus of blacks from alienating values and is incarnate in the Pan-African community in which the Spirit sustains the black oppressed in the apocalyptic struggle for freedom.

My Christian commitments have been defined in a Pan-African hermeneutic that identifies paradigms explaining the biblical base of my sense of the diversity of God. The Creator-Liberator, Incarnate Sufferer and Revolutionary signify distinct Presences in the God revealed in the struggles of the oppressed.

I turn now to the final chapter, in which I will further explore the meaning of God. Seeking to show further the development of this theology from Crummell and Blyden, I will focus again on Providence.

7.

The Providence of God: Invisible Source of a Visible Generation

Pure atheism, without affirmation of the infinite Other, is not sufficiently critical; it permits the fetishization of a future system. Only if it is affirmed that the divine is other than all possible systems will liberating revolution be possible. Hence disbelief in the fetish — atheism — must be affirmed as the exteriority of the absolute of the Origin. The center set itself up as divine: it rejected the anthropological exteriority (the Amerindian, the African, the Asian) and hence also absolute Exteriority. Antifetishism is negation of the negation of absolute Exteriority. To affirm absolute Exteriority is to close the road to a future tautological negation of the liberating affirmation. It is...the necessary hypothesis of all revolution.

— Enrique Dussel

Christ's blackness is ....literal in the sense that he truly becomes One with the oppressed blacks, taking their suffering as his suffering and revealing that he is found in the history of our struggle, the story of our pain, and the rhythm of our bodies.

— James Cone

Now when these African ideas are transported into the correspondingly Christian analogous themes, the statement "grace is familiar" (in the African sense) would imply not only that grace is communal and ecclesial, but also "ancestral," and as such Christian (Christ is the Ancestor par excellence), paradisal (suggested by mythical time), heroic (suggested by the idea of ancestral heroes), friendly, initiative, and therefore sacramental, paschal, pentecostal, pneumatic, eucharistic, dynamic, fecund, eschatological, etc.

— Charles Nyamiti

I will in this final chapter further explore the meaning of God, thereby valorizing the continuity of the legacies of the ancestors and liberating conceptions of Providence from the misconceptions of Blyden and Crummell.

Imago dei: The Invisible Source of Creation and Liberation

The *imago dei* signifies special providence as in "when God speaks through a prophet or works through some other specific action."[1] *Imago dei* here signifies neither the mythic account of free will, nor an original physical or spiritual likeness between the creature and God, nor the pristine perfection of the creature. The *imago dei* conveys the integrity of a spirituality unvitiated by modern values of oppressors. By way of the *imago dei*, God liberates the African people through the redemptive actions of popular culture. Preserving creation, God concurs with the people's struggle. Concurring with the divine telos of liberation, African people are nurtured in miraculous modes of resistance bearing God's image. These modes of resistance are miraculous as they occur despite the awesome ambit of the oppressor's power. The Pan-African community was supposed to capitulate to European domination. Yet God has sustained African people in the memory of their essential identities, a memory that is integral to their liberation struggles.

I relate the *imago dei* to what Enrique Dussel calls *exteriority*. According to Dussel: "The oppressed...of dependent nations... preserve in their own culture the maximum exteriority of the de-facto worldwide system; only they, given their metaphysical alterity, can project a real and new alternative for future humanity."[2] Exteriority signifies a peoples' assertion of their humanity, their otherness.[3] Insofar as exteriority implies a regeneration of pre-oppressive values, it is inextricable from an eschatological imagination regarding the image of God.

By way of this imagination, blacks overcome the alienation Dussel describes as the totalization of exteriority. He writes:

> The other, who is not different (as totality asserts) but distinct (always other), who has a history, a culture, an exteriority, has not been respected; the center has not let the other be other. It has incorporated the other into a strange, foreign totality. To totalize exteriority, to systemetize alterity, to deny the other as other, is alienation. To alienate is to sell someone or something, to pass it on to another proprietor. The alienation of a people...makes [them] lose their Being by incorporating them as a moment, an aspect, an instrument of another's Being.[4]

In the providence of God, African people have resisted totalization in an ancestral spirituality that renews, reforms, recreates and restores African people to the integrity of their persons. This revolutionary spirituality is the gift of the Invisible Source (God) of a visible regeneration (liberation). Indeed, a goal of Providence is penultimate liberation, which must be continuous with the legacies of ancestors created in the beginning.

According to Dussel: "To draw near [to humanity, to oneself] is to arise from beyond the origin of the world. It is an 'archaic' act (if *arche* is the origin anterior to all other origins). It is anteriority anterior to all other anteriority."[5] The gift of the *imago dei* precedes alienating values of oppressors who turn from the Creator in their subjection of the other. Nothing they value in oppressing renews the vision of the humanity of God.

The meaning of the *imago dei* is extended in the deprivileging of the Semitic, Hellenistic, medieval, and modern symbols that have monopolized its significance. Blacks resistant to this paradigm shift are bound to incur the alienation seen in the legacy of Crummell, for instance. In his legacy, despite the good he would do, Christianity legitimated a praxis of imperialism. When the oppressed, however, recognize the absurdity of this contradiction, they "shorten the distance" to life-sustaining values. "Praxis," explains Dussel, "is this and nothing more: an approach to proximity."[6] Failure to probe the meaning of ancestral legacies is an exercise in alienation from the image of God made flesh and blood in the Pan-African experience.

I have shown that Crummell's and Blyden's notions of Providence sought to answer the problem of theodicy by equating redemption with liberation from ways of the ancestors thought to be antiprovidential. Crummell, as well as Blyden, however, correctly asserted that God has been working redemptively in spite of slavery and colonization. For them, God wrought a profound good from oppression. They rightly did not attribute human sinfulness to God. Indeed, Providence's relation to theodicy is made clearer in terms of sin. Ruled out here is a demonic, preternatural metaphysics that posits the unity of evil and good in assessing the structure of the world. Although wickedness and goodness are real contradictions within human experience, God, who is ultimate benevolence, transcends that experience. Sin, expressed mythologically in terms of the Fall, is a human departure from God, who creates and liberates. The Fall tells the truth of a propensity toward sinful values inimical to liberation.

Few events reveal this more clearly than the history of the inhumane treatment of the Pan-African community. Not that Africa was a paradise before the intrusion of the Europeans. Human sinfulness is universal. The Fall signifies that humans, atomistically, tend to maintain the disequilibrium of sin. No one is free from sin's microdimension. Still, I am mostly concerned with a macrodimension — European civilization's oppression of people of color and the poor. White supremacy evinces the ostensible triumph of the original turn from the Creator. The macrodimension of sin is the apotheosis of a deformed orientation — *cor curvum in se*. Sin is that unsightly religion of the deified heart, which sought to crush African people beneath the juggernaut of slavery, colonialism, and institutionalized racism.

Euro-Christians, in their praxes of mission, have too often evinced that their god is Western civilization. As dogma is an epistemological foundation of these alienating praxes, it serves white supremacy, not God. In the words of Boulaga: "Christian discourse...[functions] as interdict....Christian practice will be reduced to the monotonous proclamation of the difference of the divine, ceaselessly described by way of contrast with and opposition to the human being, altogether as if there were no gift to God not snatched from human beings, to the latter's annihilation."[7] Such proselytizers fail to see the confusion of Subject and object in their vociferous interdict. They fail to see how they are playing God.

Blacks who have internalized values of an alienating Christianity also reveal a macrodimension of sin. An example of this is the parasitic neocolonialism through which elitist blacks manage the oppressed. The indigenization of the macrodimension of sin in Africa exacerbates the problem of famine and multiplies the deaths of the peasants. In the United States, the black middleclass' contentment with their alienation from the black underclass reveals a sinful orientation toward self-hatred and economic opportunism. Blacks' insensitivity to the pain of other blacks only evinces the immense proportion of the radical alienation wrought by the praxis of white supremacy. The self-serving interest of the black middleclass also reveals their alienation from the struggles in Africa. Wanting in on the material profits of Western capitalism, they tend to condone an economic matrix which produces the politics of starvation in Africa. They are alienated from the source of ancestral legacies and concomitantly estranged from the Source of regenerative Providence.

James Cone rightly asserts that sin "represents the condition of estrangement from the source of one's being[;] for Blacks this means a desire to be white. It is a refusal to be what we are. Sin for blacks is loss of identity."[8] Valorization of the African heritage, however, increases appreciation of the "source of one's being." Indeed, consciousness of the revolutionary potential of African values facilitates a praxis of liberation. The late Amilcar Cabral put it this way:

> A people who free themselves from foreign domination will be culturally free only if, without complexes and without underestimating the importance of positive

> accretions from the oppressor and other cultures, they return to the upward paths of their own culture, which is nourished by the living reality of its environment, and which negates both harmful influences and any kind of subjection to foreign culture. Thus, it may be seen that if imperialist domination has the vital need to practice cultural oppression, national liberation is necessarily an act of *culture.*[9]

In theological terms, opposition emerges from the communion of the ancestral past and the redemptive present, which conditions an eschatological imagination that liberates the image of God from alienation. Providence has decreed that an eschatological conception of the *imago dei* will bear God's perfected humanity in Christ, the Ancestor who, overcoming sin, reveals God's blackness.

The Blackness of God: The Visibility of the Incarnate Sufferer

The blackness of God signifies a christological position made paradigmatically clear in the work of James Cone. For Cone, the blackness of God is an idiom that valorizes orthopraxis. That is, the black oppressed, in struggling for liberation, bear a cross analogous to that of the Incarnate Sufferer, who, electing the poor, died for the sake of Justice. The blackness of God, moreover, is an idiom emergent from Cone's analysis of socioeconomic contradictions of North America. Cone's identification of white supremacy with sin led him to demarcate sharply the revelation and hiddeness of God in the United States. God is revealed in the context of black socioeconomic suffering; God is hidden in the unfair socioeconomic privilege of white affluence. Indeed, the blackness of God contextualizes the significance of the body of Christ, which is the universal presence of the oppressed, under, around and through the geopolitical spaces of oppressors. That God is black is a metaphor, reflecting the global presence of the Incarnate Sufferer. God is revealed in diverse contexts of oppression. God is among the Black underclass of North America; God is among the poor of Africa, for instance. Indeed, the blackness of God signifies the process of Africanization gaining theoretical clarity in the work of the new guard. (Recall my discussion of the new guard in Chapter 1.)

Providentially, the blackness of God is a malleable, trans-contextual idiom. The ubiquitous Incarnate Sufferer bestows true humanity on the black oppressed in a way that is liberating for them across contexts. Negating the parricide of self-hate and the absurdity of oppression, the black God raises christological reflection in a spirituality independent of the alien metaphysics of oppressors. Spirituality in this sense refers to a gift of an exterior metaphysics. As Dussel explains, metaphysics "is to know *how* to think about Being from the exteriority that judges it — just as the periphery of the world judges the center that pursues the philosophy of domination [emphasis added]."[10]

The legacies of the ancestors constitute a metaphysics signifying the communion between the divine and the human, the invisible and the visible. "There is no need," writes Boulaga, "to break with one's solicitude for the dead or any other ancestral traditions. The message of Christ is not in competition with [ancestral traditions]. On the contrary, this message has come to fulfill the dream of a life in all its fullness, a life destined to triumph even in the collapse of the framework of a way of life that has been consecrated from time immemorial."[11] God is black among the African peasantry because Christ is revealed in legacies expressive of the emergence of life from death. God is black among the North American underclass because Christ sanctifies the pariah stigma revelatory of God's identity as the Oppressed One. Christ's redemption of the Pan-African community negates the macro-dimension of sin.

The memories of innocent ancestors swinging from Southern trees and the amputated limbs of Africans entombed in Leopold's Congo provide insight into the sin of crucifixion and illumine the horror of unmerited suffering. Memories of the crucified dead are inextricable from the body of Christ revealed in the shed blood and torn flesh of the black oppressed. Jesus Christ, identical in Providence with God the Creator-Liberator, is as close to black people as their ancestors are. Ineffably close to the invisible, the ancestors in Christ bear the image of the suffering humanity of God.

Here, the humanity of God signifies a sacrifice that effects the perfect equilibrium between the human and the divine, joining the sky and the earth without confusing their distinct redemptive significance. In Christ the visible and the invisible are perfectly balanced and his immolation imbues flesh and blood with redemptive power. Christology, then, in terms of the fusion of the invisible and the visible, conveys a meaning not unlike that of African traditional religion. This meaning is brought out by the former Archbishop of Lusaka, E. Milingo.[12] According to Milingo: "The Church must insert herself [sic] into the communities of people as part of the same drive by which Christ himself, through his incarnation, allowed himself to be bound by the social and cultural conditions of the people with whom he lived."[13]

Archbishop Milingo shows clearly the redemptive meaning of the humanity of God in his charismatic ministry sensitive to the communion between Christ and the ancestors. His grassroots appeal is based on his opposition to what Boulaga calls "middle-class Christianity." According to Milingo:

> We are marrying Jesus with our ancestors. Some of my readers will think that I am merely making a comparison between the two, and leave it at that. But Jesus has all that our ancestors have and more. I have only to convince my people that they should put their full confidence in Jesus. I have no objection if at the same time they will carry along their ancestors, who will contribute to their welfare along with Jesus. I cannot imagine that my grandmothers and grandfathers are in hell. If the redemption brought by Jesus was effective for Isaac, Abraham and Lot, should it not be effective for my ancestors? Certainly they too were somehow included in the redemption wrought for the whole race by Jesus Christ.[14]

What God does not assume is not redeemed. If christology entails the amelioration of a fallen condition; if the resurrection has redemptive meaning at once retroactive and proleptic; if the redemptive meaning of human history is fragmented in the multiple reflections of Christ's body — then the ancestors share the redemption wrought in Christ. The resurrection symbolizes the rise of African people crucified without warrant.

The divinity of Jesus enshrines human belief in the ultimacy of God. Customarily, views of ultimacy that are more cyclical than rectilinear are equated with heathenism and thought to be incompatible with the redemptive significance of Christ. I should like to discuss the political significance of this view.

That the divinity of Jesus must be conceived in Western terms is a fetish traceable to a Hegelian trajectory that has conditioned a Western eschatology. Teleology is equated with Europe, "deteriology," with Africa.[15] According to Hegel:

> The peculiarly African character is difficult to comprehend, for the very reason that in reference to it, we must quite give up the principle which naturally accompanies all our ideas — the category of Universality. In Negro life the characteristic point is the fact that consciousness has not yet attained to the realization of any substantial objective existence — as for example, God, or Law — in which the interest of man's volition is involved and in which he realizes his own being. This distinction between himself as an individual and the universality of his essential being, the African in the uniform, undeveloped oneness of his existence has not yet attained; so that the knowledge of an absolute Being, an Other and a Higher than his individual self, is entirely wanting. The Negro...exhibits the natural man in his completely wild and untamed state. We must lay aside all thought of reverence and morality — all that we call feeling — if we would rightly comprehend him; there is nothing harmonious with humanity to be found in this type of character. The copious circumstantial of accounts of Missionaries completely confirm this....[16]

From this perspective, still significantly in force, divinity and the humanity of African people are inimical. It bears repeating that such perspectives imply that Western civilization is divinely providential.[17]

Harold Turner, the author of the well-noted *History of an African Independent Church: The Church of The Lord (Aladura)*, argues that certain African independent churches have been redeemed by the virtues of Christianity bearing "the spirit of modernity."[18]

According to Turner, Eurocentric Christianity overcomes the stasis of localized religions allegedly incapable of innovations necessary for "progress."[19] Turner's position reminds me of Wyatt Macgaffey's explanation of Robin Horton's notion of conversion:

> Traditional African religions...are organized at two levels. The higher level, the domain of the Supreme Being, contains universalistic propositions, but is little developed because, at this stage in history, the African thinker's experience is largely bounded by the local community. Particularistic propositions appropriate to local experiences, represented in terms of lesser spiritual beings, enrich the lower level of the religious system. As the course of history breaks down the boundaries of the local community, [traditional] intellectuals need to develop this universalistic level of their thought and for this purpose they draw upon Christianity and Islam, universalistic religions with well-developed theologies of the Supreme Being. This movement leads to conversion.[20]

According to Turner, conversion entails five transitions:

1. from a *cosmos* based on necessary internal relations to one revealing contingent relationships;
2. from dealing with *power* through magic and ritual to dependence on science and faith;
3. by the addition of history to myth, as a new category for dealing with *time*;
4. from a *society* that is closed, unitary, and sacral, to one that is open, pluralist, and secular;
5. by seeing *evil* as involving moral rather than ritual pollution, and as located internally in the individual as well as externally in evil forces.[21]

In each transition, emphasis is placed on a Eurocentric view of inculturation. Little attention is given to acculturation. Recall that inculturation signifies Christianization of ancestral legacies, whereas acculturation is the spontaneous force of ancestral legacies that de-Europeanize Christianity within the grassroots stratum of national culture.

Turner's Eurocentric valorization of inculturation reveals the hegemonic function of cultural reproduction. Inextricable from his view is the assumption that black humanity needs the tutelage of Western missionaries.[22] Turner claims that when Africans of the independent churches are no long tied to the ancestral land and its sacred powers

> and places; [they] are free to spread far and wide according to their own choices and ambitions, and some have become remarkably international. Their places of worship are church buildings, to be erected anywhere required, and not confined to the local sacred places given by tradition or determined by the spirits. There is a new element of contingency, openness, and responsibility, replacing the fixities and fatalities of the old cosmology, a change of attitude that is a necessary prerequisite for development.[23]

To be sure, Turner's essay is more sociological than theological; but his sociological assumptions have theological implications. Turner put it this way: "Eschatology in primal religions is characteristically either absent, underdeveloped, or clearly conservative, with paradise understood as restoration of something lost in the past, as following the models of the culture heroes, and maintaining reciprocity with the ancestors."[24] For Turner, Western eschatology "neither dominates the dealing with history nor is confined to the images of the past."[25] For Turner, Western "eschatology has a new freedom to deal with the future."[26] Evidence of the redemption brought by such an eschatological view, asserts Turner, is an independent church, namely The Church of The Lord, Throughout The World, whose "leader travels in a Mercedes-Benz, and [whose] leading layman is a millionaire."[27] According to Turner: "For a Church that emerged from 'the bush,' as it were, less than fifty years ago, this is an impressive record of self-development and advance in the modern manner, which has been made possible only by breaking from the old confining worldview and entering into the stream of historical development."[28] Indeed, Turner reveals that notions of eschatology are never value-free.

What is ignored is the established fact that "development" is controlled by the oppressive matrices of the center — a control calculated to prolong underdevelopment. Moreover, many African independent churches assimilate Christianity consistent with the values that Turner assumes are inevitably abandoned in "conversion" to Christianity. As Boulaga explains, profound continuity with the legacies of the ancestors

> is there — the continuity of a life undergoing a metamorphosis in depth. The continuity is not from without, via a power or a legitimacy passed down from hand to hand or church to church, in an uninterrupted spatio-temporal chain.[29]

African independent churches do not move *from* traditional values to Western values. Indeed, writes Éla, independent churches that

> develop in step with elements of African tradition are merely seeking to regain that dynamism of revelation that colonialism has prevented Christianity in Africa from expressing and assimilating.[30]

Turner's assessment of conversion obscures the traditional spiritualities that are profoundly related to a peoples' ancestral humanity.

To be sure, I do not question Turner's point that the significance

> of these new religions lies in their influence and efforts being spontaneous and locally generated, indigenous in rationale, method and form, and in the kind of new order that is envisioned; to this extent they are nearer to grass roots of local life and less Westernized.[31]

Still the West is a providential force for Turner. But that is an ahistorical claim out of touch with the grassroots reality of national cultures that are resisting Western imperialism. A Western concept of development is different from the progress of national cultures resistant to neocolonialism.

The inculturative, eschatological symbols of divinity do not sublate the redemptive acculturative milieu. The divinity of Jesus is providential to the extent that He is appreciated in grassroots terms of the invisible forces of healing and wholeness. To quote Aloysius Pieris: "The vast majority of God's poor perceive their ultimate concern and symbolize their struggle for liberation in the idiom of non-Christian religions and cultures. Therefore, a theology that does not speak through this non-Christian peoplehood is an esoteric luxury of a Christian minority."[32]

In the Pan-African experience, the divinity of Jesus may not be divided from the humanity of the ancestors.[33] Jesus Christ enriches symbols that participate in what cannot dissolve — the image of God among African people. Each child of the Pan-African experience in Christ reincarnates the love of the old Africans who — unnamed in the history of migrations from the once verdant Sahara; unnamed beneath the waters of the Atlantic and unnamed beneath the hostile soil of the Americas — are sanctified in the Providence that not only pulls us toward tomorrow, but also anchors the Pan-African theologian to God whose divinity is revealed in the redemptive legacies of the ancestors. In Christ, the ancestors come forward, rising from the macrodimension of a crucifying sinfulness, speaking through the Spirit of transformation.

Visible Continuum of an Invisible Memory

The Spirit bestows knowledge of Christ in the heart. Inextricable from this love of Christ is a providential love of blackness fructified in struggles of the African people. The Pan-African implications of this spiritual love for God and the African people were brought forcefully home to me as I read Toni Morrison's Pulitzer Prize winning novel *Beloved*. *Beloved* is dedicated to sixty million and more, a number inclusive of the old Africans who died in slave ships where the seminal Pan-Africanism emerged.

Set in the United States in the period between the 1850s and 1870s, Morrison's novel includes a depiction of a gathering of blacks in a place Morrison calls the Clearing, which is reminiscent of the hush harbors of the "invisible institution." The central character of this gathering is an elderly ex-slave woman, Baby Suggs, "holy." She possesses charismatic gifts that distinguish her as a spiritual leader of the black community of Cincinnati, Ohio. The Clearing scene resonates with the dynamic, spirit-filled spirituality of slave culture.

I do not seek to impose a Christian view of the Spirit on expressions of the African heritage for which the epistemological key lies elsewhere. Nonetheless, Baby Suggs' message relates heuristically to a pneumatological point I wish to explore.

Baby Suggs' Call to her people is as follows:

> Here...in this place, we flesh; flesh that weeps, laughs; flesh that dances on bare feet in grass. Love it. Love it hard. Yonder they do not love your flesh. They despise it. They don't love your eyes they'd just as soon pick them out. No more do they love the skin on your back. Yonder they flay it. And O my people they do not love your hands. Those they only use, tie, bind, chop off and leave empty. Love your hands! Love them. Raise them up and kiss them. Touch others with them, pat them together, stroke them on your face 'cause they don't love that either. *You* got to love it, *You*!....And O my people, out yonder, hear me, they do not love your neck unnoosed and straight. So love your neck; put a hand on it, grace it, stroke it and hold it up....More than eyes or feet. More than lungs that have yet to draw free air. More than your life-holding womb and your life-giving parts, hear me now, love your heart. For this is the prize.[34]

Although Baby Suggs focuses on the flesh, her message of the self-love that counters the heinousness of white supremacy — *cor corvum in se* — is, given the intention of *this theology*, Spirit. Baby Sugg's call to self-love is a God-given gift rooted in ancestral memories of Africa, that "other (liveable) place."[35]

The African people must love themselves tenaciously because the swelling ranks of white supremacists and the cancer of self-hatred growing in black hearts impede human liberation. Love-for-self is not an idolatrous love, but a prerequisite for participation in the new humanity — the promise of Beloved Community in which all humankind will celebrate the gift of Being in peaceful coexistence. Blacks' love of themselves concurs in the Spirit's providential work of regeneration.

The Spirit is God the Revolutionary, who inspires blacks to

struggle against the perversion of human sinfulness that would destroy creation in praxes of domination. The breathing of ancestral legacies into the present revolutionary struggle for liberation is the breath of the Spirit. She calls blacks to love their flesh that has been broken. The Spirit enables blacks to rise, in Christ, from the tomb of oppression. God the Revolutionary becomes real in the hearts of Pan-African Christians, revealing Christ, the Ancestor who takes on the identity of the "blameless Ethiopians."

Indeed, the legacies of the ancestors have taught posterity that "something of a more profound nature than the obsession with property was askew in a civilization which could organize and celebrate — on a scale beyond previous human experience — the brutal degradations of life and the most acute violations of human destiny."[36] The ancestors' knowledge of the wickedness of the West, writes Cedric Robinson,

> was most certainly informed by the Africanity of [black] consciousness — some epistemological measure culturally embedded in [black] minds which deemed that the racial capitalism we have been witness to was an unacceptable standard of human conduct. It was also the case that the source of [black] outrage characterized that conduct as inexplicable. The depths to which racialist behavior has fouled Western agencies transgressed against a world-consciousness rooted in [the] African past.[37]

In this Pan-African theology, then, the Spirit is interpreted as the Revolutionary providentially giving impetus to the preservation of life-sustaining values inimical to racist capitalism. In the context of the black oppressed, where else did the Spirit move but in the recesses of the humane legacies of the ancestors? The Spirit surely did not move oppressors' hearts to the life sustaining charity that is Christ. Thus:

> It was not...an understanding of the Europeans which preserved those Africans in the grasp of slavers, merchants and colonizers. Rather, it was the ability to conserve their native consciousness of the world from alien intrusion, the ability to imaginatively recreate a prec-

> edent metaphysics while being subjected to enslavement, racial domination and repression.[38]

The presence of the Spirit in black hearts mandates a return to the Source.

The Spirit of recreation is moving across the waters of the Atlantic in a transcontextual consciousness of the peasantry and the underclass. Ancestral values of healing and wholeness are in the Spirit gaining ascendancy over a privileged class who have turned their backs on the African heritage. New life is signified in the redemptive meaning of the humanity of God enshrined in the modalities of being of the black poor. In God the Creator-Liberator, the Incarnate Sufferer and the Revolutionary, the black poor receive in the heart a liberating gift of struggle that saves them from the absurdity of assuming the deformed image of their oppressors. This is the gift of self-love inextricable from the presence of God in popular culture.[39]

As God is revealed within the matrix of ancestral legacies, the black peasants will be empowered to affirm their humanity and the black underclass will be inspired to resist their thingification in the Diaspora. Black and African theologians in the Spirit must be voices in solidarity with the black poor, embodying the intrinsic relation between theological reflection and revolutionary intention. According to Dussel, the "most oppressed classes do not always have the most acute awareness, but such awareness can be reached by classes that, although objectively not the most oppressed, are the ones upon whom ideological contradictions weigh the heaviest."[40] Pan-African theologians must be "organic intellectuals" (Gramsci) dedicated to facilitating resistance to centers of domination. Indeed the "liberation of the oppressed is put into effect by the oppressed, but through the mediation of the critical mentality" of theologians who seek to interpret the pneumatological meaning of radical transformation.[41] Thus the Pan-African theologian, "as an organic intellectual, as militant, can express the criticism of a people...even if by birth, culture, or work, the [theologian] does not, from the beginning, belong to the oppressed classes."[42] A bourgeois background — pseudo or real — does not prevent intense identification with the misery of the poor. Jean-Marc Éla put it this way:

> To acquire a reformist mentality is to renounce the revolutionary ideal. You have to die to the state of having become bourgeois in order to find yourself a person with the soul of a revolutionary, poor among the poor, shoulder to shoulder with the poor along the pathways of struggle that leads to final victory...Salvation comes from the peasantry alone.[43]

In the United States, salvation must surely come from the Spirit rising in the heart of the black underclass. Black theologians must "lumpenize" themselves in identifying and struggling with the underclass. The Spirit calls theologians of African descent to egalitarian values, which undermine the exploitative infrastructures that trap the black underclass and the African peasants in abject poverty.

A Pan-African theology means little if it fails to become a living activity in the ecclesial matrix of the Pan-African experience. It must become a way of life — a living way of the Spirit. Progressive leaders of the black churches of the Pan-African community must continue to organize conferences, workshops, and other activities that link Africans to African-Americans. A praxis of liberation must be evinced in concrete transcontextual struggle.

In the United States, church programs designed to mitigate the socioeconomic struggle of the black poor must include a program for the poor of Africa. The spatial distance of the two contexts can be reduced by a reciprocity of interest that disallows focus on African-American problems to the exclusion of African problems. Africans too must be involved in the struggle for the regeneration of the black underclass. Without a commitment to an equilibrium of interests, without the practice of a struggle based on the complementarity of contexts, the legacies of the ancestors is but the reification of history and culture.

Churches across the Atlantic who find theological meaning in the ancestral connection must deepen their definition of their ecclesial identities in terms of the Pan-African connection.

Among questions relevant to the forging of a Pan-African church are:

- To what extent may progressive black churches in the United States aid the revolutionary struggles of the oppressed of Southern Africa?

- How might the churches in both places find ways to extend praxes of liberation in a way simultaneously relevant to both sides of the Atlantic?

- How might black churches develop paradigms of economic self-sufficiency which decrease the alienation of the oppressed from the meaning of their labor, thereby strengthening the struggle for a New International Economic Order?

- How might progressive clergy of socialist vision find ways to diversify agriculture in Africa, strengthening modes of subsistence production and complementing the efforts of the underclass to break the cul-de-sac of their existence?

The models for Pan-African ecclesial solidarity — the Pan-African church! — do not have to be overly-ambitious. The Spirit does not necessarily move in ways that are huge, but often in a smallness indicative of the mustard seed faith. Oppression will not be broken overnight and all at once. The struggle for a Pan-African church might take root first in one black community of the United States and in one locale of an African country. Progressive black clergy might perennially and creatively nurture exchange programs. But the struggle must at least continue with Pan-African theologies that seek clarity in the task of Pan-African struggle.

Perhaps my views appear quixotic. In the Spirit, however, nothing is impossible that is in quest of a new humanity. Women and men who, in the Providence of God, are activists with a vision of a Pan-African church are needed. I do not advocate secession from existing churches, but a caucusing of persons of an ecumenical spirit dedicated, with an ineffable urgency, to the liberation of African people. The legacies of the ancestors — those as yet unborn — are at stake.

Notes

Preface
What Africa is to Me

1. See Amilcar Cabral, *Return to the Source: Selected Speeches of Amilcar Cabral*, ed. by Africa Information Service (New York: Monthly Review Press, 1973), p.91. To be sure, Cabral's statement that Pan-Africanism is a means of returning to the source does not by itself reflect the theological consciousness I attribute to it. Cabral was not a theologian, but the Secretary-General of the African Party for the Independence of Guinea and the Cape Verde Islands (PAIGC). According to the African Information Service: "Under [Cabral's] leadership, the PAIGC liberated three-quarters of the countryside of [Guinea-Bissau] in less than ten years of revolutionary struggle. Cabral distinguished himself among modern revolutionaries by the long and careful preparation, both theoretical and practical, which he undertook before launching the revolutionary struggle, and, in the course of this preparation, became one of the world's outstanding theoreticians of anti-imperialist struggle." Portuguese agents assassinated him on 20 January 1973.

    His call to return to the source was directed to the alienated African elite. Cabral demanded that the elite uproot themselves from their bourgeois moorings and radicate themselves in the soil of the peasants. According to Cabral, "the culture of African peoples is an undeniable reality: in the works of art as well as... in the dynamic balance of economic political and social structures created by African man [sic]." (See p. 50.) For Cabral, the

African poor continue to display "the richness of their cultural values (philosophic, political, artistic, social and moral)."

In returning to the source, the elite, to quote Cabral, "acquire a clearer understanding of the economic realities of the popular masses." The elite "realize, not without a certain astonishment, the richness of spirit, the capacity for reasoned discussion and clear exposition of ideas, the facility for understanding and assimilating concepts on the part of population groups who yesterday were forgotten, if not despised, and who were considered incompetent by the colonizer and even some nationals." (See p.54.) Undoubtedly, asserts Cabral, the peasants are enriched by their contacts with the elites who facilitate the peasants' progressive assimilation of aspects of modernity. According to Cabral, the elite introduce the peasants to "the principles of national and social revolution postulated by the struggle. [The poor] thereby become more able to play the decisive role of providing the principal force behind the liberation movement." (Ibid.)

2. See Karl Barth, *The Humanity of God* (Atlanta: John Knox Press, 1960). The humanity of God is a phrase Karl Barth used to explain the christocentric way in which God is for us (*pro nobis*). For Barth, the humanity of God indicates the Chalcedonian definition of the essential complementarity of the natures of Jesus Christ. According to Barth: "It is precisely God's *deity* which, rightly understood, includes his *humanity*." (See p.46.) Barth thinks, then, that theology is really theanthropology, but only in terms of the humanity of *God*, not the divinity of man. Barth's claim that "we have no theological right to set any sort of limits to the loving-kindness of God which has appeared in Jesus Christ" reminds me of Cabral's perspective, the confusion of idioms notwithstanding. (See p.62.)

   Cabral's view of popular culture has profound implications for a theological reflection on the relation of the humanity of God to Providence. It seems to me that the humanity of God is reflected in popular culture, which gives liberation struggles transforming force. In the words of Cabral: "The value of culture as an element of resistance to foreign domination lies in the fact that culture is the vigorous manifestation on the ideological or idealist plane of the physical and historical reality of the society that is dominated or to be dominated."(See p.41.) For Cabral, culture is a revolutionary force as it heightens consciousness of the alienating mores of the oppressors' civilization. "The greater the differences between the culture of the dominated people and the culture of their oppressor," writes Cabral, "the more possible...victory becomes." (See p.48.) Undoubtedly, that difference is most graphically seen at the grassroots level, where God is incarnate. This view is but another way of valorizing the faith that God is on the side of the oppressed.

3. Although I came to this conclusion relatively independently, my views are hardly original. See for instance, Bernard M. Magubane's *The Ties That Bind: African-American Consciousness of Africa* (Trenton: Africa World Press, 1987). Of adventitious mores, Magubane writes: "White hegemonic views about Africa and about its inhabitants did not allow the black man [sic] in diaspora to have his prehistory percolate unimpeded through vital layers of the black man's [sic] consciousness."(See p.37.) This, as I will argue, is partially true of Crummell.

   Of that which deforms black consciousness in a crippling neurosis, Magubane writes that blacks whose values were Eurocentric "had to try to both be and not be black." The great tragedy of this is that too many blacks think that by assimilating European mores, they will convince whites that blacks are human beings. Allegedly, whites would treat blacks more humanely if blacks assimilate the "modernism" inherent to Eurocentric civilization. Assimilation of European mores, however, leads blacks to a vicious dead-end. The truth, writes Magubane, is that "wherever and whenever non-white people [come] into contact with the white man, they [are] accorded recognition as equals only to the extent that they [are] able to imitate the white model — an ultimately unattainable goal since it [includes] not only acquirable characteristics but genetic ones as well."(See p.131.)

4. See note 2 above. According to Cabral, in addition, "...cultural resistance and degree of retention of identity are not uniform. So even where ethnic groups have broadly succeeded in keeping their identity, we observe that the most *resistant* groups are those which have had the most violent battles with the colonial power during the period of effective occupation or those who because of their geographical location have had least contact with the foreign presence." (See p.66.)

   "Praxes of domination" is a phrase I have borrowed from the Argentinean philosopher, theologian, and church historian, Enrique Dussel. He writes in his *Philosophy of Liberation* (New York: Orbis Books, 1985): "The praxis of domination is a perversity....The master exercises power over the servant by means of oppressive praxis. It is the mediation of the system by which its structure endures and persists." (See pp.54-55.) Popular culture enables the oppressed to resist this domination.

5. See note 2 above. "Centrifugal force" is a phrase taken from Frantz Fanon, *The Wretched Of The Earth* (New York: Grove Press, 1968). Fanon's perspective on the revolutionary force of popular culture is not unlike Cabral's. Although Fanon's book was written in the context of North Africa rather than Sub-Saharan Africa, he too reveals the alienation of the elite, but in terms of a return to the source that is but a reification of ancestral legacies. Fanon put it this way:

   > The native intellectual who comes back to his people by way of cultural achievements behaves in fact like a foreigner. Sometimes he has no hesitation in using a dialect in order to show his will to be as near as possible to the people; but the ideas that he expresses and the preoccupations he is taken up with have no common yardstick to measure the real situation which the men and the women of his country know....*Culture has never the translucidity of custom*; it abhors all simplification. In its essence it is opposed to custom, for custom is always the deterioration of culture. The desire to attach oneself to tradition or bring abandoned cultures to life again does not only mean going against the current of history but also one's own people. When a people undertake an armed struggle or even a political struggle against a relentless colonialism, the significance of tradition changes....In

> an underdeveloped country during the period of struggle traditions are fundamentally unstable and shot through by *centrifugal tendencies*. That is why the intellectual often runs the risk of being out of date [emphasis added]. (See pp. 223-224.)

6. I do not obfuscate custom and culture here. For a powerful description of this dynamic spirituality, see F. Eboussi Boulaga, *Christianity Without Fetishes: An African Critique and Recapture of Christianity*, trans. by Robert Barr (New York: Orbis Books, 1984), pp. 77-83.

7. Mircea Eliade and Joseph Kitagwa, eds., *The History of Religions: Essays in Methodology* (Chicago: University of Chicago Press, 1959), p.101. According to Eliade, "it is necessary to underline the *existential value* of religious symbolism, that is, the fact that a symbol always aims at a *reality or a situation in which human existence is engaged*." For Eliade, the situation

> is above all this existential dimension that marks off and distinguishes symbols from concepts. Symbols still keep their contact with the profound sources of life; they express, one might say, the "spiritual as lived" (*le spirituel vécu*). This is why symbols have, as it were, a "numinous aura"; they reveal that the modalities of the spirit are at the same time manifestations of life, and consequently, they directly engage human existence. The religious symbol not only unveils a structure of reality or a dimension of existence; by the same stroke it brings a *meaning* into human existence." (See p.102.)

For my purposes, this situation — generic for Eliade — is the Pan-African experience. I will show that the symbol of the ancestors conveys an Afrocentric spirituality that discloses the meaning of Providence in terms of African traditional and black religions, both of which condition hermeneutics of the *imago dei* and the Incarnation.

8. I gleaned the phrase "great cultural symbols" from Charles Long *Significations: Signs, Symbols, and Images in the Interpretation of Religion* (Philadelphia: Fortress Press, 1986). Long, in drawing out the implications of Eliade's notion of "situation," writes:

"To prevent this level of experience from being subjected too quickly to the dogmatic categories of contemporaneity, we should try to understand it in culture and history where it is expressed as great cultural symbols." (See p. 49.) Indeed, I use the "legacies of the ancestors" as a symbol of a situation — i.e., a memory — that links blacks to a beginning inextricable from Africa and uncontaminated by values of white oppressors. This situation, this memory, as a spiritual structure, is a "primary prereflective experience." (See p.49.) That is, the ancestors are great cultural symbols that express the prereflective experience which, in the providence of God, links Africa and Diaspora.

I also like J. Serverino Croatto's definition of symbol (and myth) in his *Biblical Hermeneutics: Toward a Theory of Reading as the Production of Meaning* (New York: Orbis Books, 1987). According to Croatto, God "can be spoken of only in symbols (natural things transparently referring to a second meaning, which somehow transcends phenomenal experience) or myth (combinations of symbols built into an account of origins, in order to express the meaning of some present reality, institution, custom or the like)." (See p.78.)

9. Cedric Robinson, *Black Marxism: The Making Of The Black Radical Tradition* (London: Zed Press, 1983), p. 431. Robinson's words reveal his admiration of the legacy of Richard Wright, particularly Wright's essay, "Blueprint for Negro Writing."

10. My interest in perspective reflects the words of Richard Wright's "Blueprint for Negro Writing," as found in *Richard Wright Reader*, ed. by Ellen Wright and Michel Fabre (New York: Harper & Row, 1978), p.45. According to Wright, theme — perspective — for black scholars "will rise from understanding the meaning of their being transplanted from a 'savage' to a 'civilized' culture in all of its social, political, economic, and emotional implications. It means that Negro writers must have in their consciousness the foreshortened picture of the *whole*, nourishing culture from which they were torn in Africa, and of the long, complex (and for the most part, unconscious) struggle to regain in some form and under alien conditions of life a

whole culture again." (See p.47.) Indeed, my sense that the ancestors are "great cultural symbols" bears the influence of Wright's definition of *theme* for black scholars.

Introduction
Sections of the Text & Breakdown of Chapters

1. The contemporary reality of Pan-African Christians is evinced by the Pan-African Church Conference held in Atlanta in 1988. See Ndugu Ofori-Atta G. Thomas, "The First Pan-African Church Conference," in The *AME Zion Quarterly Review*, XCIX:3 (October 1988), pp. 48-52.

2. For a discussion of the origins of EATWOT, see James Cone, *For My People* (New York: Orbis Books, 1984), pp. 144-156. As Professor Cone reveals, Third World theologians, including black North American theologians, are in quest of a methodology that will deepen their epistemological break from First World and other Eurocentric theologians. Cone puts it this way in specific reference to the black North American context: "It is unfortunate that African-American churches have borrowed their theology from white fundamentalists and other denominations from which they often also derive their names... African-American churches need to break off their theological link with white fundamentalist churches and begin to develop their own theology in dialogue with their own past and with oppressed Christians of the Third World." In this book, I seek to do precisely that: link the black North American church to its ancestral past, a past inextricable from Africa. This makes dialogue with oppressed Christians of Africa imperative.

I hope that this book, in focusing on black North Americans and black Africans, will be useful in providing a paradigm for what Dr. Cone calls "a new method of doing theology." What is more, I hope that this book will prove useful in what Sergio Torres calls the quest for a "critical formulation that can be applied to similar situations, yet make allowances for diverse real-life contexts and cultures." See Virginia Fabella and Sergio Torres, eds., *Irruption of the Third World: Challenge to Theology* (New York: Orbis Books, 1983), p.12.

3. In *For My People*, Dr. Cone defines the paradigm as follows: "Through a political commitment informed by social and cultural analyses, a new hermeneutical situation is created. The Bible is no longer merely an ancient document whose meaning can be uncovered only by the historical criticism of biblical experts. Political commitment, informed by social analysis, provides an angle of vision that enables us to reinterpret the scriptures and thus bring to light the message that European and North American biblical exegetes had covered up." (See p.152.) See also Croatto in note 8, Preface.

Chapter 1
Elements of a Pan-African Theology

1. In addition to acknowledging my debt to these clergy, I thank Professor James Washington of Union Theological Seminary. In one of his classes that I attended, Dr. Washington used the phrase "Pan-African theology" in reference to the views of Crummell and James Pennington.

2. Dussel, p. 171 in note 4, Preface.

3. See my book *Black And African Theologies: Siblings or Distant Cousins?* (New York: Orbis Books, 1986), Chap. 6. Despite the differences in socio-historical experience that distinguish the theologians as African-Americans and Africans, they are significantly similar. They share: phenotypic characteristics; experiences of white supremacy; Pan-African legacies of historic black clergy; and a hermeneutical affinity based upon the complementarity of religio-cultural and social analyses. Each similarity, however, is limited by an attendant dissimilarity: phenotypic similarity is often rendered less significant by cultural differences among Africans and African-Americans; similarity in the experience of white supremacy gives way to the difference between the legacies of chattelization and colonization; hermeneutical similarity is tempered by dissimilarity of contexts. Nonetheless, an essential similarity includes other similarities and significantly overcomes dissimilarities I have

listed. These theologians share a profound sense of intimate kinship as they focus on liberation of the oppressed of African descent. They appear ready to embark upon a single enterprise.

4. In December 1986, at Union Theological Seminary, New York, black theologians from the United States and South Africa came together, revealing the incipiency of a contemporary, Pan-African theology. The conference emerged from a historic awareness of a relationship between blacks of South Africa and the United States. For more information on the conference, see Simon Maimela and Dwight Hopkins, eds., *We Are One Voice. Black Theology in the USA and South Africa*. (Braamfontein: Skotaville Publishers, 1989).

   The "new guard" classifies a group of Africans whose recently published theologies are far more radical than those of the old guard. By the 1980s the problems of underdevelopment in so-called independent black Africa caused these fresher voices in African theology to question the censure of the theme of liberation in African theology outside of South Africa. What made this censure unbearable for this new guard was what they perceived as the bourgeois values of African Christianity. These values were reflected in the old guard, who barely opposed the problems of neocolonialism and considered the meaning of liberation and Africanization superficially. The result has been the estrangement of African theology from the popular Christianity of the peasants and the workers.

   The designation, "old guard," is not pejorative, but merely refers to African-Christian worldviews published during a period extending from the late fifties to the dawning of the eighties. The African theology of the old guard is related to the ascendancy of nationalism, particularly evident after the triumph of Kwame Nkrumah in 1957. This period marks the beginning of African "independence" from colonialism, though that independence signifies little more than the African embourgeoisification of colonial infrastructures. Nationalism and the cultural expressions intrinsic to independence — *négritude*, for instance — led African scholars to "retrieve" and celebrate the so-called African personality problematically defined by scholars and statesmen such as E. Blyden, C. Hayford, L. Senghor and K. Nkrumah. The notion of African personality is anchored in the traditional values of Africa and includes dimensions of European civilization.

As early as 1956, African scholars in francophone Africa were publishing texts exploring continuities between African traditional religion and Christianity. The sixties saw an increase of works of that kind, encouraged in part by the inauguration of the All Africa Council of Churches in 1963. By the 1970s African theology had been established as the quest for theologies with African cultural meaning. Committed to an ideology of independence, African theologians had asserted that the theme of liberation was irrelevant to "postcolonial" realities. African theology was defined exclusively as a theology of indigenization (Africanization).

5. Theologians such as Harry Sawyerr and John Mbiti subscribed to a Western view of theology as the rational account of Christian faith by an elite group of sophisticated academicians. African theology was thought to include "a series of subdisciplines" like biblical studies, church history and systematic theology. In terms of systematic theology, the old guard — i.e., Sawyerr, Mbiti — sought to "Africanize" Christian symbols by placing select aspects of African traditional religion under the scrutiny of Western Christian doctrines. The old guard abstracted from specific ethnic groups customs that appeared to fit under certain doctrinal headings such as a doctrine of God, christology, and eschatology, distinguishing them from one another in order to show both their different nuances of meaning and their inextricable doctrinal relation.

The old guard placed traditional reverence for the ancestors under the authority of eschatology and in relation to the communion of saints; the traditional sense of intermediaries and sacrifice were Christianized in relation to christology; and the traditional acknowledgement of the ultimacy of a supreme being was Christianized under the symbols of a Judeo-Christian monotheism. The juxtaposition of dimensions of African traditional religion and Christian doctrines was understood as

African theology.

6. It seems to me that traditional African values were made, in the discourse, passive to Eurocentric theological values. The selected dimensions of African traditional religion served to convey to Africans what the old guard conceived, in Western terms, as the ultimacy of Christianity — an old missionary tactic. See, for instance, Harry Sawyerr, *Creative Evangelism: Towards a New Christian Encounter with Africa* (London: Lutterworth Press, 1968). Representing the old guard, Harry Sawyerr explains:

   > Whilst, therefore, we would advocate the assimilation of African religious thought-forms, in an attempt to make Christian converts accept the Gospel message and turn away from their pagan concepts and forms of worship, we recognize that they do not provide adequate material with which to express basic Christian concepts." (See p.33.)

   "Africanization," then, plays a minor role in the method of the old guard. What they did was Christianize dimensions of African traditional religion.

7. Intrinsically related to their Christianization of aspects of African traditional religion was the old guard's published expositions on African traditional religion. For all intents and purposes, those texts were propaedeutics to African theology. The old guard's discussions of African traditional religion differed little methodologically from European scholars, such as Geoffrey Parrinder, Placide Tempels, E. Evans-Pritchard, whose works are theoretically suspect, partly because their methods tended to rely on Christian, missionary worldviews as a frame of reference for the meaning and value of African cosmogonies. For critiques of these methodologies, see Luc de Heusch, *Sacrifice in Africa: A Structuralist Approach* (Bloomington: Indiana University Press, 1986). As Luc de Heusch claims, in analyzing Evans-Pritchard's *Nuer Religion*, much of Western scholarship on African traditional religion "provides us with interesting ethnographic material," testifying "to the symbolic system of

Western civilization." (See p.14.)

African theologians, like their European predecessors, tended to reduce African traditional religion to old relics that give way to dynamics of a linear, Western notion of history, itself enshrined in Judeo-Christianity. John Mbiti's important work on African traditional religion, for instance, tended to catalogue various traditional African worldviews on which he imposed a too general taxonomy and a theoretically suspect "philosophy" based on Africans' alleged myopic valorization of the past — *Zamani*. See John Mbiti, *African Religions and Philosophy* (New York: Doubleday, 1970).

For critical views of Mbiti, see Theophilus Okere, *African Philosophy: A Hermeneutical Investigation of the Conditions for Its Possibility* (New York: University Press of America, 1983); and Benjamin C. Ray, *African Religions: Symbol, Ritual, and Community* (New Jersey: Prentice-Hall, Inc., 1976) p.12-16. According to African philosopher Theophilus Okere, Mbiti "does not seem to appreciate the difference in the use of the concept [of time] in different contexts — psychological, social, mythologico-theological, scientific and philosophical. Furthermore, the accuracy of his observations and their exclusive validity for Africa are not beyond doubt." (See p.10.) According to Ray, Mbiti's *African Religions and Philosophy* tries "to be exhaustive and to cover too many societies and too many types of religious phenomena." (See p.13.) Mbiti's work, writes Ray, focuses on beliefs "without giving due recognition to the sociocultural and ritual fabric within which they are imbedded." (See p.14.)

Essentially, Mbiti's work on African traditional religion served his commitment to New Testament eschatology. See his *New Testament Eschatology in an African Background: A Study of the Encounter Between New Testament Theology and African Traditional Concepts* (London: Oxford University Press, 1971). According to Mbiti: "What I have attempted to do is not more than discuss New Testament Eschatology as an aspect of Christological Theology. That, I believe, is where Christian Theology starts and where it ends. (See p.191.) Barely discussed were the dynamic cultures, as opposed to customs, of the peasants, which unlock the meanings of autochthonous oppositions to colonial rules inseparable from Euro-Christian worldviews.

8. Traditional African worldviews were hardly giving way to European worldviews. See Wyatt MacGaffey, *Religion and Society in Central Africa: The BaKongo of Lower Zaire* (Chicago: The University of Chicago Press, 1986). As Wyatt MacGaffey shows in his work on the BaKongo, Africans have tended to "live by two sets of rules," African and European, "each associated with its own rules of etiquette, modes of public communication, language...*technique du corps.*" (See p.18.) "Such accommodations, always unstable and transitory, were dominated by the indigenous cosmology, in terms of which European doctrines and practices were understood." (Ibid.)

9. Abstracting traditional religions from their systems of economic production, social structure and political valences, the old guard gave little attention to the cosmologies which, changing in response to olden colonialism, interpret imperialism in terms of traditional modalities. In short, the old guard's analysis of African traditional religion was too controlled by Eurocentric assumptions, particularly in allowing Western Christian worldviews to obscure the intransigence of African traditional values, defiant of neocolonialism and related, therefore, to the theme of liberation.

    During the late sixties and seventies, things were disintegrating throughout black Africa. Nkrumah's dream of a United States of Africa appeared quixotic in the face of the civil wars between Biafra and Nigeria and the North and South of the Sudan. The African holocausts of Amin and Biyogo, the Tutsi slaughter of thousands of Hutu, the barrage of coup d'etats contradicted the old guard's claim that the process of liberation is irrelevant to African theology outside of South Africa. Manned by an African elite, the colonial apparatus remains. The West continues to export capital, extract resources from peasants and workers, transfer obsolete technology — all to the profit of the West and the impoverishment of Africa. Despite the civil wars raging in Nigeria and Burundi, the disunity of the Organization of African Unity and the gross excesses of the African elite; despite the liberation struggles of Angola, Namibia, Zimbabwe and Mozambique; despite the gross obscenity of the white supremacy of the Republic of South Africa — the old guard focused on indigenization. They explored neither African theology's relation to the values undergirding the oppressive matrix of neocolonialism, nor African traditional religions' resistance to that same matrix. Indeed, the old guard's vociferous rejection of the theme of liberation demanded that analysts of African theology "bracket" the black liberation theology of South Africa in writing about *African* theology.

10. In the radical discourse of the new guard, the theme of indigenization (Africanization) is no longer the focus of African theology, but hardly sublated by the intense valorization of the theme of liberation. In valuing the theme of liberation, the new guard resembles black South African theologians who oppose the Anglo-Boer regime and the homeland policy intrinsic to it. Indeed black South African theologians were the first to *prophetically synthesize the themes of liberation and Africanization.* Oppressed by apartheid and in touch with the values of traditional societies, theologians such as Takatso Mofokeng, Jerry Mosala, Bishop Tutu, Alan Boesak, and Frank Chikane all reveal specific opposition to the interrelated forces of white supremacy and multinational capitalism. Their struggle for liberation is against a form of colonial rule dominated by a peculiar breed of European settlers. The revolutionary situation of South Africa causes the theme of liberation in South Africa to be related to an escalating armed struggle.

    The new guard, like black South African theologians, reveal a commitment to a struggle for liberation related to the problems of white supremacy and capitalism. See, for instance, Jean-Marc Éla, *L'Afrique des villages* (Paris: Editions Karthala,1982), and *La ville en Afrique noire* (Paris: Editions Karthala, 1981. See also Englebert Mveng, *"Récents développements de la théologie Africaine,"* Bulletin de théologie Africaine, 5.9 (janvier-juin 1983).

According to Mveng:

> Il apparaît ainsi que sur l'ensemble du Continent Africain, la lutte pour la libération se trouve aujourd'hui à un point d'aggravation critique et dramatique: libération politique, économique et culturelle un peu partout, libération de la pression des forces extérieures conduisant à l'agonie du l'OUA, libération de l'oppression raciste en Afrique du Sud, libération du tribalisme et des nationalismes étroits sur plusieurs points du continent, lutte pour les droits et la dignité de l'homme, et la grande déception des masses devant les promesses non tenues des indépendances politiques. (Mveng p.138.)

Thus, it may be said, in general, that Sub-Saharan theologians have adopted a theological perspective in which the reciprocity of the processes of liberation and Africanization structures the discourse itself.

11. Whereas the old guard of African theology tended to correct what they perceived to be the primitive and problematic syncretism in the African independent churches, the new guard asserts that these churches are the hope of African theology.

12. The theme of liberation is indispensable for an appreciation of what African theology means today. The new guard's synthesis of liberation and Africanization signifies the intrinsic relation between a truly autochthonous struggle for political self-determination and cultural integrity.

13. For those with Pan-African values, the similarity between the new guard and the black theologians of South Africa promises the development of a theological discourse that is Pan-African in scope. Surely, African theology today can no longer be distinguished from the black theology in South Africa on the basis of the separation of theologies of Africanization and liberation. Jean-Marc Éla and Englebert Mveng makes this clear. See Éla, *"Le rôle des Eglises dans la libération du continent africain." Bulletin de théologie africaine 6*, 12 (juillet -décembre 1984); and Mveng, *"Conférence inaugurale: L'Afrique du sud, un lieu théologique,"*

Bulletin de théologie africaine 6,12 (juillet-décembre 1984).

14. On the *Husia*, see Maulana Karenga, *Selections from the Husia: Sacred Wisdom of Ancient Egypt* (Los Angeles: Kawaida Publications, 1984); and Karenga and Jacob Carruthers, *Kemet and the African Worldview: Research, Rescue and Restoration* (Los Angeles: University of Sankore Press, 1986). Developing the work of Cheik Anta Diop and Dr. Yosef ben-Jochannen, Karenga makes a case for the view that Western monotheism is the stolen legacy of ancient Egypt, an essentially black civilization. According to Karenga, the correct name of this civilization is Kemet.

Jacob Carruthers asserts that Egypt is a Greek name "based upon a gross linguistic misunderstanding." (*Kemet*, p.3.) According to Carruthers, "the formal name [of what is called Egypt] seems to have been Tawy (the Two Lands) but the commonly used name was Kemet, which means the Black settlement referring to the Black land along the banks of the Nile River" (p.3). "The people," writes Carruthers, "called themselves Kemites (the Black ones). It is thus appropriate that we honor the traditions of the ancestors by calling them by their names." (See p.3.)

Central to Kemet was the spirituality of which the *Husia* is emblematic. Karenga explains that the *Husia* "is taken from two ancient Egyptian words which signify the two divine powers by which Ra (Ptah) created the world, i.e. *Hu*, authoritative utterance and *Sia*, exceptional insight." (Husia, p. xiv.) Essential to the *Husia* is *maat* (truth and justice). According to Carruthers, "*Maat* is not only the essence of wisdom, but also the measure of prudence." (Kemet, p.19.)

Dr. Karenga's position greatly challenges black and African theologians. He writes: "The quest to restore Kemet's moral and spiritual legacy is a direct outgrowth of the struggle to develop an authentic Black Sacred text." (Kemet, p.83.) For Karenga, "the quest for an authentic African spirituality unavoidably depends on the restoration of the central sacred writings of Kemet." (Ibid, p.97.)

Although I think exploration of the role of Ancient Ethiopia

— land of the Gods — on Upper Egypt is intriguing and appropriate for Pan-African historiographers and religionists, the Kemetic tradition is not my focus in this book. Well aware of the integrity of the views of scholars like Karenga and Diop, I am nonetheless a Christian theologian. Perhaps indeed Ra influenced conceptions of Yahweh. Perhaps the resurrection motifs associated with Osiris influenced New Testament resurrection motifs. But I do not abandon my Christian identity. I do not say that my religious convictions, which constitute an Afrocentric Christianity, are more correct than the views of Karenga. In the final analysis I should hope that Pan-Africanists of various religious persuasions would do what Malcolm X urged us to do: "put our religions in the closet" in the valorization of what we have in common — a common oppressor. We must overcome spiritual bigotry for the sake of a praxis committed to the liberation of oppressed blacks of the Atlantic world.

15. See Tony Martin, *The Pan-African Connection: From Slavery to Garvey and Beyond* (Dover: The Majority Press, 1983).

16. This is not, however, a theology of a specific Pan-African ideology,such as Marcus Garvey's. Neither is it a synthesis of Pan-African ideologies such as the socialist theories of C.L.R. James, George Padmore, W.E.B. DuBois, or Kwame Nkrumah. Neither is the text a theology of the various organizations emergent from the All Africa People's Organization (AAPO), such as UAM, the PAFMECA, or the Umbrella organization, the OAU.

17. Sterling Stuckey, *Slave Culture: Nationalist Theory and the Foundations of Black America* (New York: Oxford University Press, 1987). Stuckey argues:

> The final gift of African "tribalism" in the nineteenth century was its life as a lingering memory in the minds of American slaves. That memory enabled them to go back to the sense of community in the traditional African setting and to include all Africans in their common experience of oppression in North America. It is greatly ironic, therefore, that African ethnicity, an

obstacle to African nationalism in the twentieth century, was in this way the principle avenue to black unity in antebellum America. Whether free black or slave, whether in the North or the South, the ultimate impact of that development was profound. (See p.3.)

18. See Cedric Robinson in note 9, Preface. He writes:

> The transport of African labour to the mines and plantations of the Caribbean and subsequently to what would be known as the Americas meant also the transfer of African ontological and cosmological systems; African presumptions of the organization and significance of social structure; African codes embodying historical consciousness and social experience; and African ideological and behavioral constructions for the resolution of the inevitable conflict between the actual and the normative. (See p.174.)

According to Robinson, these "were the terms upon which the response of the enslaved to the slave system would be grounded." (Ibid.)

19. See note 17. Stuckey, pp. 10-11. Robinson reiterates the point made above:

> the cargoes of laborers contained African cultures, critical mixes and admixtures of language and thought, of cosmology and metaphysics, of habits, beliefs and mortality. *These were the actual terms of their humanity*. These cargoes, then, did not consist of intellectual isolates or deculturated blanks — men, women and children separated from their previous universe. *African labor brought the past with it, a past which had produced it and settled on it the first elements of consciousness and comprehension* [emphases added]. (See p.173.)

Maroon communities were outstanding examples of New World cultures. One such culture was led by the great ancestor of black Brazilians, Zumbi.

Maroon communities brought together African people in an essential Pan-Africanism despite their diverse provenience and cultures. Other examples of revolutionary Pan-Africanism at work were the Haitian revolution and North American slave revolts. For an excellent discussion of these Pan-African communities, see Cedric Robinson, note 9, Preface. Also see Herbert Aptheker, *American Negro Slave Revolts,* (New York: Columbia University Press, 1987), p.98; ibid., *To Be Free* (New York: International Publishers, 1984) pp.11-30; Eugene D. Genovese, *From Rebellion to Revolution: Afro-American Slave Revolts in the Making of the New World* (New York: Vintage Books, 1981), pp. 52-54.

20. Stuckey, p. 48.

21. Ibid., pp. 23-24.

22. On Olaudah Equiano see Paul Edwards, ed., *Equiano's Travels* (London: Heinemann, 1977); and Lamin Sanneh, *West African Christianity: The Religious Impact* (New York: Orbis Books, 1983), pp.53ff, 68. On Cugoano, see Sanneh and Robert July, *The Origins of Modern African Thought* (New York: Frederick A. Praeger, 1967), pp. 21-22, 35-40, 44-46. On Paul Cuffe, see Sheldon H. Harris, *Paul Cuffe: Black America and the African Return* (New York: Simon and Schuster, 1972); and P. Olinsanwuche Esedebe, *Pan-Africanism: The Idea and Movement* (Washington, DC: Howard University Press, 1982), pp.9-10.

23. See Harris in note 22.

24. That Cuffe's proximity to slave culture increased his commitment to Pan-Africanism is a view related to Stuckey's persuasive paradigm of black nationalist theory. According to Stuckey, the undeniable presence of Pan-African values in slave culture was decisive for the emergence of black nationalist and Pan-Africanist ideologies. He writes: "Black nationalist theory in its truest, richest form is found, of course, in slave folklore, the foundation of which...is African." (See p.81.) Black nationalists' awareness of the *otherness* of the slave community heightened their consciousness of the distinctiveness of blacks, giving impetus to black nationalist consciousness as embodied in Cuffe, David Walker, Henry H. Garnet, W.E.B. DuBois, and Paul

Robeson.

25. On Paul Robeson see, Stuckey, pp. 303-358; Robeson, *Here I Stand* (New York: Othello Associates, 1957); and Martin Bauml Duberman, *Paul Robeson. A Biography* (New York: Ballantine Books, 1989.

26. My discussion of Pan-Africanism is abstracted from several sources, the ones I have noted above and the following: Imanuel Geiss, *The Pan-African Movement: A History of Pan-Africanism in America, Europe, and Africa* (New York: Africana Publishing Company, 1974); Tony Martin, *The Pan-African Connection: From Slavery to Garvey and Beyond* (Dover: The Majority Press, 1985); George Padmore, *Pan-Africanism or Communism? The Coming Struggle for Africa* (London: 1956); Colin Legum, *Pan-Africanism: A Short Political Guide* (New York: Frederick A. Praeger, 1965); W. Ofuatey-Kodjoe, ed., *Pan-Africanism: New Directions in Strategy* (New York: University Press of America, 1986); Elenga M'buyinga, *Pan Africanism or Neo-Colonialism: The Bankruptcy of the O.A.U.* (London: Zed Press, 1982); Okechukwu Mezu, *The Philosophy of Pan-Africanism* (Washington, DC: Georgetown University Press, 1965); Albert Tevoedjre, *Pan-Africanism in Action: An Account of the UAM* (Cambridge, Mass.: Center for International Affairs, Harvard University, 1965); W.E.B. DuBois, *Dusk of Dawn: An Essay Toward an Autobiography of a Race Concept* (New Brunswick: Transaction Books, 1984; ibid., *The World and Africa* (New York: International Publishers, 1981); Richard West, *A History of Sierra Leone and Liberia* (New York: Holt, Rinehart and Winston, 1970); Bernard M. Magubane, *The Ties That Bind: African-American Consciousness of Africa* (Trenton: Africa World Press, 1987)

27. See Geiss, pp. 177-198; Esedebe, pp. 45-110; and DuBois *Dusk of Dawn*, pp. 260-262.

28. See Geiss, pp. 229-262; DuBois, *Dusk of Dawn*, pp. 260-262, 274ff; and Magubane, pp. 127-157.

29. On Garvey, see: *Marcus Garvey, Philosophy and Opinions of Marcus Garvey or African for the Africans*, compiled by Amy Jacques Garvey with introduction by E.U. Essien-Udom, 2nd ed. (New York: Frank Cass, 1967); E. David Cronon, *Black Moses: The Story of Marcus Garvey*, (Madison: University of Wisconsin Press, 1959); Tony Martin, *Race First: The Ideological and Organizational Struggles of Marcus Garvey and the Universal Negro Improvement Association* (Dover: The Majority Press, 1986); John Henrik Clarke, ed., *Marcus Garvey and the Vision of Africa* (New York: Vintage Books, 1974).

30. See Magubane, p. 211.

31. See Geiss, pp. 305-321.

32. Ibid., pp. 284-293.

33. Ibid., pp. 385-408; Esedebe, pp. 161-193.

34. See Legum, pp. 65-92, 112-147; Esedebe, pp. 195-247.

35. See M'buyinga. Nkrumah's vision that the OAU would be a fortress against the balkanization of the African people was only a dream. Indeed, neocolonialism has successfully prevented the alliance of socialist forces captive to neither the West nor the Soviets. In his book *Pan-Africanism or Neocolonialism: The Bankruptcy of the OAU*, Elenga M'buyinga writes:

> As far as its record is concerned...the OAU [from the very start] was nothing more than the practical expression of the desires of neo-colonialist imperialism and the African bourgeoisie, who sought to prevent the development of a revolutionary wing of independent African states opposed to neocolonialism. The aim was to sap the ideological and practical unity of the independent African states and revolutionary organizations who were struggling against classical colonialism or neocolonialism. The reactionaries' tactical objective was to bring about a compromise between the anti-imperialist Casablanca Group States and the reactionary African puppets of international imperialism. Their

> overall strategy, the effects of which we see today, was to eliminate any African revolution which corresponded to the interest of African workers. The political unification of Africa, the genuine liberation of our continent and a commitment to socialist economic and social development policies, were essential to those interests then, and are even more so today. (See pp. 55-56.)

The Casablanca Group was from the start outdone by the matrix of underdevelopment that removed Nkrumah three years after the founding of the OAU. The conservative values of the Monrovia-Brazzaville "wing" (UAM) of the OAU succeeded in valorizing the distinctiveness of independent states, thus giving further institutional force to balkanization. (See M'buyinga, pp. 56-57.)

Indeed, neocolonialism, which pulls in its train precolonial conflicts, makes Nkrumah's dream of African union quixotic. But Nkrumah, nonetheless, saw clearly that a union based on African interest alone *would* check the opportunism of neoimperialism. Undoubtedly, for instance, the Mozambique National Resistance (MNR) — that is RENAMO — and the National Union for the Independence of Angola (UNITA) are successful in destabilizing the anti-apartheid revolutionary peasant parties because of the continent's vulnerability to outside manipulation. As M'Buyinga explains:

> Since 1975, Mozambique, Angola and countries like Tanzania have given a great deal of assistance to the anti-colonialist guerrillas in Southern Africa. But one cannot avoid the fact that, after 1963, the Pan-Africanist revolutionary current of the period 1958-62 was forced on the defensive" (See p.57.)

36. See in note 26, Ofuatey-Kodjoe, the essay by Alex Willingham, "Afro-American Pan-Africanist Ideology." According to Willingham, the neo-Pan-Africanists did not advance a radical praxis of Pan-Africanism for three reasons:

> (1) initial nationalist sentiment, even in its efforts to be international, developed without reference to the Pan-African tradition as such (2) accordingly, the writings of the Neo-Pan-Africanists do not engage the speculations of [C.L.R.] James and [George] Padmore except in passing manner, and (3) other Pan-

> Africanists devoted primary attention to institution-building and little time to theoretical analysis at all. This [disjunction] between the works of traditional Pan-Africanism and the Neo-Pan-Africanists continues to present a problem for political theorists concerned with evaluating these matters. In fact unless one is willing to limit criticism to a call that traditional Pan-Africanism be followed more faithfully, then evaluative work must be directed at two different forces where the assumptions prevailing in the one of either case may not have been accepted by the other. Neo-Pan-Africanists in particular have an automatic defense then against the limitations we may find in Padmore or James. (p.117.)

Willingham's point is not unrelated to may own criticism of Crummell and Blyden. That is, theory in Pan-African praxis must develop dialectically — the Pan-Africanist must reread the thoughts of the ancestors in an effort to overcome alienation and forge a dynamic continuity. He or she thus brings forward the best of Pan-African insight for posterity.

37. Ibid. See Ofuatey-Kodjoe's essay, "Pan-Africanism, In Crisis: the Need for a Redefinition," p.16.

38. C.L.R. James, *A History of Negro Revolt* (London: Haskel House, 1938), p.5.

39. According to Geiss, "Pan-Africanism has hardly ever been a clearly defined, precise or rational concept. On the contrary, it has been (and still is) a matter of hazy, vague emotions....Nevertheless it is possible to isolate a rational kernel from the chaos...even though this rational element is all to often subordinated to a feeling of resentment and despair at the injustice prevalent in...White domination." (*The Pan-African Movement*, p.5.) I, however, can not understand what is irrational about feeling resentment at domination. Geiss' influential book is emblematic of Eurocentric hermeneutics that would deny blacks the struggle for self-definition. Should blacks accept Geiss' perspective, they would be alienated from the redemptive implications of Pan-Africanism.

Geiss claims that the irrationality of Pan-Africanism is a

product of a refusal to accept "the world to come of age" (Bonhoeffer). He writes that Pan-Africanism emerged as the formation of a privileged bourgeois intelligentsia was accelerated by modern development. According to Geiss, "The spread of democratic ideas heightened the self-awareness of [blacks] and made them feel twice as painfully the iniquities of racism and colonialism." (See pp.199-220.) Undoubtedly, ancestors of Pan-Africanism, revealing a certain alienation from the African heritage, were an elite group influenced by Eurocentric, democratic values. Black frustration, then, at being denied full access to bourgeois culture — I do not refer to Padmore or James — gave impetus to Pan-African associations often removed from the realities of the popular masses. Thus Geiss correctly notes the influence of "modernity" on Pan-Africanists. However, his Eurocentric view truncates the integral vision of Pan-Africanism and represents an alienation from ancestral legacies of the oppressed.

As I have argued, the essential Pan-Africanism was not a product of "democratic ideas" of Europe or of blacks' assimilation of a Pan-German or Pan-Slavic movement. The essential Pan-Africanism emerged not from the elite, but from the slaves close to the African sources of black humanity. In resisting their oppressors, the slaves sought not integration into the matrix of Eurocentric democratic principles, but their own, Afrocentric autonomy. In Africa, fundamental Pan-Africanism also emerges from the most oppressed. Indeed, elite ancestors of Pan-African theology — such as Attobah Ahuma and Majola Agbebi — able to overcome in varying degrees an alienation from ancestral legacies had been impressed by the integrity of the African culture of the popular folk.

Geiss thinks, however, that modernity and the technology and the mores intrinsic to it " *dissolve* the old tribal society." (See pp.427.) The fact is that the "old tribal society" — as if the term itself captures the totality of traditional Africa — has not withered away in the advance of an oppressive post-modernity. Indeed, the popular masses, in their own self-sufficiency of insight (Lincoln), do not forsake ancestral legacies as they resist the dehumanizing crises of post-modernity.

Geiss' perspective is unmasked by Amilcar Cabral. According to Cabral, apologists for Eurocentric hegemony attempt to "repress the cultural life of the colonized people." (See Cabral p.45, note 1, Preface.) Inseparable from this praxis is the "cultural alienation of a part of the population, either by so-called assimilation of indigenous people, or by creating a social gap between the indigenous elites and the popular masses." (Ibid.) Geiss fears a progressive alliance of classes of oppressed people. What Geiss deems irrational is the consciousness inimical to a process of "deepening the divisions in the society," inimical to the process whereby the elite assimilate "the colonizer's mentality, considers itself culturally superior to its own people and ignores or looks down upon their cultural values." (See Cabral, p.45.) The revolutionary implications of this consciousness are indeed irrational to the alienating center.

Using Cabral to critique Geiss is quite appropriate. According to Cabral:

> A reconversion of minds — of mental set — is...indispensable to the true integration of people into the liberation movement. Such reconversion — re-Africanization, in our case — may take place before the struggle, but it is completed only during the struggle, through daily contact with the popular masses in the communion of sacrifice required by the struggle. (See p.45.)

The re-Africanized seek to re-appropriate ancestral values in a movement that resists the oppressor. Alienated from the realities of Pan-African expression, Geiss misunderstands blacks' interest in the meaning of the continuity of the African heritage. It is Geiss' *Eurocentrism* that causes him to argue that the African heritage should be abandoned, not the African heritage, in all its relativity, itself. It is precisely *Geiss's aversion to what he believes* to be without value that causes him to label concerns to explain the ongoing significance of the African heritage, "irrational." Whether preoccupations with the African heritage are irrational is not essentially related to his position. Adjudication of rationality is often but the projection of one "grammar" of existence upon another "grammar." The grammars have no necessary, metaphysical connection: Geiss's view of the African heritage and African heritage itself are not necessarily related. Geiss, however, writes as if his view were of itself common sense or stamped into human destiny as an *a priori*.

40. Esedebe, p.3.

41. I will say more of black oppressors in subsequent chapters. For an analysis of the oppressiveness of Eurocentric Marxists, see Robinson. Robinson shows that Marxists' tendencies to sublate black radicalism to an allegedly objective social science that appears to overcome the "dinosaur" of nationalism are themselves products of varieties of "white" nationalism.

According to Robinson:

> It appears that with respect to actual nationalist movements of their time, in Germany, Poland, eastern or southern Europe, neither Marx nor Engels achieved an extraordinary comprehension or fully escaped the parochialism of the day. Rather, their historical method provided them with a means of supporting their predispositions on the historical worth of peoples and the varying capacities of the several European national movements. Their own nationalism...made them generally unsympathetic to the national liberation movements of peoples (e.g. the Russians and the Slavs) which historically threatened what Marx and Engels believed to be the national interest of the German people." (See p.77.)

What is more, argues Robinson, this flaw in Marxist theory "that is a transmitted historical consciousness, as an aspect of class consciousness, did not equip the Marxian movement for the political forces which would not only erupt in...the Third World but within the movement itself." (See p.78.) "What the Marxists did not understand," writes Robinson,

> about the political and ideological phenomenon of nationalism is that it was not (and is not) an historical aberration (of proletarian internationalism). Nor is it necessarily the contrary: a developmental stage of internationalism. Nationalism defeated the Marxism of the Second International (World War I), but ironically, was the basis of the Third International (the Russian revolutions; Stalin's socialism in one country; the conditions for

> membership in the Comintern), yet its primary world-historical significance was denied. It remained for most northern Marxists a secondary phenomenon (to the class struggle). (See pp.79-80.)

George Padmore and Richard Wright show clearly the difference between employing Marxist theories and subscribing to the alienating agendas of Soviet nationalism.

These black scholars show clearly that culture, qua "race" and nationalism, is not epiphenomenal to the hegemony of private property and the matrix of exchange value. For Wright, as for George Padmore, dogmatic Marxists are too often unaware that African people reveal a dimension of historical experience of which a white Marxist would be ignorant because they lack existential insight and epistemological resources. For Wright, Marxism masked "the complexities of history and social experience. Its truer function was the social and intellectual cohesion of the petit bourgeoisie." (Robinson, p. 433.) George Padmore, in addition, thought that Marxists were quick to subsume the Pan-African experience in theories of the internationalization of the workers for the sake of a *Soviet Nationalism*. (See *Pan-Africanism or Communism*, p.372.) According to Padmore, blacks "are very much alive to the fact that [Soviet]...interest in them is dictated by the ever-changing tactics of Soviet foreign policy rather than by altruistic motives." (See p.289.) Politically aware intellectuals, in touch with the folk, asserts Padmore, "know that the oppressed Negro workers and peasants are regarded by the Communists as 'revolutionary expendables' in the global struggle against Western Capitalism." (See p.289.)

42. See note 3 of the Introduction. See also: Joe Holland and Peter Henriot, *Social Analysis: Likening Faith and Justice* (New York: Orbis Books, 1985).

43. Juan Luis Segundo, *The Liberation of Theology* (New York: Orbis Books, 1976), p.75.

44. According to Magubane:

> The study of black nationalism in its dialectical relationship with African consciousness should explore the empirically and theoretically determined thought of blacks in a single worldwide system, and better still in the structure of worldwide society; and should try to reveal the thought of the Afro-American as the ideology of the black man [sic] in the epoch of Western imperialism. The historical reality of capitalist imperialism attempted to expel the black man [sic] from history with its insistence upon his innate and immutable inferiority. Black nationalism and African consciousness (whether negative or positive) have a direct relevance to the Afro-American's identity, and they make up his [sic] misfortunes in the New World. (See p.10.)

Indeed, black nationalism is a polysemous term implicating distinct valences in relation to black liberation. Segregation within and emigration from the United States, cultural and political forms of nationalism and varieties of religious nationalism all signify the reality of black nationalist consciousness. Common, however, to black nationalism is the conviction that blacks constitute an atomistic mass for whom pursuit of institutional and political autonomy is indispensable for liberation. Historical evidence, moreover, indicates that black nationalist values have been meaningful primarily to the grassroots folk who embody the distinctiveness of African-American culture and are forced into the creation of separate institutions. Magubane put it this way: "Black nationalism has its greatest appeal among lower-class blacks; whether integration succeeds or fails will be decided to a large extent by the way in which the lower-class black reacts; or by what is done to him [sic]." (See p.12.)

45. For an excellent paradigm of religio-cultural analysis,which has a heuristic relation to this text, see Aloysius Pieris, *An Asian Theology of Liberation* (New York: Orbis Books, 1988).

46. See notes 6- 8 above.

47. Mercy Amba Oduyoye, *Hearing and Knowing: Theological Reflections on Christianity in Africa* (New York: Orbis Books, 1986), p.69.

48. See Wyatt MacGaffey, *Modern Kongo Prophets: Religion in a Plural Society* (Bloomington: Indiana University Press, 1983).

Chapter 2
Alexander Crummell: Two Warring Ideals in One Dark Body

1. For an excellent essay on Crummell, see Otey Scruggs, "We The Children of Africa In This Land," in Lorraine Williams, ed., *Africa and the Afro-American Experience* (Washington, DC: Howard University Press, 1981). See also, Walter L. Williams, *Black Americans and the Evangelization of Africa, 1877-1900* (Wisconsin, University of Wisconsin Press, 1982). For a thorough biographical treatment of Crummell, see Wilson Jeremiah Moses, *Alexander Crummell. A Study of Civilization and Discontent* (New York: Oxford University Press, 1989).

Alexander Crummell was born in 1819 to a family of "free" blacks who belonged to a community of "free" blacks of New York City. The community was progressive insofar as it "organized around its churches, promoted 'moral and intellectual improvement,' established organizations to further this twin objective, and contributed to the antislavery cause." (See Scruggs, p.78.) Central to the piety of that community was a sense of missionary vocation that condescendingly sought the uplift of the "culturally unrefined" black poor of the United States and the more "grossly unrefined pagan" of Africa. Crummell's elitist tendencies were part of his early socialization in a black middleclass community that unwittingly absorbed many of the values of their oppressors. The African Free Schools of New York City provided Crummell with his early education as it did that of the celebrated black thespian, Ira Aldridge, the noted black abolitionists Samuel R. Ward and the powerful freedom-fighter, Henry Highland Garnet. For an intriguing account of the friendship between Crummell and Garnet, see Alexander Crummell, *Africa and America: Addresses and Discourses* (New York: Negro Universities Press, 1969), pp. 268-305. After graduation from Oneida Institute, Crummell was refused admission to the General Theological Seminary in New York City. Crummell went on to study for the Episcopal priesthood at the Andover Theological Seminary.

2. W.E.B. DuBois, *The Souls of Black Folk* (New York: New American Library, 1969, p. 234.

3. Ibid, p. 242.

4. Magubane describes the ACS as follows:

> In December 1816, the American Colonization Society was formed by prominent white people, among whom were included some slaveholders. Its object was to transport free blacks to Africa on the grounds that they were incapable of serving useful lives in the United States. The society appealed to slaveholders by informing them the removal of free blacks would make more secure the institution of slavery. (See note 3, Preface, p. 67.)

Indeed, colonization was first and foremost the plan of whites whose benevolence towards blacks was questionable, to say the least.

The distinction Edwin Redkey, the author of *Black Exodus: Black Nationalist and Back to Africa Movements* (New Haven: Yale University Press, 1969), has made between colonization and emigration is useful at this point. Emigration may be traced to sentiments among illiterate slaves and literate Islamic slaves more African than African-American. Africa for these slaves was their true home and they naturally wished to return. (See Redkey, p. 16.) After manumission of certain blacks in the

North after the colonial war, emigration surfaced as a popular theme in "free" black communities (p.17). Many of these non-slaves, though indigenous to the Americas, felt an antipathy between their blackness and the place of their birth. Their desire to return to Africa, however, is best expressed in terms of colonization. Blacks, then, had concluded long before the formation of the American Colonization Society (ACS) that they were unequivocally an African people.

5. Hollis Lynch, *Edward Wilmot Blyden: Pan-Negro Patriot* (New York: Oxford University Press, 1970), p. 41.

6. Crummell, p. 413.

7. Ibid., p. 416. *In The Future of Africa* (New York: Scribner, 1862), Crummell put it this way:

> God never allows any evils on earth to be entirely aggregations of evil, without their incidents of good. So here, in this matter, God has raised up, even in their lands of servitude, a class of black men who have already gone from America, from the British West Indies, and from Sierra Leone; the pioneers of civilization and Christianity, to the land of their fathers. Thus God overrules the wrath of man. Thus from blasting, deadly evil, is He ever educing good. Thus does [God] pluck the sting of malignant intent out of the disastrous histories of men; and transforms those into benignant providences.(See, p. 125.)

8. Ibid., pp. 3-4.

9. Crummell, *Africa and America*, pp. 407-409.

10. Ibid., p. 409.

11. Ibid., p. 264.

12. Ibid.

13. Crummell, *The Future of Africa*, p. 59.

14. Ibid.

15. Ibid., p.60.

16. Myth, as a religious creation, signifies essential values intrinsic to human cultural development. The creation myth of Genesis suggests that humankind has evolved from common ancestors whose prehistory entails the development of stone cultures and the diffusion of migrations. To the extent that Christian anthropology has come of age, appreciation of the lithic code beneath the myths is indispensable for contemporary doctrines of humanity.

17. See note 4 above.

18. Crummell, *Africa and America*, p. 137.

19. Crummell, *The Future of Africa*, pp. 15-16.

20. Crummell, *Africa and America*, p. 139.

21. See J. Gus Liebenow, *Liberia: A Century of Survival, 1847-1947* (Philadelphia: University of Pennsylvania Press, The University Museum, 1947).

22. See Raymond Leslie Buell, *Liberia: a Century of Survival, 1847-1947* (Philadelphia: University of Pennsylvania Press, The University Museum, 1947). Buell writes:

> The slave trade having already become illegal, [the United States] Congress passed an act in 1819 instructing the American Navy to seize any American vessels engaged in the slave trade, and instructing the President to return all Negroes thus seized to Africa. During this period American naval vessels cruised off the west coast of Africa looking for slavers. The Negro slaves thus seized on the high seas and the freed slaves in America were the two sources from which the Liberian Republic emerged. (See p.20.)

According to Buell: "Altogether the American Navy carried over 5,000 captured slaves to Liberia; the remainder of about 15,000 consisted of freed Negroes from the United States." (See, p.21.) For an account of the way in which Sierra Leone mitigated the slave trade, see Sanneh, *West African Christianity: The Religious Impact*, pp. 53-105.

23. See Padmore, *Pan-Africanism or Communism? The Coming Struggle for Africa*, and DuBois, *Dusk of Dawn*, pp. 116-133. On DuBois, in this regard, see also Cedric Robinson, "DuBois and Black Sovereignty." *Race and Class* 32:2 (October-December 1990).

24. Imanuel Geiss — see note 39, chapter 1 — records the observations of McCants Stewart. Writing in the nineteenth century, McCants Stewart writes:

> the relations between the native and the Negro emigrant from America has been that of master and slave. The former American slave treated the African freeman as if he had no rights which were worthy of respect!...The natives of Liberia have been to the emigrants from America just what these ex-slaves were to the whites of the South. They have been defrauded, beaten with stripes, and made to feel that they were inferior beings (pp. 124-125).

On the rise of Colonel Doe and the overthrow of the Tolbert regime, see David Lamb, *The Africans* (New York: Random House, 1982, pp. 126-132); and Ali A. Mazuri, *The Africans: A Triple Heritage*, (Boston: Little, Brown, 1986), pp. 292-3.

25. Crummell, *Africa and America*, p. 130.

26. Ibid., p. 131.

27. Ibid., p. 131.

28. Ibid., p. 185.

29. Ibid., p. 186.

30. Ibid.

31. Ibid. In the essay "The Regeneration of Africa," Crummell writes that "the deportation of the whole Negro race, in this land, is not a necessity, nor a requirement, considered with respect to [Africa's redemption]. God does not work out His great ends in this manner. It is by *'remnants'* that He achieves the marvels of...providence and...grace. It is 'the called,' 'the elect,' 'the chosen,' few, indeed they may be, whom [God] selects and puts in fit places, and sets to their proper work, for His own glory." (See, p.449.)

32. Crummell, *The Future of Africa.* He writes: "The further [Americo-Liberians] push into the interior, the more abundant and more valuable do these gifts of nature become." (See p.86.)

33. Ibid., p. 90.

34. Ibid. Crummell writes: "It is a matter alike of policy and of duty for us to attempt, though at a humble distance, the same legal reformation among this people that the English have, with great success, effected in India." (See, p.49.)

35. Crummell, *Africa and America,* p. 170.

36. Ibid., p. 171.

37. Ibid., p. 185. Crummell quotes Mill: "To characterize any conduct whatever towards barbarous people as a violation of the 'Law of Nations,' only shows that he who so speaks has never considered the subject. A violation of great principles of morality it may easily be; but barbarians have no rights as a nation, except a right to such treatment as may, at the earliest possible period, fit them for becoming one. The only moral laws for the relation between a civilized and a barbarous government are

the universal rules of morality between man and man." (See, p.185.)

38. Crummell, *The Future of Africa*, p. 18.

39. Crummell, *Africa and America*, p. 92.

40. Ibid.

41. See note 66 below.

42. Crummell, *Africa and America*, p. 124.

43. Ibid., p. 125.

44. Crummell, *The Future of Africa*, p. 19.

45. Ibid., p. 19.

46. Ibid., p. 20.

47. Ibid., p. 23. For Crummell: "...the English language is the enshrinement of those great charters of liberty which are essential elements of free governments, and the main guarantees of personal liberty." (See, p. 25.)

48. Ibid., p. 23.

49. Ibid.

50. Ibid., p. 24.

51. Ibid. Crummell writes: "Of all races of men, none, I ween, are so domineering... none have a more contemptuous dislike of inferiority; and yet in this race the ancient spirit of freedom rises higher than their repugnances. It impels them to conquer even their prejudices: and hence, when chastened and subdued by Christianity, it makes them philanthropic and brotherly."

(See, p.24.)

52. Ibid., pp. 24-25.

53. Ibid., p. 15.

54. Liebenow reveals that despite the superior war technology of the settlers, the Africans were effective guerrillas. He writes: "On occasion...the natives' superior skill in guerrilla warfare, enhanced by arms secured from outside forces, tipped the scales temporarily in favor of the tribal element [sic]. In such cases Liberian authority was established only after many years of fighting and considerable loss of life and property by both sides. The Gola [people] in the early period and the Krebo and Kru [people] as late as the early decades of the present century are outstanding examples of tribal resistance to Liberian occupation." (See p.20-21.)

55. See Virginia Fabella and Sergio Torres, eds., *Irruption of the Third World: Challenge to Theology*, note 2, Introduction.

56. See Jacques Derrida, *Of Grammatology* (Baltimore: The John Hopkins University Press, 1976). It seems to me that Derrida criticizes, by implication, the hegemonic valorization of the English language. According to Derrida such valorization is but an ethnocentrism related to a

> logocentrism: the metaphysics of phonetic writing (for example, of the alphabet) which was fundamentally — for enigmatic yet essential reasons that are inaccessible to a simple historical relativism — nothing but the most original and powerful ethnocentrism, in the process of imposing itself upon the world in one and the same order. (See p.3.)

This order entails: (1) "*the concept of writing* in a world where the phoneticization of writing must dissimulate its own history as it is produced"; (2) "*the history of* (the only) *metaphysics*," not unlike Hegel's deification of European consciousness, i.e., the logos, "the history of truth, of the truth, [which] has always been...the debasement of writing, and its repression outside 'full speech'"; and (3) "*the concept of science* or the scientificity of science — which has always been determined as *logic* — a concept that has always been a philosophical concept, even if the practice of science has constantly challenged its imperialism of the logos, by invoking, for example, from the beginning and ever increasingly, nonphonetic writing" (Derrida, p.3).

I think Derrida discloses the oppressive mythology of the center, which Crummell internalized. As Derrida — it seems to me — suggests it will not do to totalize the plurality of human experiences in a notion of unity that dissimulates European hegemony, as if Eurocentric civilization, with all its epistemic contradictions and hubristic forgetfulness, were providential, as if it realized the alienated Logos "grown of age" in space and time.

In other words, Derrida writes:

> To free unity from the concept of man is undoubtedly to renounce the old notion of peoples said to be "without writing" and "without history"....Actually, the peoples said to be "without writing" lack only a certain type of writing. To refuse the name of writing to this or that technique of consignment is the "ethnocentrism that best defines the prescientific vision of man" and at the same time results in the fact the "in many human groups, the only word by which the members designate their ethnic group is the word 'man.'" (See pp. 83-84.)

57. Amilcar Cabral explains national culture as follows:

> In order for culture to play the important role which falls to it in the framework of the liberation movement, the movement must be able to preserve the positive cultural values of every well-defined social group, of every category, and to achieve the confluence of these values in the service of the struggle... both for the preservation and survival of the cultural values of the people and for the harmonization and development of these values within a national framework." (See Preface, note 1, p.48.)

Essential to national liberation, which seeks a certain dynamic equilibrium among social groups, is an option for the poor. Cabral writes: "Identification of a section of the indigenous *petite bourgeoisie* with the mass of the people has an essential prerequisite: *that, in the face of destructive action by imperialist domination, the masses retain their identity*, separate from that of the colonial power." (See p.64.)

58. Cabral, p. 49. On the Mozambique Liberation Front (FRELIMO) see Giovanni Arrighi and John S. Saul, *Essays on the Political Economy of Africa* (New York: Monthly Review Press, 1973), pp. 378-379; and Basil Davidson, *Let Freedom Come: Africa in Modern History* (Boston: Atlantic Monthly Press, 1978), p. 351, 361, 396.

59. Cabral, p. 47.

60. Crummell, *The Future of Africa*, pp. 29-30.

61. Ibid., p. 31.

62. Ibid., pp. 179-191; 220.

63. Ibid., p. 179.

64. Ibid., p. 179-180.

65. Crummell, *Africa and America*, p. 418.

66. Crummell, *The Future of Africa*, p. 182.

67. Crummell, *Africa and America*, p. 419.

68. See C.L.R. James, *The Black Jacobins: Toussaint L'Overture and the San Domingo Revolution* (New York: Vintage Books, 1963).

69. See Stuckey, *Slave Culture: Nationalist Theory and the Foundations of Black America*, especially chapter one. See also: Lawrence Levine, *Black Culture and Black Consciousness* (New York: Oxford University Press, 1977), pp. 3-135; Paul D. Escott, *Slavery Remembered: A Record of Twentieth-Century Slave Narratives*

(Chapel Hill: University of North Carolina Press, 1977), pp. 101-117); Zora Neal Hurston, *The Sanctified Church* (Berkeley: Turtle Island, 1983), p. 103; John W. Blassingame, *The Slave Community: Plantation Life in the Antebellum South* (New York: Oxford University Press, 1979); W.E.B. DuBois, *History of the Negro Church: Africa to 1890*, as found in Julius Lester, ed., *The Seventh Son: The Thought and Writings of W.E.B. Du Bois, Volume I* (New York: Random House, 1971); J.L. Dillard, *Lexicon of Black English* (New York: Seabury Press, 1977), pp. 111-128.

70. See Crummell, p. 437. He writes: "The black Christian emigrant...is indigenous, in blood, constitution, and adaptability [to Africa]. Two centuries of absence from the continent of Africa has not destroyed his physical adaptation to the land of his ancestors. There is a tropical fitness, which inheres in our constitution, whereby we are enabled, when we leave this country to sit down under an African sun." (See p. 442.) White abolitionists such as Thomas F. Buxton and Henry Venn also advocated employment of indigenous missionaries. Venn and Buxton wrongly thought that blacks were more resistant than whites to hinterland diseases. The Europeans thought that their praxis would develop legitimate trade which would replace the slave trade still illegally in practice. The practice was advocated in terms of "Euthanasia in mission" and "the Bible and the Plough." Both abolitionist worked under the auspices of the Church Missionary Society (CMS), which, until Venn's death, advocated that blacks be the means of Christianization. Whites like Venn envisioned not only the euthanasia of mission, but also the euthanasia of imperial control, as did Johnson. Crummell also had in mind the euthanasia of white control of Africa. See July, *The Origins of Modern African Thought*, pp. 177-195.

71. Crummell, *The Future of Africa*, p. 220.

72. E.A. Ayandele, *Holy Johnson: Pioneer of African Nationalism, 1836-1917* (New York: Humanities Press, 1970).

Johnson asserted:

> In the work of elevating Africans, foreign teachers have always proceeded with their work on the assumption that the Negro or African is in every one of his normal susceptibilities an inferior race, and that it is needful in everything to give him a foreign model to copy; no account has been made of our peculiarities; our languages enriched with traditions of centuries; our parables, many of them the quintessence of family and national histories; our modes of thought influenced more or less by local circumstances, our poetry and manufactures, which though rude, had their own tales to tell....God does not intend to have the races confounded, but that the Negro or African should be raised upon his own idiosyncracies....the result has been that we, as a people,...have lost our self-respect and our love for our own race, are become a sort of nondescript people...and are, in many things, *inferior to our brethren in the interior countries. There is evidently a fetter upon our minds even when the body is free; mental weakness, even when there appears fertility* [emphasis added]. (See p. 65.)

According to Ayandele: "By 1901 [Johnson] was convinced, after some study of Yoruba, Edo and Ibo societies, that the Christian doctrines of Atonement, the mediation of Christ and the Incarnation 'are to be found embedded in their [African] religious system.'" (See p. 301.) In regard to Johnson's Pan-Africanism, see p. 308.

73. Ibid., p. 301.

74. Ibid., p. 304.

75. See Crummell, *The Future of Africa.* Crummell appears to have been convinced that African traditional religion constituted the ritualization of sin. I do not see where he found anything redemptive about the religion. He writes: "We do not merely trust in and hope for the triumphs of the Gospel; we KNOW that all the rudeness and barbarism of surrounding heathenism shall vanish from this neighborhood; that the Church of God shall supplant the disorganized paganism of this people." (See p. 188.) On the other hand, Crummell does not completely castigate his ancestors.

Revealing again his contradictions he writes:

> Our ancestors were unfortunate, miserable, and benighted; but nothing more. Their history was a history not of ignominy and disgrace, but of heathenism and benightedness. And even in that state they exhibited a nobleness of native character, they cherished such virtues, and manifested so much manliness and bravery, that the civilized world is now magnanimous enough to recognize such traits; and its greatest men are free to render their warm eulogies." (See p. 219.)

76. Crummell, *Africa and America*, p. 427.

77. Crummell, *The Future of Africa*, p. 286-287.

78. Ibid., p. 288.

79. Ibid., pp. 286-287.

80. See J. Ki-Zerbo, *General History of Africa. I: Methodology and African Prehistory* (Berkeley: University of California press, 1981). See also John Jackson, *Man, God and Civilization* (Secaucus: Citadel Press, 1970), pp.37-59.

81. Ibid.

82. See Jackson, *Introduction to African Civilizations*, pp. 60-152; St. Clair Drake, *Black Folk Here and There, Vol. I* (Los Angeles: Center for Afro-American Studies University of California, 1987), 121f; and Martin Bernal, *Black Athena: The Afroasiatic Roots of Classical Civilization, Volume I* (New Brunswick: Rutgers University Press, 1987).

83. Chancelor Williams, *The Destruction of Black Civilization: Great Issues of a Race from 4500 B.C. to 2000 A.D.* (Chicago: Third World Press, 1976), pp. 915-200.

84. Crummell, p. 342.

85. Ibid., p. 354.

86. Ibid., p. 334-5.

87. On Ottobah Cugoano, see July, *The Origins of Modern African Thought*, p. 37.

88. Crummell, p. 351.

89. Ibid.

90. Ibid.

91. See Carter G. Woodson, *The History of the Negro Church* (Washington, DC: The Associated Publishers, 1972). Woodson writes: "Crummell was a native of New York, but a descendent of a Timanee chief." (See p. 155.) See also, Walter L. Williams, *Black Americans and the Evangelization of Africa, 1877-1900*. According to Walters, "Alexander Crummell's father was from Sierra Leone." (See p.96.)

92. Ibid., p. 107.

93. Michael Kwamena-Poh, et. al., *African History in Maps* (Burnt Mill: Longman Group Limited, 1984), p. 10.

94. Ibid.

95. Lynch, p. 269. See also Martin R. Delany and Robert Campbell, *Search for a Place: Black Separatism and Africa, 1860* (Ann Arbor: The University of Michigan Press, 1969), p. 61, 105.

96. Cyril Griffith, *The African Dream: Martin R. Delany and the Emergence of Pan-African Thought* (University Park: Pennsylvania State University Press, 1975), p. 103.

97. Ibid., p. 104.

98. Delany and Campbell, p. 106.

99. Crummell, p. 113.

100. Ibid. He writes: "And thus by these adventures, vast millions of that continent have been brought into contact with civilized men; with the fabrics of civilized nations; with the quickening ideas of superior men." (See p. 114.)

101. Ibid., p. 222.

102. Ibid., p. 218.

103. Crummell, *Africa and America,* p. 46.

Chapter 3
Edward Blyden: Blameless Ethiopian

1. Lynch, *Edward Wilmot Blyden: Pan-Negro Patriot* p. 250.

2. Esedebe, *Pan-Africanism: Origins and Meaning.* Tarikh 6,3 (1980). p.10.

3. Born 3 August 1832, on what was then the Danish island of St. Thomas, Blyden claimed to be of direct Igbo descent (eastern Nigeria). Both of his parents were "free" and literate members of the Dutch Reformed Church. A pastor of that church, John P. Knox, impressed with Blyden's intellectual gifts, took him to the United States, trying unsuccessfully to enroll him at Rutgers Theological College. Other attempts to enroll Blyden in American seminaries were also unsuccessful. His rejections from seminaries and the enactment of the Fugitive Slave Law of 1850 turned Blyden away from the United States. Prominent Presbyterians associated with the ACS convinced Blyden to emigrate to Liberia, an independent state as of 1847. Fully subscribing to the ideology of the ACS, Blyden embarked for West Africa, 21 December, 1850. He arrived in Monrovia on 26 January, 1851. For a biography of Blyden, see Lynch. See also Blyden, *Liberia's Offering* (New York: John A. Grey, 1862), pp. i-iv.

4. Lynch, pp. 14-15.

5. Ibid., p. 5.

6. Lynch, p. 15. On the Vai see T. Obenga, "Sources and Specific Techniques Used in African History: General Outline," in *General History of Africa, I: Methodology and African Prehistory*, p. 79.

7. See Lynch, p. 15.

8. Ibid., p. 19.

9. Lynch., p. 62.

10. Ibid., p. 60-1.

11. Lynch, ed., *Black Spokesman: Selected Published Writings of Edward Wilmot Blyden* (London: Frank Cass, 1971), pp. 152-153).

12. Quoted in Lynch, *Edward Wilmot Blyden: Pan-Negro Patriot*, p. 56; cf. H.H. Foote, *Africa and the American Flag* (New York, 1884), p. 207.

13. Lynch, p. 56.

14. Ibid., p. 57.

15. Aloysius Pieris, *An Asian Theology of Liberation* (New York: Orbis Books, 1988). According to Pieris:

> Technology is a [humanly] induced cosmic process, which is a conscious [i.e., self-reflective] continuation of [infrahuman] biological evolution and, like the latter [i.e., like biological evolution], becomes humanized [i.e., liberative] only by its metacosmic orientation [i.e., by the revolutionary thrust of religion toward ever nobler levels of human existence]. (See p. 108.)

16. Lynch, p. 63. Pieris puts it this way:

> If...the law of evolution has prescribed in the book of nature the revolutionary imperative to humanize technology through religion, then a dehumanized technocracy is indeed a reversal of the evolutionary trajectory, a cosmological disaster, an irreligious underdevelopment though boorishly advertised in our countries as "international culture," modernization, and progress — if not also as preevangelization! (Ibid.)

Pieris' critique of the technological values of the West is part of his valorization of non-Christian religions. Similarly, Blyden's warnings against the technological advances of Europe were related to his defense of African culture.

17. Lynch, p. 63.

18. Ibid., p. 72.

19. Ibid.

20. July, *The Origins of Modern African Thought*, p. 219.

21. July, p. 218.

22. Lynch, p. 62.

23. On Diop's two cradle theory, see his *Cultural Unity of Black Africa* (Chicago: Third World Press, 1978) and *The African Origin of Civilization: Myth or Reality* (Westport: Lawrence Hill, 1974), pp. 251-252.

24. Lynch, p. 61.

25. Blyden, *Christianity, Islam and the Negro Race*, p. 110.

26. Lynch, p. 62.

27. Blyden, p. 111.

28. July, p. 213.

29. Blyden, p. 67.

30. One such progressive theologian is Jean-Marc Éla. See his book *African Cry* (Maryknoll, New York: Orbis Books, 1986). Éla writes:

> One cannot help but notice that the traits by which African identity is defined belong to a Western conceptual heritage. In a sense, the sources of blackness are European. The Senghorian portrait [influenced by Blyden] of the Negro is permeated with the Western thought of the eighteenth and nineteenth centuries — Rousseau's noble savage is here, Kant's Negro, the African described by Hegel and Govineau, and finally, Levy-Bruhl's formalizations of the 'primitive mentality.'" (See p. 123.)

Éla takes up his critique of *négritude* in another of his books, *L'Afrique des villages* (see note 10, Chapter 1). Éla points out again that *négritude* is very much akin to white Westerners preoccupation with a pristine Africa. He explains this as follows:

> Dans une Afrique en ébullition, les villages retirés des centres urbains constitueraient le refuge ou le paradis des ethnologues en quête d'un monde intact et pur, ayant échappé au "péché originel" de la "civilisation." On en voit qui débarquent, fiches perforées en main, à la conquête d'une terre vierge où chacun se réserve sa petite tribu où le Blanc n'a pas encore mis le pied, pour la découverte de "l'Africain authentique." (See Éla, *L'Afrique des villages,* p. 11.)

Éla asserts that this *négritude* refuses to examine the contradictions of the rural areas. *Car, pour la plupart des gens de la brousse, le village n'est pas une réserve des traditions et du folklore mais le lieu du calvaire d'un peuple.* (Ibid., 10.)

In a way somewhat different from Éla, Barthélemy Adoukonou, another very progressive African theologian, in his book *Jalons pour une théologie africaine: Essai d'une herméneutique chrétienne du Vodun dahoméen. Tome I: critique théologique* (Paris: Éditions Lethielleux, 1980), also argues that *négritude* is an alien-

ated discourse.
He writes:

> Si jusqu'à un certain point l'Afrique ne retrouvera sa danse et sa musique, son esthétique et sa poétique de l'homme, que dans et par la traversée douloureuse d'une histoire aux morsures sévères, nous nous demandons si la note de "danger," de violence, de subversion, appartient constitutivement à la "Beauté Noire." [Stanislas] Adotévi [who has written a significant critique of négritude] pour sa part, croit pouvoir assigner à l'esthétique nègre biblique, "Black is beautiful" un impératif catégorique de terreur: "Le Nègre doit devenir dangereux!" (See p. 31.)

Regarding Stanislas Adotévi — to whom Adoukonou refers above — see his book *Négritude et négrologues* (Paris: Union generale d'éditions, 1972).

Éla, Adoukonou and Adotévi give ample evidence that the caricature of the legacies of ancestors in Blyden's thought — i.e., his anticipation of *négritude* — is hardly providential.

31. Blyden, p. 95.

32. July, pp. 102-103.

33. Lynch, p. 106.

34. Lynch, pp. 107-109.

35. See Edwin S. Redkey, ed., *Respect Black: The Writings and Speeches of Henry McNeal Turner* (New York: Arno Press and The New York Times, 1971). Turner was born 1 February 1934, in South Carolina. It is said that Turner's maternal grandfather was an African prince brought to North America in the latter part of the eighteenth century. South Carolina was then a British colony in which it was the practice to manumit royalty. Thus Turner was born a "freedman." According to Edwin Redkey, however, Turner's "free" status was derived from his white grandmother.

    Although Turner was not a slave, he was forced to toil like

one. At fifteen, as the result of the benevolence of a few whites, Turner learned to read. He also began to preach in his teens. As a young adult he joined the AME church and was transferred to Baltimore by Bishop Daniel Payne. In Baltimore, Turner furthered his education at Trinity College.

Influenced by Alexander Crummell, Turner advocated emigration to Africa prior to the civil war. During the war he hoped blacks would be treated fairly and thus accepted Lincoln's commission to be Chaplain of the First Regiment of black soldiers. After the war Turner clearly saw that little would change for blacks. He turned to Africa. Calling the American flag a dirty rag, Turner believed Africa was the only place blacks could be free. So much did Turner respect what is black that he had this to say when the Supreme Court ruled in 1883 that the Civil Rights Act of 1875 was unconstitutional: "If the government that freed [blacks] cannot protect that freedom [then blacks] should no longer enlist in the armies of the government or swear to defend the United States Constitution, [which is] a dirty rag, a cheat, a libel and ought to be spit upon by every Negro in the land," (*Respect Black*, p. 63). According to Turner, "If the Court's decision is right and is accepted by the country, then prepare to return to Africa or get ready for extermination." (Ibid.) The ACS made him an honorary Vice-President for life. Touring Sierra Leone and Liberia, Turner visited Africa for the first time in 1891. He visited South Africa in 1898.

36. Lynch, p. 108.

37. Blyden, p. 132.

38. Ibid., p. 12.

39. See Blyden's essay, "Mohammedanism and the Negro Race," in *Christianity, Islam and the Negro Race.*

40. See Williams, *The Destruction of Black Civilization.*

41. Blyden, p. v.

42. Ibid., p. 22.

43. Ibid., p. 6.

44. Ibid., p. 33.

45. Ibid.

46. Ibid., p. 45.

47. Ibid., p. 32.

48. Ibid., p. 33.

49. Ibid., p. 32.

50. Blyden, *African Life and Customs* (London: C.M. Phillips, 1908), p. 73.

51. Ibid., p. 69.

52. Ibid., p. 8-29.

53. Sanneh puts it this way in his book, *West African Christianity: The Religious Impact*:

> The fact of the matter is that Africa has imposed its own character on the two religions [Christianity and Islam], subjecting them to its own historical experience and immersing them to its cultural and religious traditions. Far from allowing Christianity or Islam to siphon off those elements which constituted its own spiritual integrity, Africa has dissolved much of what came to it and reconstituted the resultant phenomenon as a reinforcement to pre-existing principles of the religious life. Therefore, the most fundamental question that has faced the two missionary religions in Africa is whether and how they can reciprocate with African religions in a mutually recognizable idiom.(See p. 249.)

54. Blyden, *Christianity, Islam, and the Negro Race*, p. 26.

55. Ibid., pp. 31-32.

56. Blyden, *African Life and Customs*, p. 64.

57. I will discuss Long's position in Chapter 5.

58. Blyden, p. 63.

59. Blyden, *Christianity, Islam, and the Negro Race*, p. 55.

60. Ibid., p. 58.

61. Ibid., p. 55.

62. Ibid., p. 64.

63. Boulaga, *Christianity Without Fetishes: An African Critique and Recapture of Christianity*, p. 56.

64. Blyden, "The Aims and Methods of a Liberal Education," in *Christianity, Islam and the Negro Race*.

65. Ibid., p. 85.

66. George James, *Stolen Legacy*, (San Francisco: Julian Richardson Associates, 1976), pp. 163-174.

67. Blyden, p. 117.

68. Recently James' thesis has been discussed by Martin Bernal in his *Black Athena*. Bernal discusses what is well-known in the Black community: James' perspective, like that of Diop, ben-Jochanan, Karenga, and Jackson, has been discredited by white academia as poor scholarship. White academics reveal here a racist intransigence to the possibility that dynastic Egypt was a black creation which essentially influenced ancient Greece. The genealogy of this intransigence is traceable to the eighteenth

and nineteenth centuries which saw the burgeoning of apologetics for slavery. According to Bernal a racist Enlightenment historiography overturned the Ancient Model in favor of the Aryan model. The Ancient Model, put forward by scholars such as Flinders Petrie, reflects a position similar to James's. The Enlightenment, however, put forward the aryan model — the notion that Greek civilization could not have been seminally influenced by Africa. According to Bernal:

> The paradigm of "races" that were intrinsically unequal in physical and mental endowment was applied to all human studies, but especially to history. It was now considered undesirable for races to mix. To be creative, a civilization needed to be "racially pure." Thus it became intolerable that Greece — which was seen by the Romantics not merely as the epitome of Europe but also as its pure childhood — could be the result of the mixture of native Europeans and colonizing Africans and Semites." (See p. 29.)

Bernal writes:

> If I am right in urging the overthrow of the Aryan Model and its replacement by the Revised Ancient One, it will be necessary not only to rethink the fundamental bases of "Western Civilization" but also to recognize the penetration of racism and "continental chauvinism" into all our historiography, or philosophy of writing history. The Ancient Model had no major "internal" deficiencies, or weaknesses in explanatory power. It was overthrown for external reasons. (See p. 2.)

James's and Bernal's views seem more than credible to me.

69. Lynch, pp. 149-150.

70. Ibid., p. 152.

71. Ibid.

72. Ibid., p. 151.

73. Ibid., p. 165, see also Chapters 6 and 7.

74. Ibid.

75. See Éla, *African Cry*.

76. Blyden, p. 139.

77. See James Cone, *God of the Oppressed* (New York: Seabury Press, 1975). According to Cone: "We must probe our history,deep into its African roots, and ask about the relationship between the African shout and the Baptist moan, the river Jordan in the spirituals and the river spirits of West African religion. What is the relationship of African behavior and slave behavior? In what sense did our survival in slavery depend upon our recognition of the essential African culture of our lives and the building of the liberation program upon that structure?" (See p. 214.)

78. Blyden, *African Life and Customs*, p. 35.

79. Ibid., p. 44.

80. Ibid., p. 37.

81. Ibid., pp. 37-38.

82. Ibid., p. 46.

83. See Lynch, *Black Spokesman*, pp. 315-334. On the partition of Africa, see Walter Rodney's essay in DuBois: *On the Importance of Africa in World History* (Harlem: Black Liberation Press, 1978). According to Walter Rodney, the partition of Africa and European imperialism must be distinguished in order to intrinsically link the former to the latter. Imperialism, writes Rodney,

> derived from the expansion of the capitalist economy, while par-

tition was determined by (a) the nature of African formations, (b) the element of racism within the capitalist superstructure, and (c) the opposition of Africans to European incursion." (See p. 12.)

Partition among expansionist powers was the outcome of fencing for geopolitical advantage. Partition facilitated the hegemonic entrenchment of capitalist modes of production in Africa to the profit of the West and impoverishment of Africa. African labor was more easily exploited under the auspices of metropoles arbitrarily designing spaces of investment. As Rodney explains in terms of Lenin: "...the division of economic territory was the central factor, and the correctness of that position is powerfully evident today in Africa when imperialism has almost completely changed its *form* of political partition, the better to pursue the *substance* of economic exploitation." (See p. 14.)

84. See Blyden, *Christianity, Islam and the Negro Race*. Blyden gushes over Lord Lawrence as follows: "The greatness of Lord Lawrence was English greatness. He cannot be regarded as an isolated phenomenon in the modern history of England. He embodied in himself the characteristics of the English people. He was the result of the soundness of the central character of England." (See p. 302.) Like Crummell, in addition, Blyden was also enamored of the English language. (See p. 368.)

85. Lynch, *Edward Wilmot Blyden*, p. 191.

86. Ibid., pp. 198-199.

87. Ibid., p. 200.

88. Ibid., pp. 197-198.

89. Ibid, pp. 192-193.

90. Gwendolen M. Carter and Patrick O'Meara, eds., *African*

Independence. The First Twenty-Five Years (Bloomington: Indiana University Press, 1986), p. 22.

91. Ibid., p. 3.

92. Ibid., p. 24.

93. Ibid.

94. Lynch, p. 197. Blyden's friend, William Grant, put it this way at the dawning of olden colonialism:

> It continues to be a standing blot upon the intercourse of Europeans with Africa, that every steamer that comes to the coast...brings in large quantities of that which is comparatively worthless to be exchanged for that which is valuable and useful....If the articles given were simply worthless but harmless gew-gaws in exchange for articles of value, the morality of the transaction would even be reprehensible, but how much more when the articles are not only of trifling value...but often positively destructive. [Europeans] take home that which builds them up in wealth, often leaving to the African that which impoverishes and destroys him. It is a sad reflection that, in many cases, European commerce has left its African customer as naked as it found him...they will never secure a footing in Africa for their ideas of civilization, until the commercial relations between the...European and the...African are placed on a more equitable footing. (See July, p. 142.)

In the period of neocolonialism, Ali Mazrui puts it this way:

> It is not technological change with Africa that has affected recent African history most, it is technological development in the West. And Africa itself has contributed, unwittingly, precisely to that process in the West....the West has contributed far less to the industrialization of Africa than Africa has contributed to the industrial civilization of the West. (See *The Africans*, p. 164.)

Blyden failed to appreciate the relation of the Partition to what Walter Rodney called the interest "in the raw materials of the continent" and the attendant export of "capital...sent to transform Africans into workers and peasants producing for the capitalist market." (See DuBois, p. 9.)

95. Lynch, p. 215.

96. Ibid., p. 233.

Chapter 4
Social Analysis: At the Crossroads of the Hermeneutic Circle of the Pan-African Experience

1. See notes 2 and 3 of the Introduction. In *Irruption of the Third World: Challenge to Theology*, Sergio Torres explains that a Third World Theology, which includes Pan-African theology,

> is contextual, liberational, biblically-based, and ecumenical; it is inductive in method, starting with the faith experience of the poor and oppressed, and it rejects traditional Western theology as inadequate for the Third World. The context is understood to include both the socio-economic-political and religio-cultural dimensions; liberation is both personal and societal; the text and context are related dialectically in biblical reflection. (See p. xv.)

2. Segundo, *The Liberation of Theology*, p. 39.

3. See Sergio Torres and Virginia Fabella, *The Emergent Gospel: Theology from the Developing World* (London: Geoffrey Chapman, 1978). Here Gustavo Gutiérrez, in his seminal essay, "Liberation Theology and Progressivist Theology," asserts: "From the start liberation theology has maintained that active commitment to liberation comes first and theology develops from it." (See p. 247.) As Gutiérrez explains in the revised edi-

tion of *A Theology of Liberation* (New York: Orbis Books, 1988), "It is clear from what I am saying that when I call reflection in the strict sense a second stage of theological work, I am by no means saying that it is secondary. Discourse about God comes second because faith comes first and is the source of theology." (See p. xxxiii.)

4. Fanon, p. 250.

5. Douglas Glasgow, *The Black Underclass: Poverty, Unemployment and Entrapment of Ghetto Youth* (New York: Vintage Books, 1981), pp. 170-171.

6. Ibid., p. 312.

7. See Ivan Frolov, *Dictionary of Philosophy* (New York: International Publisher, 1984), p. 28. According to Frolov: "The principle idea of [Comte's] sociological doctrine was the assertion that it is useless to seek to change the bourgeois system by revolutionary means." (See p. 78.) My use of equilibrium, however, signifies a critical focus on inner contradictions — the ideological valences of geopolitical spaces and the social moorings which produce them. Fundamental here is not the dissimulation of the history of class struggle, but critical consciousness of them. Equilibrium, then, refers not to the disingenuous attempt to balance and neutralize inimical social forces, but to the heightening of their opposition for the sake of transformation. Thus, equilibrium signifies a balanced perspective that contradicts bourgeois attempts to obfuscate social contradictions in the valorization of the status quo.

In terms of a transcontextual perspective, equilibrium connotes a balancing of the disparate contexts of Africa and Diaspora. Here, though, balance signifies a consciousness that invites rather than neutralizes differences. Only a critical view of the dissimilarities of the Pan-African community facilitates valorization of its similarities, thereby enabling a Pan-African praxis.

8. Segundo, p. 13.

9. Magubane, in his book *The Ties That Bind: African-American Consciousness of Africa*, puts it this way:

> The Pan-African consciousness has always been a determined effort on the part of black peoples to rediscover their shrines from the wreckage of history. It was a revolt against the white man's ideological suzerainty in culture, politics and historiography. *The meaningfulness of these ideas...cannot be assessed from the number of believers, but rather through the historical understanding which they provide for the blacks' striving.* The various manifestations of African consciousness which originated among black peoples in diaspora prepared a position in the African mind from which white hegemony was to be continually attacked. Pan-African consciousness proclaimed the idea of black emancipation as a necessary state for the full development of blacks everywhere. Black consciousness of Africa is truly the prehistory of African nationalism. The black man [sic] in his diaspora, rejected with almost physical horror the lies prevalent in the lands of his [sic] captivity about Africa and its past. The black could not accept their scorn and indifference, and his anguish was to be the spirit behind the development of Pan-African consciousness [emphasis added]." (See p. 230.)

The African theologian, Barthélemy Adoukonou, in his book *Jalons pour une théologies africaine: Essai d'une herméneutique chrétienne du Vodun dahoméen. Tome I: critique théologique*, defines the genealogy of this Pan-African consciousness in a way different from Magubane. More so than Magubane, Adoukonou provides insight into the *spirituality* of Pan-Africanism.

That is he — to quote Magubane again — provides insight into "the spirit behind the development of Pan-African consciousness." According to Adoukonou:

> La protestation de l'esclave et son cri de désespoir vers le ciel afin que les dieux tranchent et en dernière instance afin que le seul Dieu créateur prononce un jugement et accorde la communion de paix, devaient s'articuler culturellement dans les Négro Spirituals et le Jazz, puis dans le grand mouvement politique du Panafricanisme.

> Né dans la diaspora nord-américaine vers le milieu du 19e, le mouvement panafricaniste suscita une aspiration vers la patrie à laquelle la foi Vodun donna une transfiguration religieuse: l'aspiration vers l'ailleurs de félicité dans l'union pacifiante avec Dieu, les Voduns et les ancêtres.

I will draw out the implications of Adoukonou's statement in the following chapters, but with a focus on the BaKongo — as opposed to the Fon — legacy.

10. Holland and Henriot, *Social Analysis: Likening Faith and Justice*, p. 89.

11. A classic text that reveals the way in which slavery is the unwithered root of black marginalization is DuBois' *Black Reconstruction in America, 1860-1880* (New York: Atheneum, 1962).

12. As Douglas Glasgow explains, in his *The Black Underclass: Poverty, Unemployment and Entrapment of Ghetto Youth*, the underclass have no upward mobility. He writes:

> Because of industry's limited expansion and increased use of technology, rather than people, to improve productivity, entry-level and blue-collars jobs — the traditional means of absorbing new and less experienced works — have dwindled considerably. No substantial change in this trend appears imminent, since industry continues to seek profit through automation, computer technology, and the like. Thus, as the need for the vast unskilled workforce of earlier periods diminishes, those on the bottom of the ladder become unneeded labor and therefore permanent members of the underclass." (See pp. 10-11.)

See also Theodore Cross, *The Black Power Imperative: Racial Inequality and the Politics of Nonviolence* (New York: Faulkner Books, 1986). According to Cross, "black families [have] accounted for about 11 percent of all families in the [United States] but over 28 percent of all families classified as living in poverty." (See p. 225.) Concentrated in areas such as New York City, the black underclass have no capital and pay incredibly exorbitant sums of money for pathetically shabby services. "In effect, then," writes Cross, "the poverty figures actually underestimate the real gap because the limited money available to poor blacks buys less than the same amount of money in the hands of poor whites living in less expensive locales. For this reason alone, the official poverty gap, showing over three times as many black families in poverty as white, should be regarded as an extremely conservative figure." (See p. 229.) Even blacks of underclass communities who manage to work cannot escape the ghetto. Blacks, in fact, earn a much greater percentage of their income through wages and salaries than do whites. The staggering fact is that *"not only do blacks comprise a disproportionately large section of the poor, but they also make up a disproportionately large number of the working poor."* (Cross, p. 232-233.)

Added to this problem is the routinization of the welfare bureaucracy which, though ostensibly fighting poverty, benefits the petty bourgeoisie that administers "manpower training programs, education, and health services." (See Cross, p. 230.) The violence of this system increases the number of poor black families. In 1984, writes Cross, *"nearly half of all black families were poor"*; by the 21st century the number will be more staggering." (See p. 234.)

See also Dorothy K. Newman, et al., *Protest, Politics, and Prosperity: Black Americans and White Institutions, 1940-75* (New York: Pantheon Books, 1978).

13. Indeed, the incredible violence of black on black crime in places such as the Northeast section of Washington, D.C., Harlem, and Watts is very much like Fanon's description of the internecine violence of a Third World context. He writes:

> The settler keeps alive in the native an anger which he deprives of an outlet; the native is trapped in the tight links of the chains of colonialism. But...the settler can only achieve a pseudo-petrification. The native's muscular tension finds outlet regularly in bloodthirsty explosions — in tribal warfare, in feuds between

sects, and in quarrels between individuals. (See p. 54.)

Fanon's description of the ramifications of a settler-society is analogous to the ramifications of the powerful society of the whites of North America. Undoubtedly that society is the essential cause of the black rage that succumbs to the drug addiction that numbs the pain of oppression and gives the immediate gratification of hedonistic materialism. Inextricable from this dead-end of drug addiction and obscene greed is the incredible violence that perennially subjects the black community to enormous fatalities. And the greatest number of fatalities are black males.

14. See Martin Luther King, Jr., *Where Do We Go From Here: Chaos or Community* (Boston: Beacon Press, 1968), pp. 3-4; 67-101).

15. My sense that the Civil Rights and Black Power movements were dismantled reflects public knowledge, because of the Freedom of Information Act, of the FBI's infiltration of black organizations during the sixties. For more information see George Breitman, et al., *The Assassination of Malcolm X* (New York: Pathfinder Press, 1976), pp. 178-190; David Garrow, *The FBI and Martin Luther King, Jr.: From "Solo" to Memphis* (New York: W.W. Norton & Company, 1981), pp. 182-183, 187-188; Assata Shakur, *Assata: An Autobiography* (Westport: Lawrence Hill & Company, 1987), pp. vii-viii.

According to Breitman:

> The FBI and the CIA claimed...that all they wanted to do was collect "intelligence" about Black organizations for possible use in prosecution of lawbreakers. But that was just the pretext. Their aim was to smash the Black movement by any means possible." (See p.10.)

Breitman, like Garrow and Shakur, refer to the FBI's Counterintelligence Program or COINTELPRO. This document reveals that the status quo, as reflected in the FBI under Hoover's direction, sought "to expose, disrupt, misdirect, discredit, or otherwise neutralize the activities of black nationalist, hate-type organizations and groupings, their leadership, spokesmen, membership, and supporters." (See Breitman, p.10.) FBI agents were directed to infiltrate black organizations in order to "exploit through counterintelligence techniques the organizational and personal conflicts of the leadership of the groups" and "capitalize upon existing conflicts between competing black nationalist organizations" and to "prevent the rise of a black 'messiah' [i.e., Malcolm X?] who could unify, and electrify, the militant black nationalist movement." (Ibid.)

After the assassination of Malcolm X — I am not saying that the FBI killed Malcolm — Hoover's chief target was Dr. King. I am not saying that the FBI killed Martin. I am saying that the FBI was effective in infiltrating the rank and file of the black resistance, and that the FBI was motivated by the conservative values that have dominated North American politics since the rise of the Republican Party. It seems to me that the victory of the conservatives is but the ugly triumph of the conspiracy against the black rebellion of the sixties — the institutionalization of what Dr. King called the white backlash.

Theodore Cross, in his *The Black Power Imperative: Racial Inequality and the Politics of Nonviolence*, puts it this way:

> In the early 1980's, blacks found themselves even further removed from the centers of political power. A new, conservative government had come to office on a platform that was openly unsympathetic to the political objectives of a vast majority of black people. The Reagan administration curtailed enforcement of laws against discrimination. It proposed to turn over the enforcement of civil rights laws to the states. It sought to reestablish a "right" of white children to the freedom to attend racially segregated schools. It gave comfort to racial traditionalists who attacked the motives and achievements of Dr. Martin Luther King....President Reagan played to the millions who continue to remain...racially prejudiced. In the mid-1980s, blacks people stood by wholly powerless to prevent the implementation of government policies that made it considerably easier not to have to live next door to blacks....Whites were no longer required "to pay in pain for holding of blacks in their place." (See pp. 619-620.)

Holland and Henriot define conservative hegemony as follows:

> The New Right...has pursued a devious strategy. Rather than focus on the deep structural causes of people's anxiety, it is catering to their fears. It promises to provide law and order, to defend the family, to restore the "American dream." However, in actuality, this New Right is a vicious force ultimately undermining all of these values.
>
> By catering to fear, the New Right hopes to drive a strategic wedge between the middle class on one side, and labor unions and the poor on the other. Labor unions and the poor are being used as scapegoats for the social problems that are threatening the security of the middle class. (See p. 82.)

Holland's and Henriot's analysis here tends to obscure the intrinsic relation of white supremacy to the New Right. In fact, large numbers of the white poor support right-wing rhetoric largely because that rhetoric conveys a myth in which patriotism and white supremacy are identical. The triumph of George Bush in 1988 is further evidence of the ossification of white supremacist values.

16. Convincingly, Sterling Stuckey, in his book *Slave Culture: Nationalist Theory and the Foundations of Black America*, asserts:

> the cyclical pattern that saw integration and nationalism vying for ascendancy owes much...to a misreading or neglect of the past — a problem endemic to integrationist leaders in black America from 1830 onward. The period from 1830 to 1860 prefigured similar struggles among black Americans in the twentieth century. Those early years were years in which integrationists — spiritually rootless leaders with little sense of the relationship between their people's liberation and the historical process — were countered by nationalists, who marked out the material and to some extent the spiritual lines along which genuine liberation might be attained. The integrationists' contribution to liberation theory in the slave era was almost non-existent; its essential hollowness was its bequest to the post-emancipation era. (See p. 231.)

I think, in addition, that E. Franklin Frazier, the distinguished African-American sociologist, has provided significant insight into the hollowness of integrationist strivings. See Frazier's seminal *Black Bourgeoisie: The Rise of a New Middle Class* (New York: The Free Press, 1966) According to Frazier, the antipathy of the black middleclass toward the black underclass is a product of an insidious ambivalence.

He writes:

> The repressed hostilities of middleclass Negroes to whites are not directed towards other minority groups but toward themselves. This results in self-hatred, which may appear from their behavior to be directed towards the Negro masses but which in reality is directed against themselves. While pretending to be proud of being a Negro, they ridicule Negroid physical characteristics and seek to modify or efface them as much as possible. Within their own groups they constantly proclaim that "niggers" make them sick. The very use of the term "nigger," which they claim to resent, indicates that they want to disassociate themselves from the Negro masses." (See p. 226.)

Caught in a crippling twoness, the black middleclass gravitate toward the whites, who do not want them, and away from the underclass, whom the middleclass despises. Caught in the middle, the middleclass creates a pathetic world of Negro respectability.

I very much agree with Frazier's assessment. My own impression of my class — black, upwardly mobile professionals — is that the majority strive for the material gains of North American capitalism and barely consider the plight of the underclass. They are indeed "exaggerated Americans" — absurd caricatures of the Euro-Americans whom they pathetically emulate.

Douglas Glasgow wrestles with the problem of the alienation between the two classes, but in a way more sympathetic to the middleclass. Middle-income blacks, he writes,

> are also aware of the underclass impact on community life. Some seek relief through flight to suburbia. But wherever they live,

> because all Black life is in some way intrinsically bound together — whether through the church one attends, maintenance of family ties and old neighborhood friendships, or the necessary use of institutions — contact with the underclass is inevitable. Still others try to escape by becoming absorbed in mainstream institutions and life. Yet a growing number maintain in-city residence, refusing to seek relief through flight. Although the class of educator blacks...has the ability to respond more effectively to community its members are usually busy meeting the demands of their professional roles and of mainstream life. And, as a result, their expert knowledge has been little used to treat the ills of the Black community itself. Even though the more recent growth of the Black middle-income group has in large measure been the consequence of the social upheavals of the 1960s, their involvement in mainstream activities nearly eliminates their ability and, in some cases, desire to attend to the crises of the underclass. (See p. 14.)

17. Robinson, *Black Marxism* p. 431. For Richard Wright, the recreation of meaning was authentic and politically empowering to the extent that such recreation valorized the distinctiveness of the black experience. Wright thought that within the folk memory was a conglomeration of modalities which, like a gestalt, told the truly indigenous story of a people torn from Africa and brutalized in North America. Identifying the contradictions of class, which inform social analysis in Pan-African theology, Wright explains that:

> Two separate cultures sprang up: one for the Negro masses, unwritten and unrecognized; and the other for the sons and daughters of a rising Negro bourgeoisie, parasitic and mannered." (*Richard Wright Reader*, p. 40.)

For Wright, black nationalism was most profoundly evinced in the culture of the black poor — what he called "Negro folklore." (See p. 41.)
Black folk culture, asserts Wright,

> contains in a measure that puts to shame more deliberate forms of Negro expression, the collective sense of Negro life in America. Let those who shy at the nationalist implications of Negro life look at this body of folklore, living and powerful,

> which rose out of a common life and a common fate. Here are those vital beginnings of a recognition of value in life as it is *lived*, a recognition that marks the emergence of a new culture in the shell of the old. And at the moment when a people begin to realize a *meaning* in their suffering, the civilization that engenders that suffering is doomed. (See p.41.)

In view of conditions of the black poor today, Wright's point is no less relevant, Harold Cruse's criticism of Wright notwithstanding. The culture of the underclass today contains the gauge of black progress and the *meaning* of black oppression. A praxis of liberation undefined by the black poor is stillborn.

18. See Malcolm X, *The Autobiography of Malcolm X* (New York: Ballantine Books, 1965). Minister Malcolm writes:

> "Conservatism" in America means "Lets keep the niggers in their place." And "liberalism" means "Lets keep the knee-grows in their place — but tell them we'll treat them a little better; let's fool them more, with more promises." With these choices, I felt that the American black man only needed to choose which one to be eaten by, the "liberal" fox or the "conservative" wolf — because both of them would eat him. (See p. 373.)

"Shorn of all hyperbole," Malcolm's words reveal his critical awareness of the structure of American politics, which is so paternalistic that blacks really have no hope of being integrated into either political culture.

19. Although blacks must fight their marginalization through the quest to own their communities, which means the collective ownership of *land*, black nationalism is allegedly a misnomer. If, it is asserted, black nationalism does not reflect the reality of a sovereign, modern state, the term, is misused, an oxymoron really. From that perspective, black nationalism has no historic reality apart from the settler colony, Liberia. Such arguments, however, ignore the reservoir of meaning of the term in relation to the contradictions of North America. The structure of American political society is such that blacks, especially the underclass, *must* struggle against the ugly hegemony of clusters

of European-Americans who systematically deny to blacks the ethnocentrism they lavishly grant to themselves. I do not argue that blacks must — indeed can — follow the example of the ethnic groups of Europe, and Asia, and "pull themselves up by their bootstraps." The conspiracy against blacks in America, from chattelization to now, has been far too effective for blacks to emulate those who, regardless of their sufferings, have not been as "lumpenized" and discombobulated as African-Americans. Nonetheless, the exigencies of the North American experience has forced blacks to ban together in the realization that struggle waged exclusively in terms of their self-interest, symbolized as the nation, is indispensable for survival. If blacks do not take responsibility for themselves, who will?

The great ancestor of all committed black scholars, Dr. DuBois, put it this way in *Dusk of Dawn*:

> I tried to say to the American Negro: ...there are certain things you must do for your own survival and self-preservation. You must work together and in unison; you must evolve and support your own social institutions; you must strive to transform your attack from the foray of self-assertive individuals to the massed might of an organized body. You must put behind your demands not simply American Negroes, but West Indians and Africans, and all the colored races of the world." (See p. 304.)

Black nationalism here, then, means neither migration nor emigration, nor that blacks are now and have been a nation in the postmodern sense. Black nationalism signifies an intense and ambivalent valorization of black autonomy. One valence, one axis of meaning, emerges from the recognition of the pervasiveness of the white supremacy through which white ethnic groups transcend their old world animosity as they express contempt for blacks and other people of color. To think that the majority of whites will let blacks into their "family businesses" is quixotic. The other valence, the other axis of meaning, emerges from reverence of ancestral legacies which heighten appreciation of the continuity of generations perpetuating the dynamic distinctiveness of black life in North America. For another classic expression of the *meaning* of black nationalism, see Carter G. Woodson, *The Mis-Education of the Negro* (New York: AMS Press, 1972).

20. Malcolm X, *Malcolm X Speaks* (New York: Grove Press, 1965), p. 4.

21. See DuBois, *Black Reconstruction*; and Robert Allen, *Reluctant Reformers: The Impact of Racism on American Social Movements* (Washington, D.C.: Howard University Press, 1974), pp. 247-280.

22. Malcolm X, p. 26.

23. Indeed, black nationalist theory best facilitates the reconciliation of the black underclass and the black middle class, which would strengthen a praxis that seeks the liberation of the Pan-African community. If Pan-African theologians do not work first within the context of the poor to whom they are most essentially related, how can they develop a transcontextual praxis? Neither the confrontation of problems particular to indigenous contexts nor their transcendence in a Pan-Africanism that strengthens the liberation struggle of those diverse contexts would be possible. Black nationalism is inextricable from Pan-Africanism. As Stuckey reveals, the connection between black nationalism and Pan-Africanism is logical and deeply historical. It is logical because the powers colluding in the marginalization of the black poor of the United States are part of a matrix that maintains neocolonialism in Africa. It is historical because black theorists, such as W.E.B. DuBois and Paul Robeson, quick to point out this relation, have been grounded in Pan-Africanism. Malcolm X, essentially in touch with the realities of the black underclass, put it this way:

> ...it is time for all Afro-Americans to become an integral part of the world's Pan-Africanists, and even though we might remain in America physically while fighting for the benefits that the Constitution guarantees us, we must return to Africa philosophically and culturally, and develop a working unity in the framework of Pan-Africanism. [As found in Yuri Smertin, *Kwame*

Nkrumah (New York: International Publishers, 1987) pp. 156-7.]

Indeed, Malcolm X reveals the continuum of a social analysis in the tradition of DuBois and Kwame Nkrumah.

Soviet Marxist, Yuri Smertin, claims that Malcolm's Pan-Africanism has "*nothing* in common with the anti-imperialist, anti-racist pan-Africanism professed by W.E.B. DuBois...and Nkrumah [emphasis added]." (See p. 157.) Given the progression of Malcolm's thought in the last months of his life, this view is unwarranted. Malcolm was neither racist nor pro-imperialist during that brief period, a period indispensable for a correct appreciation of his legacy. I believe, moreover, that the captivity to Soviet nationalism, qua white supremacy, undergirds Smertin's claim that:

> Demagogically utilizing Nkrumah's prestige and a few of his ideas the neo-pan-Africanist [presumably including George Padmore] have increased their ideological penetration of Africa. The threat this poses does not just consist in the fact that they advocate an unrealistic policy whereby various peoples with the same color of skin are declared to have the same set of goals. The main point is that these petty bourgeoisie nationalists, most of whom are opposed to communism, are objectively conduits of U.S. influence in Africa." (See p. 158.)

Although it is possible for intelligence agencies to infiltrate black nationalist organizations, and though Padmore mistakenly welcomed the support of the United States during the period he advised Nkrumah, Smertin, like Imanuel Geiss, reduces Pan-Africanism to caricature. Malcolm X, for instance, is the finest example of what could be termed neo-Pan-Africanism — an advance of the imperialist, chauvinistic Pan-Africanism of Garvey, notwithstanding Garvey's seminal grass-roots appeal.

In general, though, Marxists allege that Pan-Africanism is isolationist and thus unprogressive. The progressive consciousness of Pan-Africanism is lost on Marxists, who represent the radical wing of integrationist perspectives. Indeed, the radical wing is as flawed with paternalism as the bourgeois, liberal wing.

24. See: Basil Davidson, *Can Africa Survive?: Arguments Against Growth Without Development* (Boston, Atlantic Monthly Press, 1974), and *Modern Africa* (New York: Longman, 1985), pp.170-221; Lamb, *The Africans*; Mazrui, *The Africans*; Elenga M'buyinga, *Pan-Africanism or Neo-Colonialism*; Carter and O'Meara, *African Independence*; Yolamu Barongo, ed., *Political Science in Africa: A Critical Review* (London: Zed Press, 1983); Lloyd Timberlake, *Africa in Crisis: The Causes of Environmental Bankruptcy* (Philadelphia: New Society Publishers, 1986); Mahmood Mamdani, *Imperialism and Fascism in Uganda* (Trenton: Africa World Press, 1984); William J. Pomeroy, *Apartheid, Imperialism and African Freedom* (New York: International Publishers, 1986); Margaret Jean Hay and Sharon Stichter, eds., *African Women South of the Sahara* (New York: Longman, 1984).

25. See Éla, *African Cry*, p. 74. According to Éla, moreover:

> The decade of decolonization was marked by a style of government whose repression by torture is becoming more and more common in black Africa. The human rights situation may very well be one of the main reasons for the emigration of the intellectual, and this deprives Africa of an indispensable capital in this time of consolidation of its independence. Not many highly qualified persons can resist the temptation of exile abroad when the alternative is exile at home. When torture and repression have gone beyond all bounds, some regimes suddenly find themselves with nothing but a handful of illiterate peasants and foreign technologists exploiting the country's resources. (See pp. 70-71.)

26. Timberlake, *Africa in Crisis: The Causes of Environmental Bankruptcy*, p. 34.

27. Ibid.

28. Jean-Marc Éla draws out the implications of this statement in his article, "Santé de l'homme et Royaume de Dieu dans

l'Afrique d'aujourd'hui." *Bulletin de théologie africaine* 5:9 (janvier-juin, 1983). Éla focuses on his context, North Cameroon. He explains:

> Comme on le voit au Nord-Cameroun, toute l'économie d'une région est dominée par un seul produit exportable sans que les problèmes nutritionnels [which is the problem of famine] trouvent leur place dans une planification effective. Les priorités agricoles, les investissements, la recherche, l'industrie et les transports, l'encadrement des paysans restent subordonnés à la volonté et aux intérêts des agro-buisness au moment où les carences alimentaires compromettent le développement de l'enfant noir. Pendant que 22,1% des jeunes enfants souffrent de sous-alimentation chronique, les dignitaires du régime spéculent sur les produits de l'agriculture, réalisant en une seule opération des sommes que l'homme des champs ne peut rêver de toucher au cours de sa misérable existence de "damné de la terre." (See p. 67.)

Indeed, the machinations of *agro-business* and the greed of "the dignitaries" are ramifications of the imperial West — the chief cause of famine. As Éla indicates, famine is but the accentuated form of *sous-alimentation chronique*; and indeed the children suffer most from this radical form of undernourishment.

29. Lamb, p. 21.

30. Ibid.

31. See Gwendolen M. Carter and Patrick O'Meara, *International Politics in Southern Africa* (Bloomington: Indiana University Press, 1982); Henry F. Jackson, *From the Congo to Soweto: U.S. Foreign Policy Toward Africa Since 1960* (New York: Quill, 1984). The misery of the peasants is exacerbated by the internationalization of finance capital in the neocolonial era. Here, the export of capital is led by the United States which, manipulating the Congo crisis in favor of Tshombe and Mobutu, emerged in the sixties as the dominant Western power in Africa. Smertin, in his book *Kwame Nkrumah*, is correct that "western 'aid' [such as the Peace Corps] primarily goes towards

developing the infrastructure essential for the further exploitation of [African] countries by imperialist monopolies." (See p.75.)

According to Smertin, moreover:

> The ideological subversion the imperialist powers carry out in Africa has become a form of neo-colonial expansion. These activities include the dissemination of the bourgeois value system, the activities of religious organization, control of the mass media, the retention of the key positions in the educational system and much more. Particular vigor in this area is displayed by the U.S., which, for historical reasons, did not initially have as much political or ideological influence in Africa as did Britain or France. By the start of the 1960s, immediately following the national liberation of most of the African countries, more than 600 missionary, educational, philanthropic and other private and government-sponsored U.S. organizations were at work in Africa." (See p. 80.)

Kwame Nkrumah writes in his *Africa Must Unite* (New York: International Publishers, 1970): "Dating from the end of 1961, U.S. has actively developed a huge ideological plan for invading and utilizing all its facilities from press and radio to Peace Corps." (See p. 21.) The imperial aggressiveness of the United States is waged to off-set the spread of the Soviets who have aided the peoples' revolutionary parties of Southern Africa.

The Soviet Union, however, is also an imperial opportunist — a point that Smertin ignores. True. The Soviets have been instrumental in arming the revolutionaries of Southern Africa, but never in a way free from vulgar geopolitical interest. According to David Lamb, Soviets are blatantly contemptuous of the African people. (See Lamb, *The Africans*, pp. 186-187.) Soviet interest in Southern Africa focuses on "impeding Western access to the raw materials of Southern Africa and in disrupting Western sea lanes around the southern end of the continent." (See Carter and O'Meara, p. 15.) The freedom struggle of the African people is expendable to the Soviets, who still wish to be recognized in Europe as a global power.

In his *Imperialism and Fascism in Uganda*, Mahmood Mamdani put it this way: "When the Soviet Union turned to Africa in the sixties, it found the continent already overrun by imperialists powers. This situation called for methods of penetration different from those adopted by the early imperialists. An appropriate strategy was devised and suitably modified whenever local conditions called for it." (See p. 68.) Notwithstanding the high regard DuBois and Nkrumah had for the Soviet Union, Mamdani is of the following opinion:

> Where...progressive movements...continued to believe that the Russia of Khrushchev and Brezhnev was a continuation of the Russia of Lenin and Stalin, the Soviet Union cultivated them discreetly. Where there were no such movements, the Soviet Union sought friends within the state machinery. This strategy was most successful where there were local conflicts to exploit. Here, the Soviet Union could pick a side, arm it fully, and call for a military solution. In the process, it would create a highly militarized state and turn it into a "natural ally." But should the wind change, so would the alliance. Examples are numerous: first Egypt, then Libya; at one time Somalia, later Ethiopia." (See p.68.)

32. Engelbert Mveng, "Récents développements de la théologie africaine." *Bulletin de théologie africaine* 5:9 (janvier-juin, 1983). Mveng explains that *pauvreté anthropologique* is inextricable from black misery and goes beyond the negation of Africans' fundamental rights, cultures and religions. *Pauvreté anthropologique*

> demolishes African institutions and civilizations, it denies Africans their right to existence, to love to hope; it accompanies the massive conspiracy perpetrated by all those who are interested in Africa. This form of misery particularly dogs the black race in Africa, the United States, the Caribbean, and Latin America [my translation]. (See p. 141).

Indeed this pernicious form of poverty has Pan-African implications, though I use it here primarily in reference to the African peasants. Mveng undoubtedly has the peasant in mind as he asserts that anthropological poverty, i.e., *pauvreté anthropologique*, essentially pertains to *l'Eglise des pauvres, des faibles, des opprimés. C'est les coeur même de la problématique d'une théologie de la Libération.* (Ibid.)

33. See Ebitini Chikwendu, "The African Peasantry: Neglected by African Political Science," in *Political Science in Africa: A Critical Review*, p.41.

34. Ibid., p. 42. See also Éla, *L'Afrique des villages* (Paris: Karthala, 1982. Éla discusses precolonial Africa as follows:

> The image of an ancient communitarian Africa masks the internal tensions and conflicts through which the precolonial society was constructed and maintained. The existence, from the middle ages until the seventeenth century, of the grand African empires — Ghana, Mali, the Songhay empire; and many others, Zimbabwe, Kongo, Bornu, Kanem, etc. — entailed a mass of enslaved rural producers [*suppose une masse de producteurs ruraux asservis*] whose status was somewhere between the Roman slaves of antiquity and the serfs of medieval Europe. The significant concentration of riches in these empires is unthinkable without a class that could afford them while exploiting others. In every case, this class was comprised of the nobles, the kings and the merchants; that is, the members of the privileged classes, who sold the young people of the exploited classes to the slavetrading Arabs and Europeans. Now colonialism has exacerbated life in rural society, a life that had already begun to disintegrate as a result of the slave trade [my translation]. (See p. 22.).

35. Ibid.

36. See Rukudzo Murapa, *"Pan-Africanism: Nkrumah and Padmore," in Pan-Africanism: New Directions in Strategy*, Ofuatey-Kodjoe, ed. (New York: University Press of America, 1986), p.72.

37. Éla, *African Cry*, p. v.

38. See note 33 above, Chikwendu, p. 42.

39. Ibid., p. 43.

40. Fanon, p. 61.

41. Smertin, p. 151.

42. Ibid., p. 152.

43. Robinson, *Black Marxism.* He explains:

> Marxists have often argued that national liberation movements in the Third World are secondary to the interests of the industrial proletariat in the capitalist metropoles, or that they need to be understood only as the social efflux of world capitalism. Such movements require fitting in at the margins of the model for socialist revolution. (See p. 84.)

44. According to Robinson:

> The limits of Western radicalism as demonstrated in Marxist theory, the most sustained critique of the modern era, are endemic to Western civilization. Those limitations relate directly to the "understanding" of consciousness, and the persistence of racialism in Western thought was of primary importance. It would have been exceedingly difficult and most unlikely that such a civilization in its ascendancy as a significant power in the world would produce a tradition of self-examination sufficiently critical to expose one of its most profound terms of order. Racialism...ran deep in the bowels of Western culture, negating its varying social relations of production and distorting their inherent contradictions. The comprehension of the particular configuration of racist ideology and Western culture has to be pursued historically though successive eras of violent domination and social extraction which directly involved European peoples during the better part of two millennia. Racialism insinuated not only medieval, feudal and capitalist social structures, forms of property, and modes of production, but as well the very values and traditions of consciousness through which the people of these ages came to understood their worlds and their experiences. *Western culture, constituting the structure from which European consciousness was appropriated, the structure in which social identities and perceptions were grounded in the past, transmitted a racialism which adapted to the political and material exigencies of the moment* [emphasis added]." (See p. 82.)

"White niggers," so to speak, were in existence long before the term was applied to liberal whites, such as those who supported the Civil Rights movement in places such as Philadelphia, Mississippi in 1964.

45. Éla, p. 45.

46. Ibid.

47. Barthélemy Adoukonou, *Jalons pour une théologie africaine: Essai d'une herméneutique chrétienne du Vodun dahoméen*, p. 25. Adoukonou explains that, while the Latin American theologians have demonstrated the importance of Marxist thought, the importance itself has to do with *Justice, Paix, Solidarité*. Marxist thought is epiphenomenal to those virtues. *L'Africanisme du dedans* — as Adoukonou understands it — allows the Pan-African theologian to appreciate that there are other ways of getting to the roots of injustice.
Adoukonou writes:

> Il serait peut-être plus fécond et rationnellement plus rigoureux de s'appliquer à savoir ce que veut bien dire radical. Si "radical" veut dire "qui a trait à la racine," alors nous retrouvons dans ce que nous avons appelé la "pensée par principe," ce que les Fon du Dahomey appellent connaissance de la "chose génératrice de la chose," (Nujonu), de la réalité féconde, qui donne à homme d'être lui-même et d'être à son tour dans la vérité et donc fécond, "autoritaire" (Nu-gbo). Au nom de la foi chrétienne, qui fait un devoir à l'homme d'être créateur authentique, et au nom de la forme de pensée qui est propre à l'Afrique, telle qu'elle nous apparaît en milieu Adja-Fon, nous nous refusons à la dogmatique marxiste, qui interdit de penser jusqu'à cette radicalité où l'homme devient lui-même source de pensée neuve et créatrice. (See p. 24).

For Adoukonou, then, the freedom to think radically, which by definition is in opposition to alienation, need not be defined Eurocentrically — that is, in terms of *la dogmatique marxiste*. Rather, radical African thought — *l'Africanisme du dedans* — is here derived from insights of the Fon of Dahomey, i.e., the traditional religion of Vodun, and Christianity. These insights posit that creative solutions to inequity derive ontologically from God.

48. Éla, p. 45-46.

49. Robinson, p. 81.

50. See Mamdani, *Imperialism and Fascism in Uganda*, p. 95.

Chapter 5
The Religio-Cultural Circle of the TransAtlantic World

1. See Young, *Black and African Theologies*, pp. 63-69.

2. Several books reflect my discussion of African traditional religion. My discussion of the BaKongo is taken from works by Wyatt MacGaffey, *Modern Kongo Prophets: Religion in a Plural Society* (Bloomington: Indiana University Press, 1983), and *Religion and Society in Central Africa: The BaKongo of Lower Zaire* (Chicago: University of Chicago Press, 1986. My discussion of the BaKongo also reflects the book by Robert Ferris Thompson, *Flash of the Spirit: African and Afro-American Art and Philosophy* (New York: Vintage Books, 1983), pp. 103-158. Other books on African traditional religion are: Daryll Forde, ed., *African Worlds: Studies in the Cosmological Ideas and Social Values of African Peoples* (Oxford: Oxford University Press, 1976); Robert C. Mitchell, *African Primal Religions* (Illinois: Argus Communications, 1977); James Fernandez, *Bwiti: An Ethnography of the Religious Imagination in Africa* (Princeton: Princeton University Press, 1982); John S. Mbiti, *African Religions and Philosophy* (New York: Anchor Books, 1970); Benjamin C. Ray, *African Religions: Symbol, Ritual, and Community* (New Jersey: Prentice-Hall, 1976); Melville J. Herskovits and Frances S. Herskovits, *An Outline of Dahomean*

Religious Belief (New York: Kraus Reprint Co., 1976); Meyers Fortes, *Oedipus and Job in West African Religion*, with an essay by Robin Horton (New York: Cambridge University Press, 1983); Dominique Zahan, *The Religion, Spirituality and Thought of Traditional Africa* (Chicago: University of Chicago, 1983); E. Thomas Lawson, *Religions of Africa* (San Francisco: Harper & Row, 1984); Noel Q. King, *African Cosmos: An Introduction to Religion in Africa* (California: Wadsworth Publishing Company, 1986); Geoffrey Parrinder, *West African Psychology* (London: Lutterworth Press, 1976); T.O. Ranger and I.N. Kimbambo, *The Historical Study of African Religions* (Berkeley: University of California Press, 1976); Evans M. Zuesse, *Ritual Cosmos: The Sanctification of Life in African Religions* (Ohio: Ohio University Press, 1979); Luc de Heusch, *The Drunken King, or, The Origin of the State* (Bloomington: Indiana University Press, 1982), *Sacrifice in Africa: A Structuralist Approach* (Bloomington: Indiana University Press, 1985); Anita Glaze, *Art and Death in a Senufo Village* (Bloomington: Indiana University Press, 1981); Chris Ifeanyi Ejizu, *Ofo: Igbo Ritual Symbol* (Nigeria: Fourth Dimension Publishing, 1986); Victor Turner, *The Ritual Process: Structure and Anti-Structure* (Ithaca, New York: Cornell University Press, 1989, *The Forest of Symbols* (Ithaca: Cornell University, 1989.

3. As MacGaffey, an authority on the BaKongo, explains, much interpretation of traditional religion reveals a colonial world-view. According to MacGaffey, "colonial perspectives tend to conceal much of what actually happened in colonized Africa, which was a matter of contrasts and discontinuities. The colonial world of the BaKongo, which the prophets [of the independent churches] interpreted, was a matter of contrasting realities, kept separate by political action." (*Modern Kongo Prophets*, p. 16.)

4. Professor O.U. Kalu puts it this way:

> The study of African Traditional Religion acquired a new lease on life two decades ago as Africans themselves started a massive attempt to re-understand their cultures. Unfortunately, much

emphasis was not paid to methodology and some of the early scholars came from Christian theological and educational backgrounds. The net effects were an enumerative, descriptive approach tainted with Christian bias. Some declared that the study of African Traditional Religion was designed to isolate cultural elements which could be baptized into Christianity as a means of reinvigorated evangelism. Much debt is owed to the pioneers but after two decades, a new direction is emerging from younger scholars. (See Ejizu, *Ofo: Igbo Ritual Symbol*, p. xi.)

5. As MacGaffey explains: "Descriptions of a 'primitive' religion as lacking dogmas and theology often imply that it is the task of the anthropologist, self-appointed tribal scribe, to supply the credal texts that the infrastructure of the society in question cannot produce. To assume the presence of such an implicit text...is to assimilate the religion in question to [an alien] epistemological practice." (See *Religion and Society in Central Africa*, p. 251.)

6. Ibid., p. 1878.

7. Éla, *African Cry*, p. 130.

8. Fanon, *The Wretched of the Earth*, p. 224.

9. Boulaga, *Christianity Without Fetishes*, p. 77. MacGaffey puts it this way: "...abstract oppositions composing the structures clothe themselves in new metaphors for new situations. The continuity of ritual from the earliest recorded times to the present is, I have argued, a function of the continuity of the basic institutional fabric of the village, despite its incorporation in more conspicuous, pretentious, and usually more violent political forms." (See pp. 189-190.)

10. See MacGaffey, *Modern Kongo Prophets*.

11. MacGaffey, *Religion and Society in Central Africa*. He writes of the metaphoric and metonymic dimensions of Bakongo traditional religion as follows:

> In Kongo thought, human life is a progress in space and time from the other world, through this world, and back again. Rituals recapitulate this movement in particularistic form. The elements of the ritual process are microcosmographic space; the sequence of events in time, which is also a social process or rite of passage, moving the principal actors from one status or condition to another; invocations and songs, which describe what is going on, usually in elliptical and multivocal language; and visible objects, which "repeat" the message of the verbal formulae. The visible objects include human bodies and certain complex artifacts that, as insignia associated with the persons involved, express the particular powers attributed to them by the ritual. The elements of the objective complexes are significant either *metonymically*, in that they link the owner of the object, by contiguity, with the paradigmatic spirits from whom power is obtained, or *metaphorically*, in that they express the uses to which that power is to be put by analogies constructed in natural materials. *Metonymy expresses succession and metaphor exchange* [emphasis added]. (See p. 12.)

MacGaffey explains that the metonymic orientation of ritual is vertical, patrifilially hierarchical, extending from the invisible to the visible by way of contact with powerful spirits or by ingestion of substances related to the spirit world. The horizontal orientation is metaphoric and is expressed by way of the exchange of properties, such as "human bodies, medicines, and magical charms." (See p. 12.)

12. Discussion of the visible begins with humans who tap and master both hidden powers and more empirical forces in order to promote equilibrium or disaccord. Of the two ends, promotion of equilibrium is most characteristic of African traditional religion. Running the risk of a vulgar reductionism, we may say that African traditional religion has very practical ends. African religions are largely concerned that humans survive and, what is more, thrive in harsh environments. That is not to say that Africans have no sense of ultimacy, or highly evolved spirituality. Nonetheless, harshness of environment, with other historical factors, forced migrations hundreds of years ago. The desiccation of the Sahara, drought and famine, wars and conquests, impelled Africans to continually move until they found

an area conducive to extension of their cultures. Once settled, the ancestors handed down to their progeny myths and attendant rituals that anchored traditional societies to the land. Myths and rituals embody archetypical symbols which frame worldviews, linking traditional societies to specific cosmogonies. Structuring the scope of ritual and thus traditional life, myths reveal Africans' traditional sense of ultimacy. Zuesse puts it this way:

> The personal egoistic sphere, the social sphere, and the transcendental cosmic one must all be brought together. [African traditional religions] generally do this through ritual, and through the ritual type of instruction which emphasizes the concrete and transforms it into a symbol....The entire purpose of [African traditional religions]...is to anchor the [initiated] *in* this world, at the same time as the instruction renders this world of multiplicity transparent to eternal meaning. A different mode of concentration is evoked by transcendental truths, one must learn to enact the world differently. One must see every thing as symbol. (*Ritual Comos: The Sanctification of Life in African Religions*, p.8.)

Rituals, and the myths in which they are grounded, recount opposing forces of which humans must be scrupulously aware in order to maintain equilibrium. Humans must know what is taboo and avoid disruption of community. Both proper propitiation of elemental forces and practices of right ritual recreate and renew harmony within the localized cosmos and peace within the community. Religious preoccupation with warding off disease is directly related to environments infested with deadly parasites; concern with rain is directly related to drought. Efforts to maintain fecundity not only signifies the quest to promote fertility, but also the abundance of game, roots and grain. Rites of healing not only prevent and cure diseases, but imply the opposition to witches and the appeasement of ancestors. In short, Africans have traditionally shaped their ritual life according to the vicissitudes and nuances of their natural environments — the visible, of which they are at the center.

Tangible things mask supernatural realities valuable to humankind. It is humans who must master the land; they alone must control their milieu. Imparted knowledge of the sacred taboos, the medicines, and the magic allows them to do so. Equipped with the energies inherent in all those things, they master and manipulate lesser entities: fauna, some of which have totemic significance; flora, with medicinal or poisonous properties. Indeed, humans know the meaning of the hemispheres: West is often evil; East is often good. North is often male; South is often female. In fact, traditional civilizations construct their edifices with a sense of space and direction that is the microcosmos. Related to the religious value of architecture and a certain spatio-temporal religious sensibility is intercourse between the sexes. Entrances to huts may represent the vagina for instance; the forge and bellows of the blacksmith may symbolize copulation.

Evan M. Zuesse writes that there is a

> remarkable tendency to sexualize the smith's mysteries in many African cultures, but the symbolisms are...much more clear in Bantu societies. Among these cultures it is common to find that all implements in the smithing process are shaped in sexual images: the main furnace of Chokwe of Angola is shaped like a woman squatting in childbirth, as is the furnace among the Shona several thousand miles to the east; genital symbols on smithy bellows in Uganda intimate that these bellows are phallic in relationship to the fire that melts the ore. (See p. 96.)

Bearing special religious significance is woman. She carries essences of life that demand strict ritual observance. Again, Zuesse observes: "Cross-cultural studies show that while some cultures explain menstrual taboos as the result of women's 'dangerousness' and 'sacral pollution,' others explain the same power taboos as springing from women's highly sacred and positive mystical power." (See p. 67.)

Thus mundane things at the disposal of humankind are pregnant with religious meaning. The visible is a throbbing milieu saturated with an impersonal energy that humans must tap for good or evil, but especially for surviving and thriving in an often hostile environment.

13. For Africans, the *rites de passage* determine one's status in society. *Birth* entails the observance of many precautions, taboos must be observed. Only after these have been strictly employed are infants accorded the status of human. The visible is linked to the invisible, and the identity of the child must be determined for the realm of the ancestors in some sense feeds into that of the unborn. Indeed, an infant may be a reincarnated ancestor, or one of those children who come only to die. If the child is one of the former, then the reincarnated must be respectfully reintroduced into society; if the latter, precautions must be taken to insure that the infant does not return to the invisible. In the past, where twins were considered abnormal — i.e., among the Igbo — they had been ritually destroyed; where they were revered — i.e., among the Yoruba — they were, and are, celebrated. Certain societies used to destroy deformed children, albinos and the like. Among the Yoruba today, albino children and deformed are special manifestations of the orisha, Obatala.

    If birth is first in a series of initiations, then following closely behind it is *initiation into adulthood*. Circumcisions and clitoridectomies mark that initiation in many traditional societies — the death of the person to childhood and rebirth into adulthood. Among certain Niger-Congo societies of Mali, such operations are seen as the removal of vestiges of maleness and femaleness, enabling initiates to sublate their androgynous, primordial being to one which facilitates marriage and procreation. In many societies blood shed during the operation must flow liberally onto the ground to seal communion between humans and their ancestors, between the visible and the invisible. Upon thorough recuperation, initiates are accorded the status of adult. Imperative soon after is marriage.

    Marriage is critically important for traditional societies because it is indispensable for the survival of the family, its extension as a clan, the clans' extension as a village and the proliferation of villages as states, whether centralized under kingships or decentralized under councils of chiefs. Marriage also ensures continuity with the ancestors for, as already mentioned, there is an essential continuity between ancestors and the unborn.

At *death*, the living who are without blemish stand at the threshold of the realm of the ancestors. At death, as at birth, precautions must be taken, taboos must be observed. Whereas at birth care must be taken to respect the infant identified as an ancestor, at death, especially the deaths of elders, precautions must be taken to ensure their safe passage into the invisible realm of the ancestors. Improperly interred dead would cause much trouble for the living, particularly within families responsible for interment. In general, however, no one is safe. The cosmological fabric of the African traditional milieu is delicate: negative vibes here may extend to there, causing accident, sickness, and even death. Thus, as the invisible is perilously near at death, taboos are ritually evoked to avoid profanation.

14. According to MacGaffey, "BaKongo believe and hold it true that [human] life has no end, that it constitutes a cycle, and death is merely a transition in the process of change." (*Religion and Society in Central Africa: The BaKongo of Lower Zaire*, p. 44.)

15. See Robert Farris Thompson, *Flash of the Spirit: African and Afro-American Art and Philosophy.*

16. Boulaga, pp. 80-81.

17. MacGaffey, *Religion and Society in Central Africa: The BaKongo of Lower Zaire*, p. 65.

18. Ibid. MacGaffey quotes Van Wing in regard to the bakulu:

> A man who has lived honestly according to the laws and customs of his forbearers, whether he dies because witches have eaten him or is called by Nzambi [the Ultimate Being], becomes *nluku*. As the snake changes its skin so he sheds his mortal envelope (*ukibunini kigagala*) and leaves it in the grave. He goes whither the ancestors have preceded him, under the earth, near the water, "there where we live." Such is the common belief,

> expressed in the usual fashion. The *bakulu*, whether old or young, male or female, assume a white body. Each however retains his personality, his status, his taste and his occupations. (See p. 66.)

States of health and disease, feast or famine, are affected — we are to understand — by dispositions of ancestors. (Nilotic Africans, such as the Nuer and the Masai, have little use for their ancestors, focusing instead on a plethora of spirits, which, in the case of the Nuer, are seen as manifestations of a Supreme Being.) Ancestors may manifest themselves as animals, plants, or pools. Most Africans, especially those in the Niger-Congo language group, live with their ancestors. That is, ancestors are viewed as integral parts of families and therefore ethnic groups. *A fortiori*, the state of the people fluctuates according to the degree to which ancestors are respected. Ancestors anchor societies to tradition enshrined in primordial, thus mythical, archetypes that give meaning to religion and therefore society. As I have noted above, ancestors are those who, while visibly alive, were physically and socially unblemished. With the exceptions of clan heads, mythic heroes and the deified deceased, ancestors are remembered by name until the fourth generation. When they are no longer remembered by name, they become disembodied bush ghosts, or they spiral into the universal.

19. Zahan, *The Religion, Spirituality and Thought of Traditional Africa*, p. 15. Religious specialists oversee rituals. They discern the presences of ancestors and control evocations of divinities. Supplication of divinities is largely the responsibility of priest-diviners serving a particular god. Divinities and ancestors often speak through mediums whose utterances are interpreted by priests. Through the mediums of the ancestors and divinities, priest-diviners may determine that the amelioration of a certain condition requires a specific medicine. Medicines requiring herbs are usually the responsibility of herbalists. As, however, both healing and practice of good magic are intrinsic to traditional religion, roles of herbalists and priest-diviners may overlap. Priest-diviners are also, if too often pejoratively, known as witch doctors. That title, however, is to a degree under-

standable. A chief responsibility of priest-diviners is identification of witches. Although a force for good, priest-diviners understand the use of evil forces and thus can, in some sense, beat witches and sorcerers at their own game.

Witches and sorcerers are despised and feared to the point of paranoia. Whereas sorcerers learn wicked magic, witches are inherently evil. Inherent wickedness is believed to derive from their lack of something endemic to normal humans. Whereas a sorcerer may poison victims, a witch may devour victims. Witches, we are to understand, even consume their infants. Their cannibalism is spiritual. That is to say, the spiritual doubles of witches, leaving their flesh at night, consume spiritual doubles of others who are asleep.

Witches and sorcerers, herbalists and priest-diviners, all in their vocations, tap the forces of the cosmological matrix in all of its diversity. In this matrix the visible has intercourse with the invisible. The two realms are brought together in an essential symbiosis; and union of one with the other procreates fecundity or barrenness, equilibrium or disequilibrium, community or chaos.

20. MacGaffey, p. 43.

21. MacGaffey puts it this way: "The world, in Kongo thought, is like two mountains opposed at their bases and separated by the ocean." (Ibid.) Essentially, then, explains MacGaffey:

> the Kongo universe consists of two worlds, the lands of the living and of the dead, separated as a barrier that is represented as water but is also localized at crossroads on the way to the cemetery or the forest. The same contrast that divides topographic space also divides time, in such a way that at night, when the living are asleep, their village becomes the village of the dead. Each category of mankind [sic] is supposed to perceive the activities of the other in the dreams of its members. The two worlds are largely, though not entirely, symmetrical and complementary. (See p. 90.)

22. Zahan writes:

> The separation of the sky and the earth...simply constitutes the middle course enabling the mind to conceive of communication between these two realities. If a dialogue is to be established between them, "distance" becomes indispensable. Indeed, the mind can only justify the existence of intermediaries when a gap separates the communicators....Thus...these themes contain the element which establishes the possibility of religion as communication: distance. (See p. 16.)

23. This structuralists' approach is derived from my analysis of works of scholars such as Evans Zuesse, Mary Douglas and Luc de Heusch who are clearly influenced by the structuralism of Claude Levi Strauss. See de Heusch, *The Drunken King, or The Origin of the State and Sacrifice in Africa: A Structuralist Approach.* See also Robert Wuthnow, et. al., *Cultural Analysis: The Work of Peter L. Berger, Mary Douglas, Michel Foucault and Jurgen Habermas* (Boston: Routledge & Kegan Paul, 1984). Douglas, de Heusch and Zuesse focus on Bantu people related to the BaKongo. All of these scholars are interested in interpreting, by way of structuralist paradigms, African symbolic thought as expressed in myth.

    As I have noted, however, I do not claim that the hermeneutical key to African traditional religion is found totally in structuralism. Indeed, I, "one three centuries removed," have been very much edified by Barthélemy Adoukonou's position. In his *Jalons pour une théologie africaine* — see note 47, Chapter 4 — Adoukonou argues that much of structuralism exemplifies the "Friday syndrome," a syndrome abstracted from the story of Robinson Crusoe. Here, the white man "discovers" the autochthon — indeed the whole continent! — and names him — his real name notwithstanding.

    Adoukonou writes:

> "Vendredi," spirituellement engendré, nommé, assigné à tâche, perçu comme redoutable et domestiqué en conséquence, servant d'ombre négative à la positivité pleine d'une civilisation au projet prométhéen d'exploitation totale et ne pensant que sur un mode foncièrement dichotomique, l'Afrique comme l'Eglise afri-

caine s'éveille et prend conscience d'un aspect de sa servitude. (Adoukonou, p. 26.)

Indeed, the Pan-African theologian recognizes that structuralism is a species of Eurocentric *ethnologie* that developed in a colonial situation. As such it constitutes *l'Africanisme du dehors* (or a most naive *l'Africanisme du dedans*). The true *l'Africanisme du dedans*, however, which negates the "Friday Syndrome," requires a very critical orientation. In studying African traditional religion, the Pan-African theologian must demythologize much that is alleged to be African. Adoukonou writes:

> L'Africain peut-il porter sur soi le "regard astronomique" que se veut l'anthropologie lévi-straussienne, sans entrer en transe, sans perdre sa personnalité? Peut-il se tenir sur l'astre de l'Humanité adulte et raisonnable que se veut le "logos occidental" et se regarder sans ridicule? C'est donc un problème épistémologique existentiel que pose le nouvel "Africanisme du dedans" à la science de l'Autre qu'est l'ethnologie....l'ethnologie est une science sans objet parce qu'elle vise une Afrique et des Africains irréels. (See Adoukonou, p. 29.)

Adoukonou's insights make it necessary to note that the structuralism that has influenced my analysis has heuristic value only. What is at stake is the discovery and articulation of a true Africanity not unlike the one Adoukonou envisions. I seek to formulate a Pan-African theology that is *une théologie de la réappropriation culturelle critique*. The structuralist method is only a stepping stone to this. Indeed, to quote Adoukonou, *La note africaine de la théologie à écoute de l'africanisme* [even that of the structuralists], *se retrouverait dans l'originalité de l'expérience historique que faisait le Peuple de Dieu dans le creuset du destin de l'homme Noir*. (Adoukonou, p. 32.) I use the structuralists, moreover, in the recognition that *tout Africanisme des Africains doit être combat, vigilance politique* (Adoukonou, p. 29). Structuralists provide the weapons I must use for the moment.

24. MacGaffey, *Religion and Society in Central Africa: The BaKongo of Lower Zaire*, p. 45.

25. Ibid., p. 43.

26. Ibid, p. 45.

27. MacGaffey, *Modern Kongo Prophets*, p. 147.

28. MacGaffey, *Religion and Society in Central Africa*, p. 96-102.

29. Boulaga, p. 81.

30. Blyden's awareness of the African foundation of slave culture is revealed in his remark that "the slaves who were introduced during the first hundred years, we may presume, died Heathens, or with only imperfect glimpses of Christian teaching." (See *Christianity, Islam and the Negro Race*, p. 28.) For DuBois' views see his seminal *"History of the Negro Church: Africa to 1890,"* in *The Seventh Son*. See also Zora Neale Hurston, *The Sanctified Church* (Berkeley: Turtle Island, 1983); and Melville Herskovits, *The Myth of the Negro Past* (Boston: Beacon Press, 1958).

31. In his book, *Slave Religion: Nationalist Theory and the Foundations of Black America*, Stuckey records several stories the slaves have bequeathed to posterity. The story of King Buzzard, perhaps of Igbo origin, is a slave tale of an African chief who tricked his people into entering a slave trip. His betrayal is remembered in the folk legacy of blacks of South Carolina. The tale conveys the very African sense of a spirit who cannot be an ancestor and must be one of the foul smelling, terrible apparitions of the bush. Stuckey writes: "According to the Ibos, the spirit of the deceased returns to this world in the form of an animal if, before death, the deceased 'murdered' one or more human beings." King Buzzard must wander in his rotten condition forever as consequence of his betrayal. (See p.3-7.)

Stuckey also recounts the "Slave Barn," which tells the story of the hardness of suffering the Africans faced in the New World:

See dis barn here
wid its iron window

Its walls er brick?

Here wey de wail an' moan
Of Af'ica sound
Wuss dan de cry
Of Af'ica chillun
When dey bone been crack
By de lion' jaw (See p.8.)

The rest of the gripping lament conveys the strong sense in whichAfrican identity gave impetus to resistance and the way in which the Africans despised slavery (See pp. 8-9.) John Kunering pageants, in addition, reminiscent of the Egun-gun cults of Nigeria, revealed the Africanity of black Americans in a modality signifying the legacies of the ancestors. (See p. 67-77.)

32. Ibid., pp. 8, 11; 34, 92, 96, 97.

33. Herskovits, *The Myth of the African Past*, pp. 232-234.

34. Stuckey, *Slave Religion*, p. 34.

35. Ibid.

36. Stuckey writes:

> The majority of Africans brought to North America to be enslaved were from the central and western areas of Africa — from Congo-Angola, Nigeria, Dahomey, Togo, the Gold Coast, and Sierra Leone. In these areas, an integral part of religion and culture was movement in a ring during ceremonies honoring the ancestors. There is, in fact, substantial evidence for the importance of the ancestral function of the circle in West Africa, but the circle ritual imported by Africans from the Congo region was so powerful in its elaboration of a religious vision that it contributed disproportionately to the centrality of the circle in slavery. The use of the circle for religious purposes in slavery was so consistent and profound that one could argue that it was what gave form and meaning to black religion and art. It is understandable that the circle became the chief symbol of heathenism for missionaries, black and white, leading them to seek to eradicate it altogether. That they failed to do so owes a great deal to

BaKongo influence in particular, but values similar to those in Congo-Angola are found among Africans a thousand or so miles away, in lands in which the circle is also of great importance. (See p.11.)

37. Ibid., p. 22.

38. See Albert Raboteau, *Slave Religion: The "Invisible Institution" in the Antebellum South* (New York: Oxford University Press, 1980).

39. Like a divinity of the crossroads, such as Eshu Elegbara, Brer Rabbit, playing the sacred music of a fiddle, an instrument reminiscent of traditional chordophones, calls forth the invisible powers of the dead. Stuckey records the liminality of the event as follows in his *Slave Culture*: "Headless horsemen race about, a rabbit is seen walking 'on he hind legs wid a fiddle in he hands,' *and the sacred and the secular are one* in moments of masterly iconography as the 'buck and wing' is danced' on a tombstone'" [emphasis added]. (See pp. 17-23.)

40. See Stuckey, p. 10.

41. My discussion of black religion reflects many sources: Gayraud Wilmore, *Black Religion and Black Radicalism* (New York: Orbis Books, 1983); Norman Whitten and John Szwed, *Afro-American Anthropology* (New York: The Free Press, 1970); Cecil Cone, The *Identity Crisis in Black Theology* (Nashville: AMEC, 1975); Zora Neale Hurston, *Tell My Horse* (Berkeley: Turtle Island, 983), *Mules and Men* (Bloomington: Indiana University Press, 1978); Arthur Paris, *Black Pentecostalism: Southern Religion in an Urban World* (Amherst: University of Massachusetts Press, 1982); Milton Sernett, ed., *Afro-American Religious History: A Documentary Witness* (Durham: Duke University Press, 1985); Elijah Muhammad, *How to Eat to Live*, (Chicago: Muhammad Mosque No. 2, 1967), *Message to the Blackman in America* (Chicago: Muhammad Mosque No. 2, 1965); E. Curtis Alexander, *Elijah Muhammad on African American Education* (New York: ECA Associates, 1981); Clifton E. Marsh, *From Black*

Muslims to Muslims: The Transition from Separatism to Islam, 1930-80 (Metuchen: Scarecrow Press, Inc., 1984); C. Eric Lincoln, *The Black Muslims in America* (Boston: Beacon Press, 1973); Malcolm X, edited and introduction by Iman Benjamin Karin, *The End of White World Supremacy* (New York: Seaver Books, 1971); Randall Burkett, *Garveyism as a Religious Movement* (Metuchen: American Theological Library Association, 1978); Joseph R. Washington, *Black Religion: The Negro and Christianity in the United States* (New York: University Press of America, 1984), *Black Sects and Cults*, (New York: University Press of America, 1984); Arthur Huff Fauset, *Black Gods of the Metropolis: Negro Religious Cults in the Urban North* (Philadelphia: University of Pennsylvania Press, 1978); Leonard Barret, *Soul Force: African Heritage in Afro-American Religion* (New York: Anchor Press/ Double Day, 1974); Yosef ben-Jochannon, *African Origins of the Major "Western Religions"* (New York: Alkebu-Lan Books, 1970); Albert B. Cleage, Jr., *The Black Messiah* (Kansas: Sheed Andrews and McMeel, 1968); Ishkamusa Barashango, *Afrikan People and European Holidays: A Mental Genocide* (Washington, DC: IV Dynasty Publishing Co., 1980); Benjamin E. Mays, *The Negroes' God* (Westport: Greenwood Press, 1969); George E. Simpson, *Black Religions in the New World* (New York: Columbia University Press, 1978).

42. See Cone, *God of the Oppressed*, p. 253.

43. Charles Long, *Significations: Signs, Symbols, and Images in the Interpretation of Religion* (Philadelphia: Fortress Press, 1986), p. 107.

44. Ibid.

45. Ibid., p. 7.

46. Ibid.

47. See Hurston, *The Sanctified Church*.

48. DuBois, "Of the Faith of the Fathers," in *The Souls of Black Folk.* p. 292. Indeed, DuBois's classic description of the frenzy here brings to mind a sense of poetics as defined by Englebert Mveng, *L'art d'Afrique Noire: liturgie cosmique et langage religieux* (Yaounde: Editions CLE, 1974. Mveng defines what he calls *la poétique Bantou* — a religious and cosmic language that is constituted by African art. This art, this language, has its laws, but is in no sense an aesthetics. He writes:

> La poétique Bantou, nous entendons par là les lois du génie créateur de notre culture, ne peut donc en aucune façon être une esthétique. L'esthétique traduit la passivité du système sensoriel de l'homme devant sa concupiscence. La poétique, elle, se situe au moment où la spontanéité créatrice de l'homme se dresse contre le déterminisme de la nature et se constitue en liberté. Le rythme Bantou est l'expression de la liberté créatrice du génie humaine refaisant le monde pour l'intégrer au destin de l'homme. (Mveng p. 94.)

It seems likely to me that African-Americans, bearing the legacy of a Bantu people, the BaKongo, could well carry the memory of *la poétique Bantou* — "one three centuries removed."

49. Cone, Ibid.

50. Stuckey, p. 27.

51. Ibid., pp. 54-55.

52. Ibid., p. 27

53. Ibid., p. 41.

54. C. Eric Lincoln, "*The American Muslim Mission in the Context of American Social History,*" in Earle H. Waugh, et. al., *The Muslim Community in North America* (Alberta: The University of Alberta Press, 1983), p. 226.

55. Long, p. 49.

56. Wilmore, *Black Religion and Black Radicalism*, pp. 15-19.

57. Long, p. 174.

58. Ibid., p. 175.

59. Ibid., p. 176.

60. Ibid., p. 177.

61. Ibid., p. 176.

62. Ibid.

63. Ibid.

64. Ibid., p. 177.

65. Ibid., p. 179.

66. Ibid.

67. Ibid., p. 181.

68. Ibid.

69. See Note 70 below.

70. See Long, pp. 8-9. The relation of the discipline to Eurocentric consciousness is seen in Claude Welch's *Protestant Thought in the Nineteenth Century: Volume 2, 1870-1914* (New Haven: Yale University Press, 1985).

According to Welch:

> The modern study variously called comparative religion/history of religions/Religionswissenschaft/*science des religions* began to

> emerge almost simultaneously with the publication of Ritschl's *Justification and Reconciliation*. Its appearance may conveniently be dated from Friedreich Max Muller's London lectures of 1870, the contemporary work of Emile Louis Bournouf in Paris, and the major article "Religion" in the ninth edition of the *Encyclopedia Britannica* (1875) by Cornelius Petrus Tiele of Leiden." (See p. 104.)

According to Welch, history of religion was seminally influenced by "the early Romantics' vision, which freed the European mind to become not only curious about other peoples' religions, but also appreciative of them as authentic ways of expressing the human experience." (See p. 104.) Welch reveals that history of religion was also influenced by "the explosion of information" of the religious experiences of non-Europeans. (See p. 106.)

Perhaps this alleged catholicity and plethora of edifying information — undoubtedly a by-product of colonialism — accounts for Long's view that the history of religion is more conducive than systematic theology for an analysis of black religion. For Long, history of religions provided "a structure for the universal in the human world that, though created from Enlightenment understandings of the human venture, expressed an opening for the authentic expression of others." According to Long: "Religion thus became the locus for a meaning that carried an archaic form; it was a root meaning and could thus be the basis for radical critical thought." (See *Significations*, p.8.) Still, history of religion is clearly a discipline emergent from a Eurocentric consciousness, even seen in terms of Husserl's phenomenological method. Thus it is not Cone's Eurocentrism that Long finds to be problematic, but Cone's commitment to Christianity.

71. Cone, p. 214.

72. Ibid., p. 253.

73. Ibid.

74. Ibid.

75. See James Cone *The Spirituals and the Blues* (New York: The Seabury Press, 1972). Cone's interpretation of the spirituals is an attempt to African-Americanize his theology that had been captive to Eurocentric paradigms. I think the text is still of great value in the history of black religious thought. As with all pioneers, Cone worked with the materials he had at his disposal. He claims that:

> The theological assumption of black slave religion as expressed in the spirituals was that *slavery contradicts God,* and *he will therefore liberate black people.* All else is secondary. All else was secondary and complemented that basic perspective. But how did black slaves know that God was liberating them? Black slaves did not ask that epistemological question. As with all ontological assumptions, *the truth* of a presuppositional assertion is found in the giveness of existence and not in theory. (See p. 72.)

The question is, whose ontology are we talking about here? To that extent, I think Stuckey's theory is closer to the *otherness of slave* religion than Cone's ontology. That is, Stuckey leads one to — in the words of Adoukonou — *reposer la question de l'altérité d'une manière nouvelle.* Still, Dr. Cone recognized the significance of rhythms and movement that accompanied the singing of the spirituals.

76. Stuckey, p. 27.

77. Cone, *God of the Oppressed*, p. 253.

78. Cone, *For My People*, pp. 153-155.

79. Theo Witvliet, *The Way of the Black Messiah* (Illinois: Meyerstone Press, 1987), p. 185.

80. See Richard Allen, *The Life Experience and Gospel Labors of the R. Rev. Richard Allen* (Nashville: Abingdon Press, 1983), pp. 15, 73, 37-41. See also Frederick A. Norton, *The Story of African*

Methodism (Nashville: Abingdon, 1974), p. 169-170.

81. Allen, 37-41.

82. Witvliet, p. xi.

83. Ibid., p. xviii.

84. Ibid.

85. Witvliet, p. 218.

86. Ibid., pp. 224-225.

87. See Cone, *For My People*.

88. Witvliet writes that pneumatology,

> gives black theology its hermeneutical authorization to begin from the effective presence of God's Spirit in black history. It cannot itself be the foundation of this real presence. On the contrary, this presence is its foundation and is its *raison d'être*. Precisely the fact that black theology here leaves the freedom of the Spirit as a historical power intact in turn gives it freedom not just to seek traces of the Spirit within the framework of the institutional church. The black experience *in its totality* is here its sphere of activity, the blues as much as the gospel songs, the folk tales as much as the sermons, *the work of Malcolm X* as much as that of Martin Luther King, Jr [emphasis added]. (See pp. 221-222.)

89. Ibid., p. 223.

90. Malcolm X, *The End of White World Supremacy*. According to Minister Malcolm, the Honorable Elijah Muhammad's

> mission is to teach the so-called Negroes a knowledge of history, the history of ourselves, our own kind, showing us how we fit into Biblical prophecy. When you go to one of the churches you will notice that it is named after some word in their Bible: Big Rock Baptist Church, Friendship Baptist Church, Union Baptist,

> Israel Baptist, Jacob's Ladder Baptist. They find some kind of old funny word in their Bible to name their whole religion after. Their whole doctrine is based on a verse in the Bible: "He rose."
>
> The Honorable Elijah Muhammad bases what he teaches not on a verse but on the entire book. And from beginning to end, he says, he can open up the Book to prove that what they are saying in the church is wrong. You know that's saying something. (See pp. 33-34)

Witvliet's claim is all the more egregious given the fact that his pneumatological orientation is based on the Trinity — an absurd doctrine for Black Muslims. In his seminal book, *Message to the Blackman in America*, for instance, Elijah Muhammad, a former Baptist preacher, writes:

> The Christians refer to God as a "Mystery" and a "Spirit" and divide Him into thirds. One part they call the Father, another part the Son, and the third part they call the Holy Ghost — which makes the three, one. This is contrary to both nature and mathematics. The law of mathematics will not allow us to put three into one. Our nature rebels against such a belief of God being a mystery and yet the Father of a son and a Holy Ghost without a wife or without being something in reality. We wonder how can the son be human, and the father a mystery (unknown), or a spirit." Who is this Holy Ghost that is classified as being the equal of the father and the son? (*Message to the Blackman in America*, p. 1.)

Witvliet, and other Christians — such as myself — must respect the Honorable Messenger's view. "God is a man [the Asiatic Blackman] and we just cannot make Him other than man, lest we make Him an inferior one; for man's intelligence has no equal in other than man. His wisdom is infinite; capable of accomplishing anything that His brain can conceive. *A spirit is subjected to us and not we to the spirit* [emphasis added]." (See p. 6.)

91. Ibid., pp. 23-66.

92. Boulaga, *Christianity Without Fetishes*, p. 205.

93. Dereck Jewell, Duke: *A Portrait of Duke Ellington* (New York: W.W. Norton and Company, 1977), pp. 52-53.

94. Long, p. 173.

95. See Valerie Wilmer, *The Face of Black Music* (New York: Da Capo Press, 1976). Ellington asserts in 1964:

> If "jazz" means anything at all, which is questionable, it means the same thing it meant to musicians fifty years ago — freedom of expression. I used to have a definition, but I don't think I have one anymore, unless it is a music with an African foundation which came out of an American environment. (See p. 12.)

For an explanation of this metronome sense, see John Miller Chernoff, *African Rhythm and African Sensibility: Aesthetics and Social Action in African Musical Idioms* (Chicago: University of Chicago Press, 1981), pp. 48-50.

96. Regarding Adoukonou, see note 9, Chapter 4, above. See also Marshall W. Stearns, *The Story of Jazz* (New York: Oxford University Press, 1970). pp. 55-66; Derek Jewell, Duke: *A Portrait of Duke Ellington*, p. 138.

97. Stuckey, p. 95.

98. Ibid., p. 19.

99. Thompson, *Flash of the Spirit*, p. 104. See also Thompson, "Kongo Influences on African-American Artistic Culture," in *Africanisms in American Culture*, Joseph E. Holloway, ed. (Bloomington: Indiana University Press, 1991).

100. See the liner notes for the album "Mary Lou Williams and Cecil Taylor. Embraced." Pablo Records, 2620 108, 1978.

101. Ibid.

102. Cone, *Spirituals and the Blues*.

103. Joachim-Ernst Berendt, *Jazz: A Photo History*, trans. by William Odom. New York: Schirmer Books, 1979), p. 221.

104. Critics may argue that the music is patronized by the white bourgeoisie and an elite group of highly sophisticated musicians. This is only ostensibly true. The musicians are often forced out of the black community because the community itself is alienated from the progression of its own prophetic and sacred spirit. This alienation is the calculated outcome of structural forces which manipulate what they sell. Indeed many critics of the music are whites, themselves alienated from the black community,and having complicity in the conspiracy to hinder its religio-cultural and political force.

105. Valerie Wilmer, *As Serious As Your Life: The Story of the New Jazz* (Westport: Connecticut, 1980), p. 129.

106. Long, p. 183.

107. Ibid., p. 7.

108. Brian Priestly, *Mingus: A Critical Biography* (New York: Da Capo Press, 1982), p.4.

109. Ibid.

110. Ibid.

111. Dizzy Gillespie, with Al Fraser, *To Be or Not to Bop* (New York: Garden City, 1979), p. 31.

112. Ibid., p. 30-31.

113. Ibid.

114. Paris, p. 74.

115. Wilmer, p. 106.

116. See: Wilmer, pp. 31-45; Leroi Jones, *Black Music* (New York: Quill, 1967), pp. 56-58; James Lincoln Collier, *The Making of Jazz: A Comprehensive History* (New York: A Delta Book, 1978), pp. 478-493; C.O. Simpkins, *Coltrane: A Biography* (Perth Amboy: Herndon House, 1975; J.C. Thomas, *Chasin' the Trane* (New York: Da Capo, 1983; John Cole, *John Coltrane* New York: Schirmer Books, 1978).

117. Berendt, p. 119.

118. Long, pp. 27-28.

119. See notes above 65-66. In returning to his religious roots, Coltrane overcame drug addiction and alcoholism. This also marked a turning point in his music. As he kicked his substance abuse he dreamed he heard a "beautiful sound" of the God incarnate in his music. According to Coltrane:

> During the year 1957, I experienced, by the grace of God, a spiritual awakening which was to lead me to a richer, fuller, more productive life. At that time, in gratitude, I humbly asked to be given the means and privilege to make others happy through music. I feel this has been granted through his grace. ALL PRAISE TO GOD.

120. DuBois, *The Souls of Black Folk*, pp. 210-213.

121. John Coltrane, *A Love Supreme* (recording): Impulse 77, December 9, 1964. See also Simpkins, p. 181-183.

122. Long, p. 28.

123. See Cole.

124. Ibid., p. 87.

125. See Frank Kofsky, *Black Nationalism and the Revolution in Music* (New York: Pathfinder Press, 1983), p. 48-54. See also Frederick Kaufman & John P. Guckin, *The African Roots of Jazz* (Alfred

Publishing Company, 1979).

126. Long, p. 140. I think Charles Long's position regarding otherness, relativity and the hegemony of Eurocentric Christian categories, is complemented by Barthlémey Adoukonou's position regarding the "right" of African people to play their own theological game. Indeed, Adoukonou's position corresponds to the theological position I explore in Pan-African terms.

According to Adoukonou:

> La théologie étant, par définition, hospitalière de altérité, ne redoutera aucune manifestation de la différence; au contraire, elle l'accueillera comme une grâce, un don pour le service de la promotion. Elle assure les conditions fondamentales de la libre circulation des dons, des différences, car elle s'accomplit comme trans-gression de sa "localité" culturelle, anthropologique, vers l'U-topos de la Croix, seule forme historiquement donnée de l'utopie tant recherchée aujourd'hui dans le dialogue des cultures et des religions. (Adoukonou ix.)

Indeed, I explore the sense in which theology — generically speaking — should be hospitable to myriad patterns *de la différence* in the next chapter. I can only agree with Adoukonou that otherness, a metaphor for God, is a gift, the scandal of which is made clear in the crucified, i.e., immolated, God.

Chapter 6
Sky & Earth: Revelation & The Words of God

1. Boulaga, *Christianity Without Fetishes*, p. 188.

2. My view of the relativity of religious values has been strengthened by these texts: John Hick and Paul F. Knitter, eds., *The Myth of Christian Uniqueness* (New York: Orbis Books, 1988); Aloysius Pieris, *An Asian Theology of Liberation* (Maryknoll, New York: Orbis Books, 1988. With the exception of theologians such as Aloysius Pieris, Rosemary Reuther, Raymundo Panikkar, Paul Knitter, and Tom Driver, the theologians of religion appear to be too removed from the practical locus of interreligious dialogue. Among the masses of the African people, however, Western Christianity is really transformed through its essential and creative encounter with the non-Christian values of popular culture. In truly reciprocal relationships, as in the equilibrium between acculturation and inculturation, assertions of religious superiority are meaningless.

3. Raymundo Panikkar put it this way:

> Pluralism in its ultimate sense is not the tolerance of a diversity of systems under a larger umbrella; it does not allow for any superstructure. It is not a supersystem. Who or what principles would manage it? The problem of pluralism arises when we are

> confronted with mutually irreconcilable worldviews or ultimate systems of thought and life. Pluralism has to do with unbridgeable human attitudes. If two views allow for a synthesis we cannot speak of pluralism. We speak then of two different, mutually complementary, although apparently opposite, attitudes, beliefs or whatever. We do not take seriously the claim of ultimacy of religions, philosophies, theologies, and final human attitudes if we seem to allow for a pluralistic supersystem. (*Toward a Universal Theology of Religion*, p. 125.)

4. C.C. Berkouwer, *General Revelation* (Grand Rapids: Wm. B. Eerdmans, 1953) p. 12.

5. Boulaga, p. 188.

6. Mercy Oduyoye puts it this way:

> Missionary theology burst upon Africa South of the Sahara after the Protestant Reformation by way of pietists and evangelicals, whose nations were experiencing the power of steam and gunpowder. This theology clashed with African culture, which was pious in its own right, but had no steam engines and rifles and was by no stretch of imagination evangelical in the sense of going out to tell its own good news to other nations. The missionaries reflected their culture in the symbols they brought along and in their telling the story of salvation. (*Hearing and Knowing*, p. 68.)

7. Ibid., pp. 146-155. See also Joseph G. Donders, *Non-Bourgeois Theology: An African Experience of Jesus* (New York: Orbis Books, 1985.

8. Zahan, *The Religion, Spirituality and Thought of Traditional Africa*, p. 157.

9. See Éla, *African Cry*, p. 51.

10. MacGaffey, *Modern Kongo Prophets*, p. 181.

11. Boulaga, *Christianity Without Fetishes*, p. 203.

12. Itumeleng J. Mosala and Buti Tlhagale, eds., *The Unquestionable Right to Be Free: Black Theology from South Africa* (Maryknoll, New York: Orbis Books, 1986, p. 196. See also Mosala, *Biblical Hermeneutics and Black Theology in South Africa* (Grand Rapids, Michigan: William B. Eerdmans, 1989).

13. According to Mosala,

> the ideological condition and commitment of the reader issuing out of the class circumstances of such a reader are of immense hermeneutical significance. The biblical hermeneutics of liberation is thoroughly tied up with the political commitments of the reader. This means that not only is the Bible a product and a record of class struggles, but it is also a site of similar struggles acted out by the oppressors and oppressed, exploiters and exploited of our society even as they read the Bible. (See *The Unquestionable Right to Be Free* pp. 196-197.)

14. Ibid., p. 180.

15. Ibid., p. 181.

16. James Cone, *A Black Theology of Liberation*, 2nd. ed. (Maryknoll, New York: Orbis Books, 1986), p. 71.

17. Ibid., P. xxi.

18. Éla, *My Faith as an African* (Maryknoll, New York: Orbis Books, 1988) p. 99.

19. Paul Tillich, *Systematic Theology*, Volume One (Chicago: University of Chicago Press, 1951).

20. Croatto, *Biblical Hermeneutics: Toward a Theory of Reading as the Production of Meaning*, p. 78.

21. Ibid., p. 49.

22. Ibid., p. 41-50.

23. Ibid. Croatto writes: "The event is open to many readings, each of which closes the meaning, only to have it opened once more, and so on; the process can be repeated many, many times." (See p. 41.)

24. Ibid., p. 47.

25. Ibid., p. 48.

26. Ibid., pp. 50-51.

27. Ibid., p. 70.

28. Ibid., p. 58.

29. For a detailed analysis of the relation of African creation myths to Scripture, see Modupe Oduyoye, *The Sons of the Gods and the Daughters of Men: An Afro-Asiatic Interpretation of Genesis* 1-11 (Maryknoll, New York: 1984).

30. Mercy Oduyoye, *Hearing and Knowing,* p. 91

31. Ibid.

32. Boulaga, p. 81.

33. Éla, *African Cry,* pp. 90-91.

34. Oduyoye, *Hearing and Knowing,* p. 82.

35. Ibid., p. 95.

36. Ibid., 81. Although he is an African, Adoukonou, in his *Jalons pour une théologie africaine,* draws out the African-American implications of Oduyoye's explosion of the myth of "paradise regained." Adoukonou writes of the track of Pan-Africanism in the Diaspora and critiques it for its *accent prométhéen* and subscription to the illusion of "paradise regained."

> Le voeu de nouveauté et de simplicité ("sans complications") sonne comme le désir de retour dans le sein maternel de l'indifférenciation et de la sécurité. Violemment pro-jeté, mis-au-monde de la dure réalité d'une communauté humaine en différenciation progressive et accélérée, mais aussi déchirée par des prétentions de supériorité raciale, l'enfant noir voudrait revenir au jeu du libre étalement de ses possibilités natives sous le regard encourageant et réjoui de l'autorité (augere: faire croître, augmenter) de la bonne mère. Mais "l'heure du déracinement" a sonné et elle est sans appel. La personnalité est à gagner désormais sur l'axe du futur. Il n'y a pas de retour possible. (See p. 55.)

37. Ibid., p. 89.

38. See Éla, *African Cry*, p. 46. Éla's view, which opposes the Eurocentric, Marxist claim that religion is an opiate of the people, is complemented by Barthélemy Adoukonou. In his book *Jalons pour un théologie africaine*, Adoukonou also critiques that Marxist position by way of an analysis of black religion in the Americas. He writes:

> Dans la cassure de l'histoire où nous vivons, il serait surprenant qu'au moment où la réaction historiquement significative des Noirs aux Antilles et au Brésil a été de crier vers les dieux de la lutte, de la rupture, du refus, la théologie chrétienne africaine se dérobe à ses responsabilités historiques pour se réfugier dans une simple reprise des vieux mythes et symboles. "Le Vodun africain, écrit Ki-Zerbo, "avec les rites de possession et d'extase, fut conservé à Haïti comme un viatique sur les chemins de la souffrance. Néanmoins, les dieux les plus invoqués ici n'étaient plus les symboles de la fécondité ou de la prospérité agricole....C'était les dieux de la lutte, de la violence, de la rupture et du refus. Shango, dieu du tonnerre, Ogoun, dieu de la forge, Eshu, l'inévitable intermédiaire des dieux, mais aussi le principe dynamique du changement et le désir inassouvi." (See pp. 57-58.)

Like Éla, then, Adoukonou holds that Neo-African religion in the Americas was the foundation of resistance to slavery and the necrophilic values of the Eurocentric slavers. Adoukonou argues that those values constitute a tragic arrogance and evince the reality of original sin. *L'hybris du savoir, du pouvoir (technique) et de l'avoir (économique) s'est développé en structure objective de péché: la négation de l'homme par l'homme dans la traite des nègres et plus tard dans le système colonial.*

> De cela le Noir voulait s'affranchir; longtemps la religion Vodun sera la seule forme que prendre sa protestation au pays de l'esclavage. Certaine manifestations de Eshu ou Lêgba que l'on a observées en Afrique moderne témoignent aussi de ce refus. La rencontre d'une forme historiquement pure du "Je veux" (science, technique, politique de domination systématique) a donné à la religion Vodun, jadis aux Antilles, et aujourd'hui en Afrique même, l'occasion de s'exprimer et de révéler des aspects de son être: de religion d'évasion, est devenue religion prophétique à accent prononcé de libération socio-politique pour devenir dans un troisième temps une religion d'intégration sociale, comme les études de Montilus Guérin l'ont montré en ce qui concerne Haïti. (See pp. 58-59.)

39. Lawrence W. Levine, *Black Culture and Consciousness: Afro-American Folk Thought from Slavery to Freedom* (New York: Oxford University press, 1978), p. 38.

40. Cone, *The Spirituals and the Blues*, p. 53.

41. Levine, p. 37.

42. Stuckey, p. 37.

43. Ibid.

44. Ibid.

45. Long, p. 181-183; Levine, p. 43.

46. Cone, *God of the Oppressed*, p. 83.

47. Ibid., p. 83.

48. Boulaga, p. 199.

49. Ibid., p. 199.

Chapter 7
The Providence of God: Invisible Source of a Visible Regeneration

1. Alan Richardson and John Bowden, eds., *The Westminster Dictionary of Christian Theology* (Philadelphia: Westminster Press, 1983), p. 248.

2. Dussel, *Philosophy of Liberation*, p. 71.

3. Ibid., pp. 39-53.

4. Ibid., p. 53.

5. Ibid., p. 17.

6. Ibid.

7. Boulaga, *Christianity Without Fetishes*, p. 28.

8. James Cone, *A Black Theology of Liberation* 2nd ed. (Maryknoll, New York: Orbis Books, 1986), p. 108.

9. Cabral, *Return to the Source: Selected Speeches of Amilcar Cabral*, p. 43.

10. Dussel, p. 48.

11. Boulaga, p. 64.

12. See E. Milingo, *The World in Between: Christian Healing and the Struggle for Spiritual Survival* (Maryknoll, New York: Orbis Books, 1984). Although he had risen in the ranks of the Vatican, Milingo could not abandon his ancestral values. Consistent with magico-religious modalities of *Cilola*, his clan, Milingo found that he had the gift of healing and the ability to drive out evil spirits. For his valorization of the legacy of his ancestors he was forced to resign his see in 1982. According to Mona Macmillan, Milingo's only fault was "his outspoken criticism of the Missions, and that his popularity with his people threatened the Church's comfortable *status quo*." (See p. 137.) The Vatican failed to accept an *African* praxis related to the humanity of God, a christological understanding emergent from intense valuation of political struggle and cultural innovation.

13. Ibid., p. 12.

14. Ibid., pp. 87-88.

15. I take the term deteriology from John Mbiti's *New Testament Eschatology in an African Background* (London: Oxford UniversityPress, 1971). He writes:

> Thus, for the Akamba, and indeed for many African peoples as far as evidence is available, the Eschatology of man takes him back to the remotest possible point in Time beyond his point of beginning to, in reality, a point of non-being, since it takes him beyond where he is createable. Or, to put it another way, God does not recreate what at death has begun to disintegrate. *There is no teleology in African Eschatology; what there is might be called "deteriology"* — at least that is the theological and philosophical conclusion to which our analysis seems to drive us [emphasis added]. (See p.139.)

16. Georg Wilhem Hegel, *The Philosophy of History* (New York: Dover Publications, 1956), p. 93.

17. Éla writes:

> We must insist on the fallacious nature of this view of things. It regards everything as if there were a "providential" civilization: "traditional" societies, solicitous for harmony and for conformity with the past, are supposed to have need of the West in order to become dynamic, critical, and historical — all of the traits stamped with the Spirit that, since Grecian times, is incarnate in European history, as Hegel says. (*African Cry*, p. 45.)

18. See Harold Turner, "The Relationship Between Development and New Religious Movements in the Tribal Societies of the Third World," in Frederick Ferre and Rita Mataragnon, *God and Global Justice: Religion and Poverty in an Unequal World* (New York: Paragon House, 1985), p. 84.

19. Ibid.

20. MacGaffey, *Modern Congo Prophets*, p. 15. MacGaffey's definition is based upon the views of Robin Horton.

21. Turner, , p. 93.

22. Ibid., p. 85.

23. Ibid., p. 94.

24. Ibid., p. 96.

25. Ibid., p. 97.

26. Ibid.

27. Ibid., pp. 97-98.

28. Ibid., p. 98.

29. Boulaga, p. 64.

30. Éla, p. 48.

31. Turner, p. 108.

32. Pieris, *An Asian Theology of Liberation*, p. 87.

33. MacGaffey, Boulaga and Adoukonou afford us an opportunity to see the practical implications of this view in terms of the African independent churches.

As MacGaffey reveals in his study of Christianity among the BaKongo:

> Christian BaKongo interpret "salvation" primarily in a materialistic sense and see the biblical Christ as a great healer and mediator rather than a scapegoat [sic]. The cross is a map of the path leading from [the living to the dead], linking this world and the other. The insignia of Mpadi Simon's Black Church, in one version at least, superimpose an x on the cross, showing that "the path of Kimbangu" has replaced "the path of Christ." (*Religion and Society in Central Africa*, p. 120.)

Reflecting on the same issue of the independent churches, Boulaga put it this way:

> Here the one who "rises up" in the name of God is not a church reformer but a prophet — and indeed "another Christ," or at very least the personal, black emissary of the Founder [such as an Simon Kimbangu] and thus not merely of witness, commentary, and the preservation of an intangible deposit of faith. This person has the mission to do for this particular African community what Jesus did for his own people when he came to fulfill the Scriptures. (See p. 64.)

In another vein, Adoukonou explores this ancestral understanding of Christ in terms of traditional Fon values. According to Adoukonou, one, in examining the issue of revelation in Fon terms,

> est conduit à comprendre ce que signifie l'ancien (menxo) pour le Fon. Il est celui qui se tient tout près des origines, qui a "vu" la parole et dont il faut écouter la parole! Ainsi la figure de l'ancêtre

> apparaît comme une figure de révélation. Nous ne pouvons pas contester à nos pères, dans la mesure où ils étaient des sages au sens défini dans ce travail, d'avoir entendu (sè) Dieu comme s'ils le voyaient (mon) dans la forêt de signes-symbols (nusinu, vodun) qu'est le monde: cf Heb 1, 1; Rom 1. (*Jalons pour une théologie africain*, p. 307.)

Adoukonou claims that this focus on the ancestors — a way to "ambush" general revelation — is orientated to the past, which not necessary a bad thing. Thus, *On peut dire que pour eux l'eschatologie était dans le passé — parce que dans le passé s'est faite la révélation — et que devenir conforme à la figure de l'ancêtre, retourner au "pays"* [invisible] *où il est, c'est la bonne fin pour l'Adja-Fon. C'est la révélation parfaite qui se fait à Ifê, pays où sont les anciens morts.* (See p. 307.) For Adoukonou, this ancestral understanding of revelation, anchored in the legacy of eponymous ancestors, must be fructified in Christ. Here, Adoukonou makes an appeal to a natural theology — i.e., general revelation — and the special revelation of Christ Jesus.

> Si jadis Dieu a parlé à nos pères à travers des signes de la nature, aujourd'hui c'est en son Fils Jésus qu'il nous parle (Heb 1, 1-3). L'eschatologie Vodun doit se convertir en eschatologie chrétienne. Ce n'est pas finalement sur l'axe du futur qu'elle se décider; en effet, elle n'était pas limitée, simplement parce qu'elle était orientée vers la figure passée de l'ancêtre éponyme qui se trouve dans le passée; c'est à une décision de foi dans le présent qu'elle est appelée. Depuis Christ, 'eschatologie est au présent! (See p. 307.)

For Adoukonou, this call to the present does not cut the Fon off from their ancestors.

In sum, Boulaga, MacGaffey and Adoukonou give concrete examples of how, in the Pan-African experience, the divinity of Jesus may not be divided from the humanity of the ancestors. If the memory of the ancestors has been providential in retaining the Afrocentricity of the image of God, then reflection on this memory is indispensable for a Pan-African christology. Jesus Christ is believed to be the perfection of an image vitiated by sin. Given my focus on the macrodimension of sin, the perfection of the image of God in my theology must sanctify values and symbols of the African heritage. The intrinsic relation of cultural imagination and political struggle is understood christologically as the visible incarnation of a regenerative process.

34. Toni Morrison, *Beloved* (New York: Alfred A. Knopf, 1987), pp. 88-89.

35. Ibid., p. 198.

36. Robinson, *Black Marxism: The Making of the Black Radical Tradition*, p. 442. In a more theological key, Adoukonou addresses Robinson's assertion that something has been terribly wicked about Western civilization. That something — that "nastiness" — for Adoukonou, as well as Robinson, has to do with the slave trade. The slave trade, Adoukonou argues, led *en vérité à la plus terrible histoire des temps modernes et à côte de laquelle la bagatelle du nazisme ne sera qu'un jeu d'enfant* (Adoukonou 40). He writes:

> Comparés aux 6 millions de Juifs livrés au four crématoire, que dire des 100 millions d'esclaves déportes en Amérique par le même hybris de l'homme, et dont les trois quarts mouraient dans les soutes des bateaux négriers? Mais si le retour du boomerang a réveillé l'Occident épouvanté, a-t-on jamais tenté théologiquement de penser l'homme à la lumière de cette expérience douloureuse? Si nous observons la querelle tribale et ethnique qu'a été la théologie chrétienne (Réforme, Contre-Réforme, les Lumières, le Modernisme...) entre le 15e et le 20e, nous pouvons nous demander s'il ne revient pas effectivement aux peuples qui ont le plus souffert au cours de l'Histoire du mode occidental de traitement de "autre" et qui se retrouvent être aussi les prétendus "peuples ethnologiques," de reposer la question de l'altérité d'une manière nouvelle. Nous reviendrons sans cesse sur ce leitmotiv qui est le véritable fil d'Ariane de notre théologique. (Adoukonou 40-41).

37. Robinson, p. 442.

38. Ibid., p. 443.

39. Dussel explains the eschatological significance of popular culture. According to him, popular culture:

> preserves the best of the Third World and is the one whence new alternatives will emerge for future world culture, which will not be a mere replication of cultures of the center....The exteriority of popular culture is the best guarantee and the least contaminated nucleus of the new humankind. Its values, scorned today and not even recognized by the people itself, must be studied carefully; they must be augmented within a new pedagogy of the oppressed in order to develop their possibilities. It is within popular culture, even traditional culture, that cultural revolution will find its most authentic content. (See p. 90.)

Indeed, the Spirit, within modalities of peripheral culture, reactivates the redemptive catalysts of radical change. Éla, in *African Cry*, put it this way:

> The present encounter of faith and culture takes place in a context where culture is essentially defined in terms of challenge. The problem is no longer the opposition between modernism and tradition. The problem is in the battle for the liberation to which a new culture is called to give birth in dominated societies. The church must find its ways of expressing its faith in a basic articulation between popular masses, which have remained close to their mores and traditions. (See p. 130.)

40. Dussel, p. 125.

41. Ibid., p. 93.

42. Ibid., p. 125.

43. Éla, p. 58.

Index